December 2014

Dad.

Hope you will enjoy read

about the history of S

Then you can plan a visit!

♡ Hannah

1ST EDITION
B18
$15

ISLAND TIME

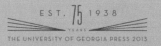

EST. 75 YEARS 1938

THE UNIVERSITY OF GEORGIA PRESS 2013

THE UNIVERSITY OF GEORGIA PRESS   ATHENS & LONDON

ISLAND TIME

AN ILLUSTRATED HISTORY OF St. Simons Island, Georgia

Jingle Davis   PHOTOGRAPHS BY BENJAMIN GALLAND

a
Friends Fund
publication

*Publication of this work was
made possible, in part, by a generous
gift from the University of Georgia
Press Friends Fund.*

Unless otherwise noted, all photographs in the book were taken by Benjamin Galland.

© 2013 by the University of Georgia Press
Athens, Georgia 30602
www.ugapress.org
All rights reserved
Designed by Erin Kirk New
Set in Adobe Garamond Pro
Manufactured by Bang Printing for Creasey Printing Services
The paper in this book meets the guidelines for permanence and durability
of the Committee on Production Guidelines for Book Longevity of the
Council on Library Resources.

Printed in the United States of America
17 16 15 14 13 C 5 4 3 2 1

Library of Congress Cataloging-in-Publication Data
Davis, Jingle.
   Island time : an illustrated history of St. Simons Island, Georgia / Jingle Davis ;
photographs by Benjamin Galland.
      pages   cm
   Includes bibliographical references and index.
   ISBN-13: 978-0-8203-4245-0 (hardback : alkaline paper)
   ISBN-10: 0-8203-4245-9 (hardback : alkaline paper)
      1. Saint Simons Island (Ga. : Island)—History. 2. Saint Simons Island (Ga. : Island)—
History—Pictorial works. I. Galland, Benjamin. II. Title.
   F292.G58D38   2013
   975.8'742—dc23   2012046534

British Library Cataloging-in-Publication Data available

For Claudia, Joe, Jim, Trina, Ervin,

Yumi, Karl, Elizabeth and the lucky 13;

for my husband, Frank Swisher,

and in memory of two beloved island natives:

my brother, Jaxon Hice, and my lifelong friend

Carolyn O'Quinn.

Contents

Preface

ANYONE WHO GROWS UP ON St. Simons learns its history by osmosis. The past is as pervasive on the island as the humid, sea-scented air. As children, my brother and I unearthed in our yard shell tools made by prehistoric Indians and found Spanish and English colonial pottery on the beach. We romped with other island youngsters over the ruins of Fort Frederica and water-skied in the river where the tiny Georgia navy won a Revolutionary War battle against the British. We waded through marshes that, we were told, once ran red with the blood of Cuban grenadiers. We climbed the steps of the "new" lighthouse, built in 1871 to replace the original, which had been blown up by retreating Confederate troops during the Civil War. We sat on the bench beside our mother while she played the organ at the historic Christ Church, and we searched for ghosts in the old church cemetery, where so many early islanders are buried.

Our maternal grandmother, one of the many Georgians who rode the ferries to St. Simons in the late 1800s and early 1900s, told us stories about the island as she remembered it from her youth. She later brought her own son and daughter back for visits. In the 1930s, our parents moved to St. Simons and built a house on property that remains in the family today. A few years later, our mother's brother—whom, in southern fashion, we always called Brother because that is what Mother called him—built a house across from us on an unpaved street that residents have fought to keep that way. Brother's house is now occupied by the fourth generation of his family and is often visited by the fifth and sixth generations. My own island house is across the street. We are no longer considered St. Simons newcomers, but our roots do not stretch back to James Oglethorpe, as those of some island families do.

Osmosis and family stories are wonderful ways to learn to love history but are no substitute for scholarly research and interpretation of what happened—or *might* have happened—many years ago. For well over a century, historians, anthropologists, archaeologists, geologists, and other experts have dug up the island's past. They have excavated relics from the woodlands, marshes, beaches, and waterways, painstakingly pieced them together, and pondered their significance. Scholars are still translating and interpreting thousands of documents, including the voluminous Archivo General de Indias of Seville, Spain, written in part by some of the earliest Spanish explorers of the Georgia coast. Their work continues to illuminate the dark corners of island history, often contradicting the work of earlier scholars. For example: when we were growing up, it was a given that the prehistoric Indians on St. Simons belonged to the Guale ("*wal*-ee") chiefdom. Later research has shown that postcontact Indians at the Spanish mission established on the island in the early 1600s were Mocama, not Guale. But were the prehistoric Indians on St. Simons Guale or Mocama? Scholars are still debating that issue. The island's Mocama mission on the south end has never been excavated, nor have the remains of three other missions established later on different parts of the island.

Island history has been recorded in dozens of personal memoirs written by ordinary and extraordinary people who stayed on St. Simons for a short time, a long time, or a lifetime. A Spanish teenager, Andrés de Segura, wrote about his experiences when he was shipwrecked on or near the island in 1595 and spent time in Guale and Mocama villages. John and Charles Wesley, British brothers who led the movement that evolved into the Methodist Church, wrote about their hard times on St. Simons almost three hundred years ago when they preached to settlers and soldiers at Fort Frederica. The esteemed English actress Fanny Kemble lived on island plantations for only a few months in 1838–39, yet her journal rivets readers today with its horrifying descriptions of slavery, especially the abuse of female slaves by white men and women. Anna Page King, who inherited and managed a giant island plantation, wrote more than a thousand letters to friends and family members, describing her busy but lonely life. Her husband, involved in national politics and nation building, was seldom at home, although he did ask John James Audubon to stay with the Kings for a month when the acclaimed ornithologist's boat ran into a storm off the island. Audubon was enchanted with St. Simons, comparing it to one of the "fairy islands of the Golden Age."

One of the most remarkable island memoirs was written by a black woman, Susie Baker, who at age fourteen spent time teaching other liberated but not yet officially freed slaves at contraband camps on St. Simons during the Civil War. Her school was one of the first schools sanctioned for black people in the Deep South.

European artists, including the French cartographer Jacques Le Moyne (c. 1533–88), the Belgian engraver Theodor de Bry (1528–98), and the German artist Philip Georg Friedrich von Reck (1710–98), are thought to have made the earliest known pictures of Indians on the southeastern coast, as well as of the native flora and fauna of the land then known as La Florida, a huge territory that stretched north to Chesapeake Bay and west past the Mississippi River. Some of the artists, such as de Bry, relied more on their imaginations and preconceptions than on their eyes. Their sketches, paintings, and etchings, widely circulated in Europe at the time, help us understand today how little accurate information was available to Old World rulers and others whose decisions had devastating and often unintended consequences in the New World.

There is no telling how much history remains undiscovered in dusty archives or beneath the sandy soil of the island itself. St. Simons boasts at least three giant shell rings built by Indians of the Late Archaic period, thousands of years ago. Only one shell ring has been examined so far by experts; the others, including one just discovered in the present century, wait to be explored and interpreted, although all three are now in danger of disappearing.

St. Simons has changed in radical ways from the island of my childhood. Yet it remains a special place, rich in natural beauty and charm, with a fascinating, many-layered history that it spreads like a banquet before everyone who sets foot on its shores. Because of its popularity, the island is in danger of being loved to death, as so many other wonderful places have been. Twelve miles long and three miles wide at its widest point, St. Simons is the largest of Georgia's developed sea islands and is the only developed island on the state's one-hundred-mile-long coast that remains more residential than resort. Unlike most Georgia sea islands, St. Simons has never been owned by a single wealthy family or been a private club. From the beginning of human occupation, it has always been a community where people lived, worked, played, and reared new generations of islanders. It is also a place where visitors, including my Middle Georgia forebears, have come to enjoy the beaches and tidal waterways, the oak-shaded woodlands, and the intriguing oyster-shell tabby ruins left by generations past.

Fortunately, St. Simons has ardent advocates devoted to the protection of its natural resources, its old communities and buildings, and its historic artifacts, sites, and documents, including those yet to be discovered. They include members of the St. Simons

Land Trust, the St. Simons African-American Heritage Coalition, Residents United for Planning and Action, the Museum of Coastal History, the Arthur J. Moore Methodist Museum at Epworth by the Sea, the Fort Frederica National Monument, the Maritime Center and Museum at the Historic Coast Guard Station, the Cassina Garden Club, the Friends of Demere Park, the Coastal Georgia Audubon Society, the Altamaha Riverkeeper, the Georgia Historical Society, the Center for a Sustainable Coast, and all the other individuals, scholars, artists, writers, musicologists, folklorists, organizations, societies, and government and nongovernmental agencies that are, have been, or will be dedicated to St. Simons's past as well as its future. The island can always use more advocates, especially with the development pressures of today.

This book, written and photographed by island natives, is intended as a tribute to all the people who have loved St. Simons over the years and those who will continue to care for the island for a long time to come.

Acknowledgments

THANK YOU TO three friends whose kindness made this book possible: John Griffin, Carolyn O'Quinn, and Keith Graham. My parents, Jean and Jack Hice; my maternal grandmother, Bess Norris Langston; and my uncle "Brother," Ed Langston Jr., all told me wonderful stories when I was growing up about earlier times on St. Simons and Sea Island. The writer and archaeologist Jerald T. Milanich, an expert on the Timucua and other Indians of the Southeast, read and commented on the manuscript, suggested sources, and provided hard-to-find illustrations. Other academics and researchers who were generous with time and expertise include Clark Alexander, coastal geologist, Skidaway Institute of Oceanography on Skidaway Island; Keith Ashley, archaeologist and coordinator of archaeological research, University of North Florida, Jacksonville; I. Lehr Brisbin Jr., retired senior research ecologist, University of Georgia Savannah River Ecology Laboratory, Aiken; Fred C. Cook of Brunswick, the archaeologist who has led more digs on St. Simons over the years than anyone else; Karl L. Davis, historian and island native; Ervan Garrison, geoarchaeologist, University of Georgia, Athens; Paul E. "Hy" Hoffman, historian, Louisiana State University, Baton Rouge; Kevin S. Kiernan, retired professor of English, University of Kentucky, Lexington; Michael A. Russo, archaeologist, Southeast Archaeological Center, National Park Service, Tallahassee; Jan M. Saltzgaber, professor emeritus of history, Ithaca College, Ithaca, New York; and Kenneth E. Sassaman, archaeologist, University of Florida, Gainesville. Hans Neuhauser of Athens is the former editor of *Right Whale News*, a publication of the New England Aquarium, Boston, whose scientists study the rare whales. He is also an expert on Georgia's preparations for the Spanish American War. Mimi Rogers, curator, Coastal Georgia Historical Society, provided a number of illustrations from the archives of the Museum of Coastal History and the archives of the Sea Island Co., shared documents, and offered her own expertise on the island's history. Andrea Marroquin of the Jekyll Island Museum offered information on the descendants of captives brought to coastal Georgia aboard the slave ship *Wanderer*. At Epworth by the Sea, Suzanne Burke Slover at the front desk and Judi Fergus, director of the Arthur J. Moore Methodist Museum and Library, along with the Reverend David Ogletree, a museum researcher, and the Reverend David Hansen, who lectures on the Wesley brothers, were all helpful, knowledgeable, and welcoming. David Grant, a marsh tackie breeder in South Carolina, directed me to a photograph of the rare horses. The writer and historian Buddy Sullivan, an expert on the history of Georgia and especially the Georgia coast, guided me to sources, provided a last-minute illustration, and read and commented on sections of the manuscript. The historian Patricia Cofer Barefoot made valuable suggestions regarding islanders to interview, and Frankie Ansley passed messages back and forth between us until our schedules meshed. Linda Wood housed and entertained me on the island and arranged meetings with friends and other long-term islanders, who provided old photographs, meals, and stories of St. Simons. They include Barbara and Freddie Pilgrim, Annabel and Paul Salter, Kaye and Earle Hartridge, and Bill Strother. Wells Kilgore of Morningstar Children and Family Services, the private facility that now occupies the site of the former Elizafield Plantation north of Brunswick, was kind enough to guide me through deep woods in the buggy swelter of a summer afternoon to photograph the tabby ruins of the plantation's old sugar mill, one of the structures misidentified in 1925 as the remains of a Spanish mission. My unofficial island in-laws, Shelley and Jim Renner, housed, fed, and entertained me many times while I was doing research on St. Simons. Jim, a geologist, also offered comments on chapter 1. Brad Wynn of the Georgia Department of Natural Resources in Brunswick provided information about the rise and fall of Pelican Spit. Denise Spear of Fort Frederica was my guide through the Oglethorpe period. My former college English teacher, the late Mary Gash of St. Simons, allowed me to read her unpublished manuscript on Christian Priber, who billed himself the "Prime Minister of Paradise." Lee Chisolm, MD, of Athens gave me a lesson on malaria and sickle cell disease. Chris Halderson, a former employee of Little St. Simons who lived on the island for several years, provided information on the island's imported white fallow deer. Old island friends and former Glynn Academy classmates were generous with stories and photographs of St. Simons. Among them are Winn Baker, Leslie Faulkenberry, Lurlyne Holland, Bill Jones III, Sudi Leavy, Dorothy

McClain, Barbara Hasell Murrah, Don Napier, Patti Parker, Bob West, Evelyn "Bootie" Wood, Bill Smith, and Bill Strother. Kathie Shinholser, who teaches the dance aerobics classes at the YWCO in Athens, and my fellow dancers—Ann, the two Barbaras, Bill, Cindy, Cynthia, Dean, Jeannie, Josie, Julia, Kitty, Lari, Larry, Linda, Lavonda, Marilyn, Martha, Melissa, Millicent, Monica, Nan, Pat, and Virginia—all helped me stay healthy and happy. Three exceptional editors: Regan Huff, C. J. Bartunik, and Laura Sutton, and one exceptional husband, Frank Swisher, all helped get the book written.

Map of the New World (Courtesy of
the Hargrett Rare Book and Manuscript
Library / University of Georgia Libraries)

Map of La Florida (Courtesy of the
Hargrett Rare Book and Manuscript Library /
University of Georgia Libraries)

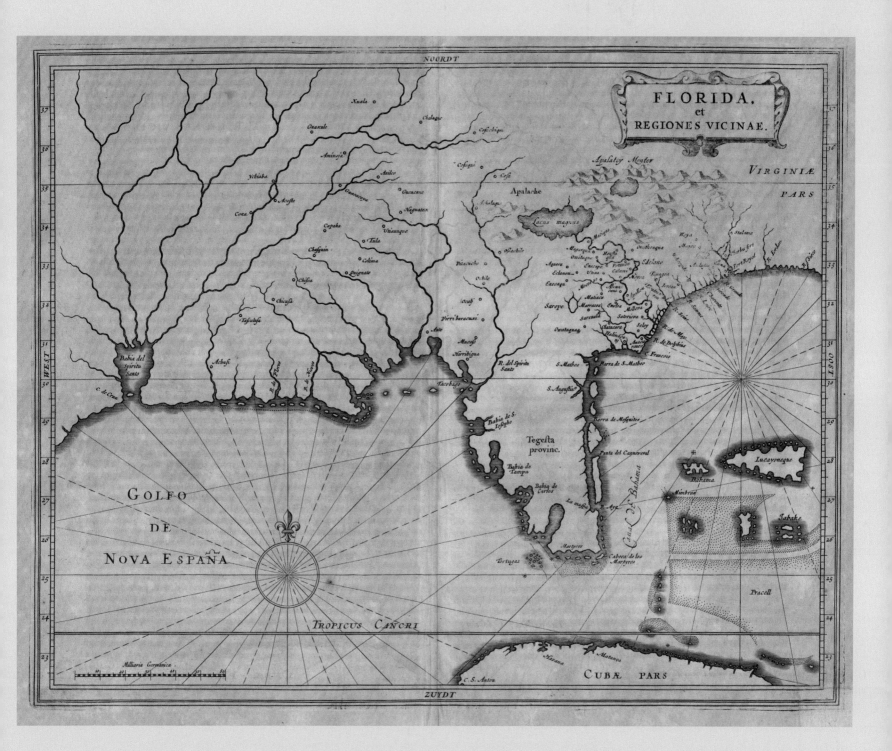

NOORDT

FLORIDA,
et
REGIONES VICINAE.

VIRGINIÆ
PARS

Apalatcy Montes

Xuala

Chalaque

Cofachiqui

Guaxule

Cofaqui

Cofa

Aminoja

Apalache

Ychiaha

Axilco

Guancane

Lacus magnus

Acofte

Cona

Canasoqua

Naguatex

Capaha

Uttanque

Chasqui

Tula

Colima

Chisca

Quignate

Picacucho

Chicasa

O chile

Tascaluca

Socab

Pirri baracuxi

Aute

Mucoço

Bahia del
Spiritu Santo

R. de Flores

R. de Nieve

Achusi

Harribigua

R. del Spiritu
Santo

c. de Cruz

Tacobaga

S. Matheo

Barra de S. Matheo

C. Francois

S. Augustin

Bahia de S.
Iosepho

Barra de Mosquitos

Tegesta
provinc.

Bahia de
Tampa

Punta del Cagneveral

GOLFO

Bahia de
Carlos

Lucayoneque

DE

La maffue

Ays

Bahama

Mimbres

NOVA ESPAÑA

Jabake

Martyres

Cabeça de los
Martyres

Tortugas

Pracell

TROPICUS CANCRI

Milliaria Germanica.

Havana

Matança

C. S. Anton.

CUBÆ PARS

ZUYDT

WEST

OOST

Canal de Bahama

CHAPTER 1   Early Time

THE AREA WHERE Georgia's modern coast currently resides has seen a multiplicity of geological and biological changes over the course of Earth's history. Long before St. Simons and other sea islands were born, Georgia's lower coastal plain lay beneath a primordial sea. During the ice ages of the Pleistocene, about two million years ago, the forerunners of today's sea islands first emerged between the rises and falls in sea level, growing, eroding, and shape-shifting. At times they became part of the mainland, miles from the shore; at other times they disappeared beneath the ocean far from land.

Paleo-Indians, the first known humans to reach the Southeast, arrived in Georgia at least twelve thousand years ago, when the land that would become St. Simons was a sand hill fifty miles from the ocean. The Paleo-Indians were nomads, moving from place to place in search of fresh water and food. Around forty-five hundred years ago, prehistoric people began to occupy the sea island later named St. Simons, leaving traces of their culture in massive shell rings, shell tools, and decorative objects made of shells and imported stone; they also left sherds of fiber-tempered pottery, which is thought to represent some of the first pottery ever crafted in the Americas.

Europeans began exploring the southeastern coast in the early 1500s, bringing radical changes to the flora and fauna as well as to the native Guale and Mocama people, who then inhabited the Georgia sea islands and coastal mainland. The Spanish dominated the area for almost two centuries. Only one of their many Georgia missions has been unearthed to date, on St. Catherines Island, north of St. Simons. By the late 1600s, the Spanish friars, along with the Guale and Mocama, were being forced south into Florida by the British. By then, the Indian chiefdoms of coastal Georgia had been decimated, primarily by European diseases.

Millions of years before the Europeans—let alone any humans—arrived, however, many now-extinct creatures, including more than twenty types of toothed whales, swam in an ancient warm and shallow sea that covered what would later become the southeastern coastal plain. The whales and many other large sea creatures were pursued by one of the most fearsome predators ever to inhabit the planet. *C. megalodon*, a monster shark, may have hunted the same way great white sharks do today, targeting its prey from below and surging upward to inflict an often-fatal first strike. The force of *C. megalodon*'s bite was five times that of *Tyrannosaurus rex* and ten times that of a modern great white shark. Fossils of *C. megalodon* teeth turn up sometimes on St. Simons, usually when sediments are pumped or dredged up for the construction of bridges and highways. Some of the fossilized teeth are enormous: one found under a causeway bridge on St. Simons suggests that it came from a fish forty to fifty feet long. During the European Renaissance, teeth of the ancient sharks were identified as the petrified tongues and teeth of dragons and giant snakes. *C. megalodon* teeth are so impressive that Georgia legislators have designated them the state fossil.

The forerunners of St. Simons and Georgia's other sea islands formed during a time of major climate change in the Pleistocene, which began about 2.6 million years ago. The titanic glaciers of Eurasia and North America advanced and retreated, in colder times trapping vast amounts of ocean water in thick sheets of ice. When the planet warmed, the glaciers melted, releasing torrents of water that lifted sea levels around the world. Between periods of glacial advance and retreat came times when sea level changed very little. During those more stable times, Georgia's ancient shorelines appeared remarkably similar to those of the coast today, with ancestor islands that were relatively short and wide, separated by deepwater sounds and backed by wide fields of marsh grass laced with tidal

Fossilized tooth of giant prehistoric shark

Sea oats bend with ice

waterways. As the sea retreated, the islands merged with the mainland, becoming the rolling sand hills of the coastal plain.

The birth of a sea island is never straightforward. Sandy shorelines such as Georgia's forced islands to roll back over themselves, their dunes invading marshes and tidal creeks. When the sea level dropped and new islands formed to the east, older beaches were replaced by marsh. Sometimes developing islands, including St. Simons, ended up as part of the mainland, only to reappear as islands when seas rose again.

An ancient shoreline called the Wicomico featured a giant island that rerouted the ocean-bound rivers of south Georgia, including the Satilla and St. Marys, and blocked the tides that flooded and nourished a seven-hundred-square-mile marsh basin. The salt-dependent marsh grasses dried and died. During the planet's last major glaciation, which lasted from about 110,000 years ago to about 12,500 years ago, the basin supported stands of oak trees. Later, when the glaciers melted and groundwater levels rose, the basin's clay lining trapped rain and groundwater. Cypress trees and aquatic plants colonized areas that stayed wet year-round. The wetlands gradually coalesced to form the Okefenokee, North America's largest freshwater swamp. Remains of the Wicomico island today form part of Trail Ridge, which flanks the Okefenokee's eastern edge and stretches 130 miles south into Florida from the Altamaha River.

Today, Georgia's ancient shorelines form terraces that descend like giant stair steps to the coast. They begin with the Wicomico, some fifty miles inland and ninety-five feet above today's sea level. To the east, successively younger terraces are named Penholoway, Talbot, Pamlico, Princess Anne, and Silver Bluff. The bulk of St. Simons is Silver Bluff, formed thirty-five thousand to forty thousand years ago, during the late Pleistocene. Parts of the modern Holocene shoreline, including Sea Island, appeared about five thousand years ago and overlap parts of the Silver Bluff shoreline. The oldest part of St. Simons is five or six feet higher than islands formed during the Holocene. The island's East Beach neighborhood sits on a Holocene fragment. Both East Beach and Sea Island are narrow fingers of land fronting the Atlantic, separated from their larger neighbor

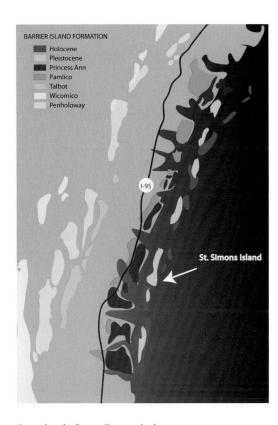

BARRIER ISLAND FORMATION
- Holocene
- Pleistocene
- Princess Ann
- Pamlico
- Talbot
- Wicomico
- Penholoway

I-95

St. Simons Island

Sea islands from Georgia's distant past are now sand hills on the state's coastal plain. (Courtesy of Buddy Sullivan, manager of the Sapelo Island National Estuarine Research Reserve, National Oceanic and Atmospheric Administration)

Devil's pocketbook (skate egg case)

by a long wedge of marsh and tidal creeks on their western sides. Both were linked to St. Simons by causeways during the twentieth century.

Georgia's lower coastal plain is defined today by its ancient shorelines. Because the old barrier island terraces are higher than the surrounding land, they long served as game trails, aboriginal footpaths, and sites for Indian villages. Modern builders are drawn to the ancient terraces: Savannah, Jesup, Brunswick, Waycross, and other towns and cities of the coastal plain are built on parts of old shorelines, as are stretches of Interstate 95 and U.S. Highway 17.

East of St. Simons, the shallow continental shelf descends gradually for seventy or eighty miles before it reaches the continent's edge, the continental slope, which begins a steeper decline to the Blake Plateau before plunging to the Atlantic abyss. The continental slope marks the western boundary of the Gulf Stream, a strong, fifty-mile-wide tropical current that runs north from the Straits of Florida along the east coast to Cape Hatteras, where it angles seaward. The stream wobbles a bit as it crosses a large feature on the Blake Plateau off Savannah called the Charleston Bump. The bump, a rocky underwater island with steep scarps, coral mounds, and extensive caves, provides habitat for a variety of deepwater species, including one-hundred-pound wreckfish. It rises from a surrounding depth of more than 2,000 feet to 1,230 feet, high enough to deflect the Gulf Stream offshore.

St. Simons is tucked into the Georgia Bight, the long incurve of the Atlantic coast that stretches from Cape Hatteras, North Carolina, to Cape Canaveral, Florida. St. Simons and neighboring islands lie at the westernmost point on the country's Eastern Seaboard; the island's longitude is about the same as that of the midwestern city of Cleveland. The bight and other natural features of the Georgia coast help shelter it from tropical storms and hurricanes, which tend to follow the Gulf Stream's warm blue waters as they churn northward. The Bermuda High, a summertime weather feature that forms annually between the southeastern coast and Bermuda, pushes cooling breezes toward land and tropical systems out to sea. Because incoming tides meet the continent first in Florida and the Carolinas, seawater is funneled into the bight, where it piles up, giving Georgia the most extreme tidal range from Texas to Maine. As ocean waves travel across the shallow bight, much of their energy is depleted before they roll gently onto the wide beaches of St. Simons. When a tropical system miles offshore adds energy to the waves, islanders turn out for a glorious day of body surfing or riding the big combers on a motley assortment of surfboards.

Although Georgia's coast is the youngest part of the state, its islands and marshes are almost as old as the hills. As the Appalachian Mountains and Piedmont eroded over millions of years, tons of minerals washed into ancient rivers that carried the sediments to the Atlantic Ocean. The heavier sand grains congregated at the ocean's edge, where they were bulldozed by wind and water into sandbars, shoals, dunes, and beaches. The shift from fresh to saltwater caused clay and finer silt to settle in sheltered, low-lying areas between the islands and the mainland, providing the muddy footing for the vast salt marshes of the Georgia coast. The processes continue today.

Like all sea islands, St. Simons is dynamic and changeable, reinventing itself according to the whims of tides, currents, winds, and sediments. A marsh today can be a freshwater slough tomorrow. The island's beaches and shoals erode and relocate. Dunes rise and fall, sometimes sweeping inland and sometimes moving offshore to merge with sandbars after storms. Channel dredging, seawalls, groins, and renourishment projects all affect the natural processes, often to the detriment of beaches and the creatures that populate them.

A large sandbar called Pelican Spit stood for at least a century at the mouth of the Hampton River, a distributary, or outlet, of the giant Altamaha River, one of the largest waterways leading to the coast in the eastern United States. The Hampton curves around the northern tips of St. Simons and Sea Island before emptying into the Atlantic. The spit, an important nesting ground for brown pelicans, avocets, black skimmers, and other seabirds, some of them rare, boasted about five acres of dry land and was a popular destination for fishermen, beachcombers, and campers. Some locals even thought the spit showed promise of becoming a small barrier island. It built up and eroded like all sea islands, but a thick cover of tough, salt-tolerant plants anchored its central dune field.

Sand whips down a windy beach

Beach erosion

Pelican Spit vanished during a series of eroding tides in the winter of 1999–2000, illustrating the ever-ephemeral nature of the Georgia coast. Human activities may have played a role, too. Shortly before Pelican Spit disappeared, sand was dredged from a shoal south of the spit to nourish Sea Island's badly eroding beach. Sand from Pelican Spit could have washed down-current to fill the depression. Less than a decade later, Pelican Spit rose again from the waves, albeit south of its former location. Although it had no central dunes and was still being overwashed by the highest tides, a few seabirds were again nesting there.

For most of the past five thousand years, sea levels have been slowly rising. Global warming, either caused or accelerated by worldwide industrialization, has increased the rate of rise in recent decades. Eventually, if the trend continues, St. Simons, Manhattan, and other coastal islands will disappear beneath the sea.

St. Simons did not exist as a sea island when nomadic Paleo-Indians arrived in Georgia about twelve thousand years ago. It was a time of dramatic climate change. The ice ages of the Pleistocene were ending, but the climate was much colder and more arid than it is today. Although St. Simons formed during the Pleistocene, the Earth subsequently entered another glaciation period. Sea levels around the world plunged, leaving the continental shelf exposed for eighty to a hundred miles east of Georgia's present-day shoreline. The Paleo-Indians left proof of their presence in Georgia in a scant handful

Young alligator on Pelican Spit

of Clovis projectile points, fluted stone spearheads made in a distinctive style. (The points are named for Clovis, New Mexico, where examples were first found.) None of the points have turned up on St. Simons, which was then a sand ridge on the mainland, left high and dry by the retreating sea. Many scientists believe Paleo-Indian sites will be found one day on the now-submerged shelf. A shrimp boat off Savannah netted a Clovis point, but since there is no way to tell whether the point came from a Paleo-Indian site or was carried there by people of a later period, it is not considered proof of occupation by the earliest-known Georgians.

The Paleo-Indians were nomadic, roaming from place to place to hunt, gather edible plants, and find fresh water and toolmaking materials. Their quarry included big game: giant ground sloths, woolly mammoths, mastodons with huge curving tusks, saber-toothed cats, and prehistoric horses, camels, and bison, all of which were nearing extinction. The demise of the great creatures was probably caused by climate change but may have been hastened by early hunters. Black-water divers retrieved the fossilized skeletons of two giant ground sloths, an adult and juvenile, in the murky waters of the Frederica River near Gascoigne Bluff. The skeletons were reconstructed at the Fernbank Museum

of Natural History in Atlanta, which now has the replica of a giant ground sloth on exhibit, along with a fossilized skull pulled from the river.

By the time Indians established permanent settlements on St. Simons in the Late Archaic some forty-five hundred years ago, the climate had stabilized and the Georgia coast looked much as it does today. Indians settled on the island primarily because the coastal estuaries offered a reliable source of protein-rich food year-round. They would have been attracted to St. Simons for spiritual reasons too. Prehistoric Indians believed that rivers, rocks, trees, and other inanimate parts of the natural world were alive and powerful. The endless green ocean must have impressed them as a sentient being of spectacular strength, beauty, and mystery. The ocean and tidewaters around St. Simons glow on summer nights with bioluminescence from thousands of sea creatures that flash distress signals when disturbed. Indians pulling nets or paddling dugout canoes at night would have been trailed by blazing paths of light. The sun played a major role in the spiritual lives of the Indians. On the island, they would have watched it rise out of the ocean every morning. The archaeologist Kenneth Sassaman speculates that the Indians might have believed the shining water was where the sun went at night.

Aside from battles against insects, the lives of Indians on St. Simons may have been easier than those of their mainland counterparts. Summers are cooler and winters warmer on the sea islands than they are just a few miles inland, because the ocean is a giant temperature modulator. Seafood is available year-round; oysters are at their peak in colder weather. The long semitropical growing season meant wild plants could be gathered through the winter. Since the ground never freezes, edible roots were harvested year-round. The acorns of live oak trees, a dominant feature of the island's forest, are less bitter than acorns of other oaks. Women gathered the acorns in autumn, pounding the meat to a powder in log mortars with long wooden pestles, another invention of the Late Archaic. They leached the powder in cold water to remove bitter tannins, then dried it for storage. Indians used the acorn meal for thickening stews or baking into small cakes.

The island's tidal realms offered a tasty bouillabaisse of fish, shrimp, oysters, clams, mussels, whelks, snails, crabs, loggerhead sea turtles, and diamondback terrapins, all relatively easy to net, hook, spear, trap, dig, pluck from creek banks, or simply pick up off the sand. On night-fishing expeditions, the Indians built fires in clay basins in their canoes to attract fish. Schooling mullet jump toward light; prehistoric people may have believed the fish that landed in their canoes were gifts from the sea. Mullet jumping, as it is called on the island, is still a popular St. Simons pastime, although modern fishermen use Coleman lanterns or battery-operated lights instead of open flames to attract the fish.

Indian spear points from
St. Simons

Loggerhead sea turtle

Indians used razor-sharp shark's teeth and the spines of stingrays and horseshoe crabs as cutting tools or projectile points. While seafood was by far the major component of the coastal Indians' diet, early islanders harvested food as well from the maritime forest, open savannahs, marshes, hammocks, and rolling sand dunes. Men hunted white-tailed deer, bear, bobcat, panther, rabbit, raccoon, opossum, and a variety of other animals in the island's woodlands. Rain- and spring-fed ponds and sloughs offered potable water as well as such tasty edibles as turtles, frogs, fish, alligators, and plants such as cattails, sweetflag, and water lilies. The late Euell Gibbons, who authored several popular books on collecting and eating wild food, including *Stalking the Wild Asparagus* and *Stalking the Blue-Eyed Scallop*, once led a field trip for members of the Sierra Club who were meeting on St. Simons. With Gibbons's help, participants collected dozens of edible wild plants from a relatively small area on Gascoigne Bluff.

The tidewater environment of the island demanded different technologies from those used on the mainland. Coastal Indians invented new tools, making scrapers, awls, and other necessities of the Late Archaic from seashells instead of stones. They crafted eating utensils, weapons, and ornaments of shells, traded shells to Indians of the interior, and buried their dead under blankets of shells. The archaeologist Jerald Milanich, who led a dig on the island's north end during the 1970s, found an infant dressed in a tiny apron of shells interred in the steps of a burial mound. Late Archaic Indians, especially those on the Gulf Coast of southern Florida, modified shells in so many ingenious ways that nothing improved on or replaced their inventions until the advent of iron tools from Europe thousands of years later.

Horseshoe crab

The Indians of the Late Archaic built some of the most distinctive features of the southern coast: giant ring-shaped, C-shaped, and U-shaped structures collectively called shell rings. Three thousand years before Mayans erected stone temples in Central America and a thousand years before Egyptians built pyramids, Indians on the south Atlantic and Gulf Coasts of North America were building structures with shells, the most durable material available. At one time, researchers linked the building of monuments to the rise and spread of agriculture. It was when agriculture took hold that Indians on the mainland built giant ceremonial mounds such as those in Georgia near Macon, Cartersville, and Blakely. By happenstance or on purpose, Indians of the southern coast created shell rings at least a thousand years before the ceremonial mounds of the mainland were built. The archaeologist Michael Russo of the National Park Service theorizes that shell rings are among the earliest large community architectural projects in North America. He and others consider them so significant that they recommend listing and preserving the structures, including the Cannon's Point Shell Ring on north St. Simons, as National Historic Landmarks.

There are about fifty known shell rings in the Southeast, as large as 820 feet in diameter. The majority are in Georgia and South Carolina; nine are in Florida. Two on the

Mississippi coast were destroyed in modern times. Many were mined by early colonists and planters, who used the shell to make tabby, a unique coastal building material, and to pave sandy coastal roads. Relic hunters have raided many of the shell rings, removing clues to their origin and purpose and to the people who built them.

Three shell rings have been identified to date on St. Simons, including one discovered in 2008 by the Brunswick archaeologist Fred Cook, who stumbled across it during a dig in the island's Oglethorpe Park subdivision. It has not been explored, but radiocarbon dating indicates the Cannon's Point Shell Ring and the West Shell Ring on north St. Simons are more than four thousand years old. The Cannon's Point Shell Ring is the oldest shell ring containing pottery of any found so far in the Southeast.

Oysters, an easily harvested and renewable resource, were the dietary staple of Georgia's coastal Indians. Consequently, oyster shells were the chief components of their shell rings. Indians piled tons of empty shells, along with fish and animal bones and pottery fragments, into rings, some fringed with smaller ringlets, around large central plazas, where feasts and other important events were held. Shell rings were often the tallest structures on the low-lying coast; one shell ring in Florida measured twenty-three feet high in places.

Experts disagree whether the shell rings were formed for quotidian or spiritual reasons or both. Cook and others believe they are kitchen middens, trash dumps where Indians discarded shells and debris that, over long periods, accumulated in circular

Cannon's Point shell ring (Mike Russo, Southeast Archeological Center, National Park Service)

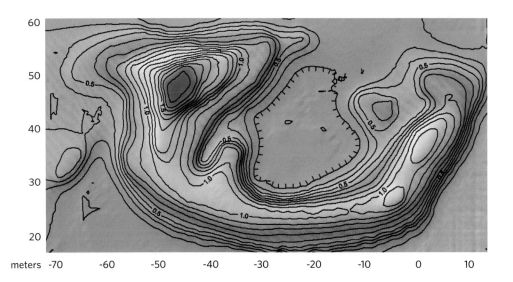

shapes because traditional Indian villages were arranged in a circle. The archaeologists Ken Sassaman and Mike Russo believe shell rings built in the Late Archaic were monumental seats of symbolic and spiritual power where Indians gathered to celebrate rituals and feasts, to see and hear their leaders, and perhaps to exchange mates or trade valuables.

Regardless of their intended purposes, shell rings served practical functions. They were lookout points and breezy retreats from summer's heat, humidity, and biting insects. Indians built houses and villages on them. When storm tides surged, shell rings offered high ground. On the flat coastal plain, even a few feet of elevation can mean the difference in being wet or dry.

Many scholars, including the archaeologist Keith Ashley, believe shell rings could function as middens or monuments, the determination to be made for each one individually. Because only a handful of known shell rings have been examined to date, future explorations, if any rings survive long enough, may yield more definitive information. All three St. Simons shell rings now lie in the marsh, although they were likely built on dry land. Experts once theorized that the rings were constructed originally in the marsh, perhaps as giant fish traps. Now experts believe that rising sea levels have created new marsh, which has invaded the shell ring sites. The shell rings on St. Simons are already threatened by rising waters, and Cook fears they could be lost completely in the next fifty years.

Pottery was another important invention of Late Archaic Indians. Plain or simply decorated, unglazed, and ranging in color from buff to orange-brown to dark gray, fiber-tempered St. Simons culture pottery is very similar—some say identical—to Stallings culture pottery, the oldest type dated so far in North America. (The latter is named for Stallings Island, near Augusta.) Stallings sherds from sites near the coast along the Savannah River have been radiocarbon-dated to about forty-five hundred years old. Some scholars believe that St. Simons culture pottery is even older.

Kenneth Sassaman is convinced that pottery originated in coastal Georgia on or near St. Simons at the beginning of the Late Archaic, then spread north to the Savannah River basin, where it gave rise to Stallings culture pottery, and south into Florida, where it preceded Orange culture pottery. There are too few radiocarbon-dated specimens from the lower Georgia coast to prove the theory, but Sassaman and others say they are confident that St. Simons culture pottery will prove to be the oldest in the Americas.

Indian women probably invented pottery as a substitute for the soapstone slabs and boiling stones used by mainland Indians for cooking. The slabs were pushed close to a fire, and food was placed on them to cook. Egg-sized boiling stones were heated in a fire,

Island shells and potsherds

then dropped at intervals into tightly woven baskets or hide containers of water to keep it simmering. Food was added to make soups and stews. There is no natural surface stone on any of Georgia's sea islands, so Indians either traveled inland to get it or traded for it with mainland Indians. Retrieving heavy cooking stones may not have been a priority for the male paddlers.

The first pottery vessels were shallow, flat-bottomed basins that might have served much the same function as cooking slabs or shellfish steamers. Boiling stones made of clay may have been used to heat earthen ovens. Over time, Indians learned to temper their pots with sand, grit, and grog (crushed pottery), building them out of clay coils and decorating them with elaborate designs. By the time of the European invasion, the art of making pottery had spread to every corner of the Americas.

There is scholarly disagreement over the identity of the prehistoric Indians who occupied St. Simons in the decades just before and just after contact. Some experts believe they belonged to the Guale chiefdom; others say they were Mocama, which translates as "saltwater people." When the first Europeans arrived, Georgia's coast was dominated by the two chiefdoms: Guale, who lived as far north as the Ogeechee River, and Mocama, who ranged south to just below today's Georgia-Florida line. The Mocama were one of the many Timucua-speaking groups that embraced nineteen thousand square miles in northern Florida and in Georgia south of the Altamaha River. Guale territory was confined to a narrow stretch of coastal Georgia. Scholars agree that the first and longest-lasting Spanish mission on St. Simons, San Buenaventura de Guadalquini, established in the early 1600s, was populated by Indians who spoke the Mocama dialect.

But the archaeologist Fred Cook believes Indians of the Guale chiefdom were on the island before the Mocama mission on St. Simons was established. Cook believes that precontact Guale occupied the coast from the Ogeechee River south to St. Simons, an opinion based in part on Indian pottery that he excavated on the island. Cook theorizes that Guale Indians on St. Simons left at some point, possibly in the wake of an Indian uprising in 1597, when the Guale fled the sea islands to escape reprisals from Spanish soldiers. He speculates that Indians on St. Simons might have been devastated by European diseases brought by early explorers. In either case, Cook says, the Spanish could have occupied the mission with a small Mocama group relocated from the mainland to St. Simons, since the Mocama proved loyal to the Spanish during the uprising.

The archaeologist Jerald Milanich, an expert on the Timucua, disagrees. He believes that the Indians on the island in the years leading up to contact were Mocama. Milanich says historic documents indicate that the prehistoric Mocama chiefdom embraced all the Georgia sea islands south of the Altamaha River, including St. Simons. Two other Mocama groups occupied a narrow strip of mainland west of the islands. Although Indians hunted and gathered food on smaller islands, such as Sea Island and Jekyll, their settlements were on the larger islands.

Although the Guale and Mocama shared many cultural similarities, they were traditional enemies and spoke unrelated languages. Descriptions and drawings made by early Europeans indicate Indians on the Georgia coast were tall, muscular, and athletic, with aquiline noses and tawny, reddish, or olive skin. The women had lighter skin. The bear grease they rubbed on themselves may have offered some protection from the sun or from mosquitoes. Both sexes tattooed and painted their faces and bodies in red, blue, and black. The chief's tattoos were always the most elaborate.

Timucua Indian (Etching by Theodor de Bry)

Black rush characterizes
the high marsh

On ceremonial occasions, important Indians were carried on litters under arching bowers of branches, accompanied by bodyguards and flanked by Indians carrying palmetto leaves to shade those of higher rank. A Guale chief was referred to by the Spanish as a *mico* (*mica* for a female chief); a Mocama chief was called the *cacique* (*caciqua* for a female chief), a title brought by Spaniards from the Caribbean, although the Spanish often used the titles interchangeably. Guale and Mocama chiefs usually inherited their titles from their maternal uncles. Women sometimes became micas or caciquas, especially after postcontact Indian populations plummeted.

Guale men and women wore their hair long, cut in front and colored with red ochre. Mocama men and women also had long hair, but men wore theirs piled on top of their heads and secured with braided grass, moss, and bear grease. Sometimes they stuck arrows into their hair for easy retrieval during hunting or warfare. Both Guale and Mocama buried their dead in graves decorated with red ochre, a burial tradition used for thousands of years in many cultures around the world.

In colder months, the coastal Indians covered their regular clothing with cloaks the Europeans called match coats. The chiefs' cloaks were often decorated with plumes and intricate painted designs. One match coat that awed the Europeans was made entirely of shimmering emerald feathers from the heads of mallard ducks. High-ranking Indians wore elaborate medallion-like necklaces called gorgets, which were made of shell or copper (acquired from the Great Lakes region by trade) and often featured elaborate carvings. Indian men and women wore bear claws, fish teeth, and dried fish bladders in their pierced ears, including bladders painted red, which Europeans called carbuncles, or rubies. The Indians carved ear pins from the hard columellas, or central columns, of whelk shells, and wore bracelets of fish teeth, shell beads, freshwater pearls, and small copper disks on their wrists and upper arms, above and below their knees, and around their ankles.

Before contact, Indians on the Georgia coast grew a few basic crops, including the three sisters—maize, squash, and beans—but agriculture was never as important on the sea islands as it was farther inland. Coastal Indians relied heavily on natural food but probably practiced swidden farming, or the practice of clearing land, planting it for a few years until the sandy soil was exhausted, and then moving on to clear and plant another tract. The health of Indians on the sea islands declined after they began growing and eating more corn and other crops favored by Europeans. The natural sugar in corn promoted tooth decay. Research on Indian skeletons and teeth indicates that when the natives ate wild food, they were not only healthier and taller but also had more robust bones.

Timucua Indians hunting alligators
(Etching by Theodor de Bry)

It is difficult to determine when the first contact occurred between Indians and Europeans on St. Simons. When Juan Ponce de León stepped off his ship in eastern Florida in 1513, he became the first European to land on the North American mainland, which he named La Florida. A few years later, another Spaniard, Pedro de Salazar, landed somewhere farther north on the coast, possibly in Georgia or South Carolina. Juan Vespucci, the nephew of the more famous explorer Amerigo Vespucci, for whom America is named, mapped the Eastern Seaboard in 1526 with maps, charts, and nautical instruments inherited from his uncle. Other explorers and slave raiders sailed along the Eastern Seaboard in the early 1500s. Whether they stopped on St. Simons is anyone's guess.

Jerald Milanich found a dog buried in a late Savannah-period charnel house on St. Simons; the Savannah period ended around the time Ponce de León made landfall in Florida. The dog had a musket ball in its skeletal remains, indicating that Europeans may have been on St. Simons not long after Ponce de León's landing. Others say the dog could have been shot at a later date and buried in the charnel house, which was from an earlier period.

The earliest European settlement in what became the United States was established probably only a few miles north of St. Simons. In 1525, two lightweight, agile sailing ships called caravels led by the Spanish slave trader Pedro de Quejo searched the coast for good land and friendly Indians. Lucas Vásquez de Ayllón, a wealthy Hispaniola lawyer, judge, and sugar planter who planned to establish a colony in North America, sent Quejo as a scout. As Spain's exploration of the New World continued, the Spanish defined La Florida as all the land from western Louisiana north to Chesapeake Bay and south to the Florida Keys. Quejo and his partner had visited the southeastern coast a few years before the Ayllón venture, kidnapping at least sixty Indians from South Carolina and selling them as slaves in Santo Domingo on the island of Hispaniola. Within five years, most were dead. On the 1525 trip, Ayllón wanted Quejo to establish peaceful relations with the Indians because his colony would need their help, especially in the early years. He told Quejo to teach the native people to grow European food plants, give them small gifts, and treat them well.

Ayllón rejected the site that Quejo chose for the colony and sent three ships to look elsewhere along the coast for a better place. Navigation logs indicate that two of the ships, including Quejo's, explored St. Simons Sound, which they named Mar Baja, or shallow sea. There is no known record of whether any of the Spaniards came ashore on the island. At the Taylor burial mound on north St. Simons, archaeologists found beads

Carolina Dogs

Carolina dog, also known as a Dixie dingo (Photo by Jackie Baxter Roberts)

DOGS WERE THE CONSTANT COMPANIONS of aboriginal people. A young German artist, Philip Georg Friedrich von Reck, who came to Georgia as a religious refugee in 1736, drew realistic sketches of Indians, animals, and plants he observed on St. Simons. His drawings and a passage in his diary suggest the close relationship between Indians and their dogs: "The fire is in the center of the house, around which they lie on the ground in the ashes with their wives, children and dogs round about."

I. Lehr Brisbin of the University of Georgia's Savannah River Ecology Laboratory monitored wildlife for years at the Savannah River Site, a 310-square-mile tract where material for nuclear weapons was manufactured. Brisbin discovered dogs running wild on the property and noticed that they looked and behaved like the wild dingoes of Australia and New Guinea, as well as the canines depicted in ancient cave paintings, on early Indian pottery, and in sketches made by von Reck and other early European visitors to the sea islands.

Brisbin says the dogs are North America's dingoes, linked in type to the oldest known dogs in the Americas, canines that crossed the Bering Strait land bridge with the first Paleo-Indians. They resemble the classic dog of the rural south, the "Old Yeller" type with short ginger or yellow fur, long muzzles, and ears that swivel like radar receivers when they hunt. They are good watchdogs but rarely bite; those that did went into Indian stewpots, which weeded out genetically inclined biters. Brisbin developed a breed from founder dogs living wild on the coastal plain in South Carolina, Georgia, and northern Florida. Named the Carolina dog, and sometimes called the Dixie dingo, it is the first recognized breed ever created from Georgia stock.

and iron and brass objects that could have come from the Ayllón ships either directly or in trade with Indians elsewhere. Barrels loaded with such items sometimes washed ashore after shipwrecks. Many scholars now believe that Ayllón and his six hundred or so colonists, including women, children, priests, and African slaves, settled near Sapelo Sound, about twenty-five miles north of St. Simons. Called San Miguel de Gualdape, Ayllón's colony, founded in 1526, predated Florida's St. Augustine by thirty-nine years and Virginia's Jamestown by seventy-one. There were other firsts: the Africans were the first brought to North America. They staged the country's earliest documented slave revolt. After one of the colonists' ships wrecked, they built the first European boat constructed in the country.

Ayllón's colony failed. Within two months, he and many others were dead of hunger, cold, sickness, or conflicts with the Guale. Survivors sailed for Hispaniola, probably leaving the Africans to fend for themselves. Their fate is unknown, although a period

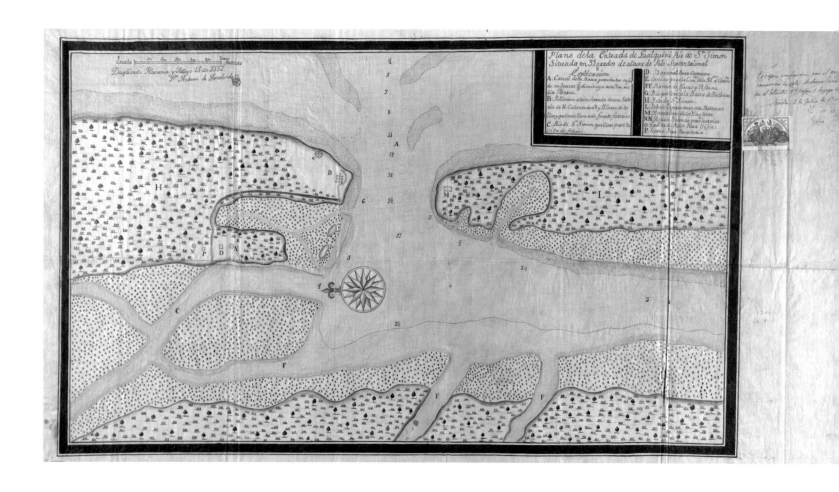

Early map of Jekyll and St. Simons (Courtesy of the Hargrett Rare Book and Manuscript Library / University of Georgia Libraries)

skeleton found in the area is thought to be that of a person of mixed Indian-African ancestry. Only 150 of the 600 colonists are known to have made it back to the Caribbean. The Ayllón colonists and many other Europeans starved to death in North America in part because they were unwilling to eat unfamiliar food. They expected Indians to give them corn, which created shortages for the Indians and sometimes provoked them to kill the demanding Europeans.

Short-lived though it was, the colony could have brought devastating changes to coastal Georgia. Anything imported by the Ayllón settlers, including European diseases, could have spread along the coast and beyond through active trade routes between pre-Columbian chiefdoms. When Hernando de Soto and his conquistadors raged through the Southeast during Soto's expedition of 1539–43, they discovered Spanish items at an Indian village in today's central South Carolina. Some historians theorize that the items came from Quejo's earlier, slave-raiding expeditions, but Soto thought the glass beads, rosaries, and iron axes were from "the government or territory where the lawyer Lucas Vázquez de Ayllón came to his ruin."

Two large towns Soto explored were uninhabited. Indians said that there had been a plague some years earlier and that survivors had moved elsewhere. Such a plague could have come from the Ayllón-Quejo expeditions. Some scholars believe the South Carolina towns were abandoned for other reasons. Indian power centers in the Ancient South shifted constantly, for a variety of reasons: chiefs died or were killed by rivals, territories expanded, elite factions competed for control, and populations increased. Sometimes internal strife prompted an entire village to pick up and move to another chiefdom.

Plants and animals introduced to North America by early Europeans had a major impact on native flora and fauna. The livestock that arrived with Ayllón was probably eaten by the starving settlers, but Soto's expedition traveled with pork on the hoof—more than three hundred pigs, which "multiplied greatly" on the journey. Soto gave breeding pairs to Indian chiefs in Georgia and elsewhere; some of the pigs escaped into the woods. The aggressive razorback hogs of the Deep South are thought to be descendants of stock imported by early Europeans. If Soto's forces left horses behind, the Indians probably killed them. They were terrified when they first saw mounted Spaniards, believing they were half human, half beast.

Following several disastrous Spanish attempts to colonize the continent, Philip II of Spain declared it off-limits to official settlements in 1561. The French were eager to move in. French corsairs were already preying on Spanish treasure ships loaded with gold, silver, and precious stones from the mines of Central and South America. The ships, collectively called the plate fleet, sailed close to the southeastern coast on their voyages home, riding the Gulf Stream north. A coastal settlement would both give the corsairs a base of operations from which to attack the treasure ships and offer a refuge for French Protestants, whose conflicts with Catholics in France were escalating toward war. Jean Ribault, a French naval officer, was chosen to establish Huguenot colonies in La Florida.

Ribault explored the Georgia coast in 1562. He named St. Simons the Île de Loire, after the Loire River in France, and may have come ashore. He established Charlesfort on what is now Parris Island, South Carolina, but about a year after Ribault returned to Europe for supplies, the Charlesfort colonists ran out of food. The desperate settlers sailed back to France, resorting to cannibalism on the voyage. In 1564, Ribault's lieutenant, René de Laudonnière, established a second French colony, Fort Caroline, near the mouth of the St. John's River in northeast Florida.

The Spanish king, incensed that hated French Huguenots were settling land previously claimed by Spain, sent his best sea captain, Pedro Menéndez de Avilés, to drive out the Protestants and establish a permanent Catholic settlement in La Florida. In 1565, Menéndez founded St. Augustine and massacred most of the French, including Ribault, but spared a few Frenchmen who claimed to be Catholic. He also spared a musician and several others who had useful skills. Laudonnière escaped the massacre by hiding in the woods. Menéndez sailed up the coast and founded the Spanish colony of Santa Elena on Parris Island at the site of abandoned Charlesfort. He passed St. Simons regularly on trips up and down the coast.

Soon after Menéndez established St. Augustine and Santa Elena, Spain began sending missionaries to convert the Indians of La Florida to Catholicism. The first Jesuit missionaries were withdrawn after several were killed by Indians. One Jesuit, Domingo Agustín Báez, compiled a grammar of the Guale language while he was based on St. Catherines Island at the mission of Santa Catalina de Guale. It was the first book written in North America. Although mentioned in period documents, the book itself has never been found.

The Franciscans, who followed the Jesuits, were more successful. Over time they established about 150 missions in Georgia and Florida, including one on south St. Simons. The island's Mocama mission was located in an Indian village somewhere between the current locations of the lighthouse and the Sea Island Golf Club. The mission village has never been located, although bits of Indian pottery showing early Spanish influence sometimes turn up in Neptune Park, in south-end neighborhoods, and on south beach.

The Spanish missions became a controversial topic in coastal Georgia in the mid-1920s when the Brunswick historian Mary Letitia Ross and her mentor, Herbert E. Bolton, a professor at the University of California, Berkeley, published their landmark book on Georgia's Spanish colonial history. Until then, little had been known about the Spanish era in Georgia. Most history books began with James Oglethorpe and the founding of Savannah in 1733, ignoring the fact that Spain, by that time, had been the dominant European presence in the Southeast for almost two centuries. By the time the first British settlers arrived in Georgia, St. Simons and the rest of the Southeast had undergone profound and permanent change. For example, the Guale and Mocama had disappeared at least half a century before the beginning of the British period.

The archaeologists Keith Ashley (kneeling on left) of the University of North Florida and Fred Cook (not pictured) of Brunswick, along with volunteers, conducted shovel tests in Neptune Park in 2012, searching for the remains of the island's first Spanish mission, San Buenaventura de Guadalquini, c. 1604.

Tabby ruins in Georgia were misidentified as ruins of Spanish missions. This illustration, published in 1925 in a book about the Georgia missions, was based on the look of Spanish missions in western states. (Illustration by Willis Physioc in *The Spanish Missions of Georgia*, by John Tate Lanning, courtesy of the University of North Carolina Press)

Bolton, Ross's mentor and coauthor, was one of the most prominent and respected historians in the country. His research embraced the Spanish history of the United States, focusing on the western Catholic missions, which Franciscan friars began establishing in 1769, some two hundred years after Spain began building missions in La Florida. Bolton encouraged Ross, his graduate student, to research the Spanish era in Georgia; she was among the first scholars in the United States to examine the state's Spanish past. Ross spent years collecting and pouring through documents from the Archivo General de Indias in Spain, working through an American woman who lived in Seville. Time has proved Ross to be an impeccable researcher who made vital contributions to the field of Georgia's early European history. But an error in *The Debatable Land* (1925), the book she coauthored with Bolton, prompted Ross to vow never to publish again.

In their book, Bolton and Ross identified some of the tabby ruins on the Georgia coast as the remains of Franciscan missions. John Tate Lanning, another brilliant Bolton student, who later taught at Duke University, perpetuated the idea a few years later with a book that included drawings and descriptions of what Georgia's Spanish missions might have looked like. The drawings were inspired by the Franciscan missions of the West, with bell towers, arched walkways, and courtyards.

Tabby ruins of the sugar mill from Elizafield Plantation, north of Brunswick. The ruins were misidentified as the ruins of mission Santo Domingo de Talaje, and a state park of the same name was established at the site. (Photo by Jingle Davis)

National newspapers and magazines, including the *Atlanta Constitution*, the *New York Times*, and *National Geographic*, produced a flurry of feature articles about Georgia's Spanish missions, illustrated with photographs of romantic, moss-draped tabby ruins, which captured the public's imagination. The oyster-shell structures were soon being touted as "a unique asset" that could be exploited to attract tourists and prospective buyers to coastal Georgia. The publicity kicked off a mini land boom in the area. In Glynn County, weathered tabby walls on the Altamaha River west of St. Simons were identified as the ruins of Mission Santo Domingo de Talaje, and the site was soon designated a state park.

But the only Spanish mission identified to date in Georgia is the one on St. Catherines Island. David Hurst Thomas of the American Museum of Natural History, in New York City, has spent several decades leading a team of archaeologists on St. Catherines, discovering and then exploring the remains of Santa Catalina de Guale, the Franciscan mission established there in the late 1500s. Thomas said the books published in the 1920s by Mary Ross and others regarding Spain's Catholic missions in Georgia caused a furor among descendants of early British settlers, who "objected to such a complimentary view" of the

Spanish era in the American Southeast. They considered their Protestant forbears the true founders of the region and the country, according to Thomas.

"Everyone *knows* that America's colonial history began at Roanoke, Plymouth and Jamestown—not at St. Augustine or on the sea islands of Georgia," Thomas writes facetiously in his book *St. Catherines: An Island in Time*. He says the identification of the old tabbies as Spanish mission ruins "positively electrified" the members of the Georgia Society of the Colonial Dames of America. The organization hired a team of experts headed by the noted historian E. Merton Coulter to investigate and refute what they called "the Spanish mission myth." Coulter enlisted the help of Marmaduke Floyd of Savannah and James A. Ford of the Smithsonian Institution, who researched the subject for a decade in the late 1920s and early 1930s. They conducted archaeological studies, reviewed documents, and interviewed coastal residents, whose older relatives had identified the tabbies as sugar mills, cotton barns, and other structures from the antebellum period. The team proved beyond doubt that not a single known tabby ruin in coastal Georgia dated to the mission period, even though the Spanish built with oyster-shell tabby in St. Augustine at the time. The Franciscan missions of the Southeast, however, were apparently all built of wood, thatch, and other materials that rotted away over time.

Tourist promoters, developers, and governmental officials were outraged to hear that Georgia's tabby ruins were not Spanish mission remains. When Floyd helped prove that the Glynn County ruins being promoted as the Mission Santa Domingo de Talaje were actually the remains of Elizafield Plantation, he was fired from his job with the state. Members of the Georgia Society of the Colonial Dames of America were vindicated, at least as far as the tabby ruins were concerned.

Ross and Bolton were harshly criticized and even ridiculed for their error. Bolton weathered the storm in faraway California, but Ross, a Glynn County native, was crushed. She believed she had ruined her own reputation as a researcher; even worse, she was sure she had tarnished the reputation of the mentor she revered. She retreated to her home in Brunswick and continued her scholarly research for another thirty years, but she kept her vow and never published another word. After her death, her valuable papers were collected in the Georgia Department of Archives and History, now located in Morrow. A waterfront park in downtown Brunswick is named in her honor.

The only Spanish mission found to date in coastal Georgia is the one Thomas unearthed on St. Catherines, but there is ample documentary evidence that a number of others were established on the mainland and the sea islands, including St. Simons.

The only "myth" about Spanish missions in Georgia was the erroneous identification of the tabby ruins as mission remains. In 2012, the archaeologist Keith Ashley of the University of North Florida and Fred Cook, along with a team of volunteers, made a number of shovel tests in Neptune Park on south St. Simons in search of the remains of San Buenaventura de Guadalquini. They found bits of Indian pottery showing Spanish influence in the park, as well as period potsherds in a nearby neighborhood. Perhaps someday a full-scale dig will determine the location of the church and other mission structures on St. Simons.

The island's mission was called San Buenaventura de Guadalquini because the Spanish traditionally named missions in honor of the saint whose day was celebrated when the first Mass was said, indicating the St. Simons mission was established on July 14, Saint Buenaventura's day. The last part of the name usually reflected the name of the mission village—in this case, Guadalquini. Guadalquini referred also to the island itself, the village chief, and the sound between St. Simons and Jekyll. Although earlier researchers identified neighboring Jekyll Island as Guadalquini and believed the mission was sited there, smaller Jekyll never had a mission because it never had a significant Indian population.

The majority of what we know today about the Guale and Mocama Indians native to coastal Georgia comes from archaeological explorations and documents written by Spanish friars, chroniclers, explorers, bureaucrats, mapmakers, and even shipwreck victims in the early years after contact. We have a record of the Timucua language and some of its dialects, including Mocama, because the dialects were translated into Spanish by a talented Franciscan friar, Francisco Pareja, who lived for decades at a Mocama mission on St. George Island in northern Florida. Pareja wrote a *Confessionario* (1613) and other treatises in Timucua for the friars to use in converting the Indians to Catholicism, hearing their confessions, and involving them in the rituals of the Catholic Church. Much of the *Confessionario* was designed to ferret out Indian beliefs and customs the Franciscans believed to be inspired by the devil. The friars were instructed to ask the Indians whether they "first made a prayer using tobacco" before every hunt, a practice of which the Franciscans strongly disapproved. The Indians were questioned about asking their shamans to pray over the first fish they caught, the first deer they killed, the first wild berries of the season, and the first of the corn crop, all customs the friars wanted to eradicate. Although the lengthy *Confessionario* was designed to strip the Mocama of traditional beliefs and customs, it provides a rich trove of information on Indian culture.

Indians on the Georgia coast played variations of a violent game called chunkey with chunkey stones similar to these.

Life changed quickly for Indians at the missions. They farmed instead of roaming the woods and waterways in search of natural food. They became more sedentary, spending hours learning prayers and receiving religious instruction. Indian men from every mission village were regularly conscripted to work for the Spanish in St. Augustine by growing crops, building roads and bridges, caring for cattle and other livestock, and training with the soldiers.

Although little is known about the daily life of the coastal Indians, an eyewitness account of Guales who lived in a soon-to-be-missionized village a few miles from St. Simons was provided by a Spanish teenager, Andrés de Segura, who later became a monk and took the name Andrés de San Miguel. He was shipwrecked on the Georgia coast in 1595 after a harrowing adventure at sea. Segura was about sixteen when he boarded a ship in Spain to seek adventure in the New World. The trip went well until a storm struck on the return voyage, two years later. The ship was damaged and in danger of sinking. After the only lifeboat was hijacked by a group of sailors, the other passengers persuaded the ship's caulker to build a boat with wood from the ship's superstructure. The resulting craft was, in Segura's words, "a long box, tall and narrow."

The leaky box was barely seaworthy. It was so unstable that the thirty men on board were afraid to move their heads for fear of capsizing. After bobbing around in the Atlantic for ten days with almost no food or water, Segura and his companions washed ashore on a small island near the mouth of the Altamaha River. He described the island in his narrative: "The soil is sandy and level and covered with tall pines and live oaks and with palm trees like those of Andalucía." Segura said he later learned the landing place was called Reynosa Island. There is no island by that name on the Georgia coast today, and no other mention of it appears. Some speculate that the island might have been Little St. Simons, Sea Island, or Wolf Island, although Wolf today is a marsh island with a narrow, treeless sand spit facing the Atlantic.

After digging a shallow beach well for fresh water and eating oysters, palm shoots, and foliage for more than a week, the castaways were rescued by Guale Indians from the mainland village of Asajo, or Asao, near today's Darien, about fifteen miles northwest of St. Simons. The village chief, Don Domingo, spoke Spanish and was about eighteen, the same age as Segura. The teenagers got along well. Don Domingo and Don Mateo, the mico of the neighboring village of Talaje, were brothers whose towns were visited often by Franciscan friars. A few months after Segura's stay, Friar Francisco de Veráscola began building the mission of Santo Domingo de Asajo-Talaje in Don Domingo's village.

Decades later, the mission was moved to the north end of St. Simons. Some scholars now believe that Don Domingo was the ringleader of the rebellion two years later that radically changed Guale chiefdoms on the Georgia coast.

In his adventure story, Segura wrote about the days the shipwrecked Spaniards spent in Asajo, which would have been similar to other early postcontact Indian villages in coastal Georgia, both Guale and Mocama. He enjoyed the Indian corn cakes, toasted in ashes and "two fingers thick," but was not a fan of red and yellow acorn cakes, because they were bitter. In addition, the Guales served the Spaniards a thick gruel of parched corn the Spanish called *atole*, which is still popular in Mexico today. The Spanish had to barter for familiar European food. The fair-minded Segura hesitated to trade "things of little value," such as two needles, for an imported Castilian chicken, but he did.

Don Domingo gave the Spaniards the best accommodations in town. He put them in the *jacal*, a large round council house with a long bench for seating and sleeping built around the circumference. The jacal was constructed of tall pines, their thicker ends buried for stability and their slender tips joined together at the top "like the ribs of a parasol." The council house was large enough to accommodate three hundred people, but the doorway was so small that adults had to stoop low to pass through. Segura said the entry was covered at night with palm fronds to keep out the cold. A small fire made of two sticks heated the structure enough to make the visitors sweat.

Council houses were the hearts of Indian villages. The chief and other leaders met there daily to discuss politics and village business, redistribute stored food during times of need, make weapons and tools, and drink cassina, the ceremonial black drink of Indians throughout the Southeast. Dances, feasts, and ceremonies were held in the council houses, echoing those held in the center of Late Archaic shell rings thousands of years earlier. Council house seating was hierarchical, with the loftiest place going to the chief and the next-best occupied by village elders according to rank. Others sat wherever they could, usually on the floor.

Indian leaders in Don Mateo's village entertained the visitors with a version of the violent ball game called chunkey, which was popular across North America. The game began when the chief hurled a heavy chunkey stone "with all his strength" down a flat course. The chief and other village leaders raced after the stone, throwing spears "all at one time and without any order." Segura thought the player whose spear came closest to the rolling stone scored, although the object in many chunkey games was to throw the

The Black Drink Ceremony

The black drink ceremony, a purification ritual, was vital to the beliefs of southeastern Indians, who drank large quantities of cassina and vomited it up. (Etching by Theodor de Bry)

INDIAN WOMEN gathered and toasted the highly caffeinated leaves of yaupon holly, *Ilex vomitoria*, a shrubby tree with bright red berries that grows wild along the southern coast. They covered the parched leaves with boiling water and steeped them like tea leaves to make the drink the Indians called *asi* or *cassina*. Coastal Indians traded the prized cassina leaves with inland chiefdoms, along with ceremonial cups made from large whelk shells. Honored visitors like Segura were offered the black drink, but it was served only to Indian men of high social standing, those who had distinguished themselves in hunting, games, or battle. Women, children, and lower-ranking men did not drink cassina.

The historian and anthropologist Charles Hudson considers the ritual use of cassina one of the defining characteristics of southeastern Indians. Hudson notes that purity was of vital importance to the Indians. High-ranking adult males took great pains to keep themselves in a state of ritual purity because anything attempted by an impure Indian was doomed to failure. Indian men were forbidden to eat certain foods or to have contact with menstruating women. Indians thought witches sometimes contaminated their food. They believed the ritual drinking of cassina was an essential part of maintaining purity.

Experts say that properly brewed cassina tastes much like coffee or Asian tea and is not emetic unless it is drunk rapidly, hot, and in large quantities. (Water can be emetic if consumed the same way.) *Ilex vomitoria* looks identical to *Ilex paraguayensis*, the species used today to brew maté, a popular caffeinated drink in Central and South America.

spear where the player thought the stone would stop. Play continued until the Indians were exhausted and dripping with sweat.

Segura witnessed one of the famed black-drink ceremonies after the game. The event followed prescribed steps as fixed and formal as those of a Japanese tea ceremony.

In the black-drink ceremony that Segura witnessed, everyone gathered in the council house. A wide-mouthed jar of cassina was placed at the feet of a carved figure painted with red ochre. Around the jar were two-liter pots filled with cassina. Segura wrote:

> Each Indian took one of these in his hand, and with reverence, they went about giving it to those who had played [chunkey], who were each seated on a bench. Each took one and drank his. As a result of this their bellies became like a drum and as they went on drinking, their bellies kept on growing and swelling. They carried this on calmly for awhile . . . when we saw that, on opening their mouths with very great calmness, each one began ejecting by way of [their mouths] a great stream of water as clear as it was when they drank it.

Segura added that the tribal leaders then knelt and spread the liquid with their hands, although he does not explain why. The vomiting was due to the quantity of liquid consumed, not from some toxin in the beverage.

Indians and many Spaniards drank smaller quantities of cassina every day for the caffeine kick and to prevent kidney stones. Segura drank it during his stay in St. Augustine. Although it smelled like lye water, it did not taste bad, he wrote. He predicted, however, that cassina would "never serve as a real treat like chocolate."

Segura was intrigued by the Indians' clothing. Guale men did not tan the hides for their deerskin loincloths, but instead rubbed them with their hands and long sharp fingernails until the skins were soft and supple. Indian women made their garments of Spanish moss. *Tillandsia usneoides* is one of the signature plants of St. Simons and the southern coast. An epiphyte, it is neither a Spanish import nor a moss. The long gray strands hanging like scraps of tattered lace from trees, fences, and utility wires get their nutrients from rainwater and air. Indians used Spanish moss for cushioning, as absorbent pads for babies' diapers and women's menses, and for braiding into cord. Warriors made fire arrows by wrapping the shafts with the dried plant. When Indians built walls with wattle and daub, they mixed the clay with Spanish moss to keep it from cracking. Before the Civil War, slaves on coastal plantations made a medicinal tea for asthma from Spanish moss. Well into the twentieth century, it was used to stuff mattresses and pad upholstery for automobile seats. Jonathan Dickinson, a shipwrecked Quaker who saw Spanish moss garments in the late 1600s, commented on their appearance: "Women natives clothe themselves with the moss of trees, making gowns and petticoats thereof, which at a distance, or in the night, look very neat." Dickinson failed to report what Spanish moss gowns and petticoats looked like up close in broad daylight.

Pre-Columbian women on the sea islands made knee-length Spanish moss garments that fastened over one shoulder, leaving a breast bare. After the arrival of the missionaries, the garments were probably redesigned to be more modest; Segura noted that they covered women from the neck to the ground. Scholars say the moss was most likely pounded to make a feltlike cloth for the garments.

Indian women smoked their Spanish moss clothing over herb-scented fires to perfume the garments and perhaps give them magical properties, although those might not have been their primary objectives. As every southerner knows, red bugs, also called chiggers, are ubiquitous in Spanish moss. Their bites itch for weeks, and the standard remedy, coating the bites with nail polish to smother the chiggers, is useless except as a

Indian women made clothing from Spanish moss. (Etching by Theodor de Bry)

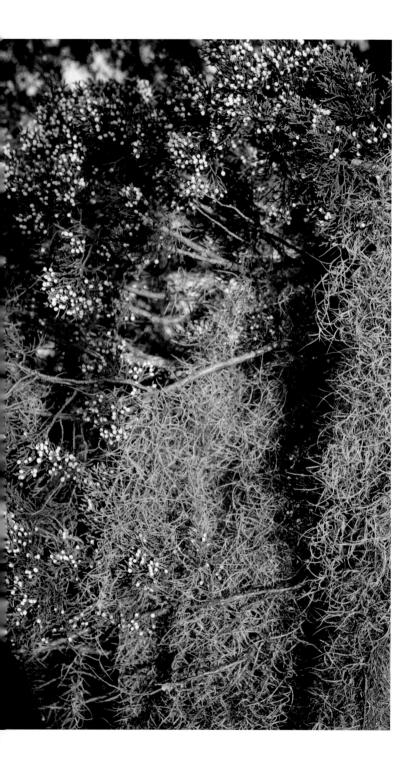

placebo. Enzymes in red bug saliva create straw-like structures through which the creatures suck up liquefied tissue. The straw, called a stylostome, causes the itching and remains long after the chigger is gone. The main reason for smoking the Spanish moss garments may have been to roast the resident red bugs.

Segura and his shipwrecked companions left the village of Asajo in early May 1595, stopped for lunch on Reynosa Island, then headed toward St. Augustine. They traveled in large Indian canoes, accompanied by the village chiefs Don Domingo and Don Mateo, who were to be baptized in the Spanish town. They stopped at the Mocama mission village of San Pedro on Cumberland Island, where they stayed for about two weeks. There, Segura met the *mico mayor*, or principal chief, of the Mocama province, whose Spanish name was Don Juan Sanchez. His wife, Segura wrote, wore a cloak "like a Spanish lady."

The chief had been away. When he returned, the Indians began wailing in high voices to welcome him back. The wailing continued as everyone proceeded to the council house, which Segura noted was larger than Asajo's and had a skylight. The Indians knelt before their chief and continued wailing. Don Juan "listened with great calmness and seriousness until, from fatigue, he got up and left." At that point, the wailers too got up, dried their tears, and left, obligations fulfilled. In St. Augustine, Segura heard Indians wailing every afternoon because their chief had died. "They had to cry for a whole year," he remarked.

Two years after Segura was shipwrecked on coastal Georgia, Indians staged an uprising that left five Franciscan friars and many Guales dead. The Guale chiefdom changed profoundly after the uprising. Villages were abandoned and new ones established. Tolomato, the former seat of power, was never rebuilt. Indians from other chiefdoms moved into the northern part of Guale territory, and the hereditary successors to the Guale chiefdom at Tolomato were all killed. Traditional accounts say Juanillo, who was next in line to become the mico mayor of the Guale, led the uprising after the mission friar demanded he give up

Spanish moss is neither Spanish nor a moss.

his multiple wives. When he refused, the mission friar, Pedro de Corpa, denied him the position of mico mayor. Juanillo is said to have left Tolomato and returned later with Indians adorned with red war paint and feather bonnets, and armed with bows and arrows and heavy clubs, to kill the friar and four others at missions north of the Altamaha River. Then the raiders paddled south to Cumberland Island to attack the Mocama mission, but were driven back by Indians loyal to the Spanish.

Historians have reported that Friar Francisco de Veráscola was killed on St. Simons at the Guale mission of Santo Domingo de Asajo, but there was no mission on the island at the time of the rebellion. Although Santo Domingo de Asajo-Talaje was moved to the north end of St. Simons more than half a century later, the mission was originally in Don Domingo's village near Darien. The five murdered Franciscans, now called the Georgia Martyrs, have been nominated for sainthood because of their defense of monogamous marriage. The Vatican is considering the petition.

Researchers in recent years have discovered documents suggesting the uprising had more to do with Indian politics and a struggle for power and land than with Juanillo's polygamy. There is evidence that non-Guale Indians from chiefdoms in South Carolina and inland Georgia participated in what is usually called the Guale Uprising or the Juanillo Rebellion.

The historian J. Michael Francis and his former graduate student Kathleen Kole, who examined documents from the Archivo General de Indias in Seville, theorized that Corpa and the other friars were killed because they meddled in Indian politics. After the uprising, there was a scramble to fill the position of mico mayor that Juanillo had been due to inherit. Even the Mocama chief on Cumberland made an unsuccessful bid, although he had no legitimate claim to an inherited Guale title. Neither did Don Domingo, the mico of Asajo who had rescued Segura and his shipwrecked companions a few years earlier. But Francis and Kole speculate that Don Domingo may have engineered the uprising and arranged to blame Juanillo in order to become principal chief of the Guale himself.

After the five friars were murdered, Spanish reprisals against the Guale were severe. The governor ordered his troops to "seize [Guale] canoes in which they go about the islands for food, and burn their villages and cut down their maize and other crops, and capture some of them." Guale on the sea islands fled to the mainland, hiding in woods and swamps for several years while Spanish soldiers destroyed their villages, cornfields, and granaries, and blocked their access to seafood resources. In the famine that followed, which coincided with a drought, a number of Guale died, and all suffered.

Two years later, a handful of Guale leaders traveled to St. Augustine and petitioned the governor for amnesty for themselves and other village chiefs, including Don Domingo. They did not, however, speak on behalf of Juanillo. The governor, eager by then to reestablish peaceful relations with the Guale, granted their request. He wrote to the Spanish king, Philip III, blaming Juanillo for the uprising and murders. Juanillo's conflict with Friar de Corpa over the former's polygamy gave the governor an easy explanation for the troubles.

There is more evidence implicating Don Domingo as the rebellion's leader than Juanillo, according to Francis and Kole. Don Domingo was identified by other Guale as the leader of the uprising. After he was granted amnesty, Don Domingo volunteered to track down Juanillo and twenty-two kinsmen and bring them to St. Augustine to be punished. Instead, he had them all killed. Don Domingo scalped Juanillo himself and forced the female relatives of Juanillo's kinsmen to scalp their loved ones in front of their children. After eliminating or intimidating any Guale with a legitimate claim to become principal chief, Don Domingo successfully petitioned the Spanish governor to award him the title.

After peace was restored in the early 1600s, the Franciscans rebuilt the Guale missions north of the Altamaha River and established San Buenaventura de Guadalquini on south St. Simons sometime around 1604. It was the northernmost of the Mocama missions. With some exceptions, the Georgia missions operated in relative tranquility for the next half century. Indian populations continued to plummet as smallpox, chicken pox, measles, and other common European diseases to which the Indians had no immunity swept through the Southeast. Some Indian towns lost 90 percent of their population to disease. In 1656, La Florida's governor observed that few Indians were left in either the Mocama or Guale provinces because of "plagues."

At the same time, marauding bands of British-sponsored Chichimeco Indians, also called Westo or Ricahecrian, began attacking interior chiefdoms in Georgia and kidnapping Indians to sell as slaves in Virginia. The attacks were vicious. The Chichimeco tortured, butchered, and burned Indians alive and enslaved hundreds more. Their reputation as cannibals terrified other Indians, especially those not affiliated with Europeans. Survivors of ravaged interior chiefdoms fled to the lower Carolina coast, where they became known as Yamasees. In 1661, British and Indian slave raiders took aim at the missions of coastal Georgia. On July 20, a massive force paddled down the Altamaha River and swept like a flood over the Guale mission of Santo Domingo de Asajo-Talaje,

which probably embraced both villages where Segura and his shipwrecked companions had taken refuge more than half a century earlier. The survivors fled downriver to Sapelo Island. They were pursued by the Chichimeco, who built a boat with wood from the mission church, but the makeshift craft sank and all aboard drowned, according to accounts of the time.

The Franciscans relocated the surviving Indians of Santo Domingo de Asajo-Talaje to the north end of St. Simons, giving the new mission the name Santo Domingo de Asajo and causing a great deal of confusion for later scholars. As the slave raids continued, two groups of unmissionized Indians fled to St. Simons for protection. One pagan settlement, San Simón, was occupied by refugee Yamasee Indians from the Georgia interior. It was located on the island's western shore, probably at the site where the fortified British town of Frederica was later founded, in an "Indian old field." The British anglicized the settlement's Spanish name to St. Simons and adopted it as the name for the island as well. Yamasee Indians also occupied the other refugee village, Ocotonico, a few miles south of San Simón. The four island missions, occupied by Indians from different chiefdoms, apparently coexisted over the next few years in peace. By that time, the Indians may have had neither the inclination nor the strength to fight one another.

After the British founded Charles Town in 1670, raids on Georgia's coastal missions intensified. English forces and their Indian allies attacked the refugee mission of San Simón, but were driven off by island Indians and Spanish soldiers. In 1684, pirates sacked and burned the old Mocama mission of San Buenaventura de Guadalquini, which had stood on the south end of St. Simons for some eighty years.

Georgia's Spanish mission period was over. Less than two hundred years after Columbus landed in the Americas, the Indians native to the Georgia coast were gone. Some of the Guale joined bands of Yamasees; most moved south with the Spanish and Mocama. After the missions were abandoned, coastal Georgia was never again occupied by its indigenous people.

The Spanish relocated the refugee Indians to northern Florida, closer to the soldiers in St. Augustine. A settlement populated in part by Mocamas from St. Simons was called Santa Cruz y San Buenaventura de Guadalquini. The remains of the mission were located in recent years on Black Hammock Island, near Jacksonville, and are still being investigated. The site is now part of the Timucuan Ecological and Historic Preserve, which is managed by the National Park Service.

Because they were directly in the path of European exploration and expansion, the Indians of coastal Georgia and Florida suffered more from contact than any other natives of mainland North America. (It should be noted that many Indian groups in the Caribbean were exterminated also, and sooner.) The Timucua were the first to encounter Europeans when Ponce de León landed on the northern Florida coast in 1513. They also have the sad distinction of being the first mainland North American Indians to become extinct. A handful of Guales retreated to Cuba, along with the Spanish, after the signing of the Treaty of Paris in 1763, which ceded the Georgia coast, among other lands, to Great Britain. The last known full-blooded Timucua joined the retreat. He died on the Caribbean island, far from his ancestral home.

Tomochichi

AFTER THE SPANISH MISSIONARIES and indigenous Indians fled coastal Georgia in the late 1600s, St. Simons was probably unoccupied for a time. Other Indian groups eventually moved to the coast, including one whose leader, Tomochichi, formed his small Yamacraw chiefdom from Lower Creek and Yamasee Indians.

By the time Oglethorpe and a group of trustees founded the Georgia colony in 1733, Tomochichi had dealt with Europeans for decades and had no reason to trust them. English traders from Carolina and Virginia routinely cheated Indians when they traded for deerskins. Tomochichi, who was perhaps in his nineties, and Oglethorpe, in his thirties, spoke different languages and were culturally poles apart. But Tomochichi agreed to allow Oglethorpe to settle Savannah on Yamacraw Bluff overlooking the Savannah River and later helped Oglethorpe negotiate a treaty by which the powerful Lower Creek confederation granted most of coastal Georgia, including St. Simons, to the British "as far inland as the tide flowed." Tomochichi traveled the length of the Georgia coast with Oglethorpe to show the general the extent of the grant.

Perhaps Tomochichi believed the idealistic general's pledge to treat the Yamacraw fairly, but he was also a pragmatic man. He understood the vulnerability of his small Indian band and probably thought his people would benefit by being allied with the powerful British Empire. Oglethorpe carried a message from Tomochichi to the trustees, saying the chief hoped the British would "love and protect [our] little families."

Oglethorpe honored the chief by taking him, along with his wife, his nephew and successor Toonahowee, his war chief Hyllispilli, and other Yamacraw Indians, to England, where they were treated as royalty. Court followers were shocked when tattooed Indian men, dressed only in loincloths, were introduced to the king and queen. Oglethorpe persuaded the Indians to don English-style garments for subsequent appearances—Tomochichi and his wife, Senauki, dressed in scarlet clothing trimmed with gold—but a British magazine reported that "their Faces were variously painted after their Country manner." While they were in England, an artist painted the well-known portrait of Tomochichi and his nephew. The portrait shows the dignified old chief, his face covered with ceremonial tattoos befitting his rank. Toonahowee holds an eagle, also a symbol of high rank. After the group returned to America, the British acquired most of the Georgia sea islands, but the Lower Creek kept Ossabaw,

The Yamacraw chief Tomochichi and his nephew and successor, Toonahowee (Courtesy of the Hargrett Rare Book and Manuscript Library / University of Georgia Libraries)

St. Catherines, and Sapelo as hunting islands. The treaty specified that the British would punish traders who destroyed Indian property or defrauded Indians after promising fair prices for trade goods.

After Oglethorpe founded the fortified town of Frederica on St. Simons, Tomochichi, Toonahowee, and Hyllispilli were frequent visitors, often bringing fresh game to the settlers and soldiers. When Tomochichi learned that his first gifts of game had been distributed unfairly, he divided subsequent offerings himself to make sure everyone benefited. The Indians shared their material possessions; selfish Indians were shamed and shunned.

Tomochichi was suffering from alcoholism when he died in 1739. Oglethorpe buried the great chief with honors in the center of Wright Square, one of Savannah's lovely green spaces. In accordance with Indian custom, Tomochichi's grave was marked with a simple pyramid of stones. The stones were removed from his grave in 1883, and a monument was erected to honor a white man: William Washington Gordon, a prominent Georgia attorney, politician, and businessman who was the grandfather of Juliette Gordon Low, the founder of the Girl Scouts of America. Gordon was best known for organizing the Georgia Central Banking and Railroad Company. During railroad construction, workers degraded and destroyed a number of important burial and ceremonial sites of the Lower Creek. It is ironic that the old chief's bones now lie beneath a monument to the man whose railroad violated so many sacred places of Tomochichi's birth confederation. In the late 1800s, Indians got little respect from white Americans, many of whom supported the government's notion that Indians were savages who should be confined on reservations.

Gordon's daughter-in-law, Nellie Kensie Gordon, tried to remedy the destruction of Tomochichi's monument. In 1899, she and other members of the Georgia Society of the Colonial Dames of America marked a corner of Wright Square with a granite boulder and a bronze plaque that reads: "In memory of Tomochichi, the mico of the Yamacraws, the companion of Oglethorpe and the friend and ally of the colony of Georgia."

CHAPTER II   British and American Time

[1736–1775]

FOR MORE THAN FORTY YEARS after pirates sacked the San Buenaventura de Guadalquini mission in 1684 and the Spanish moved the survivors to northern Florida, St. Simons remained either unoccupied or sparsely populated by Indian groups. In 1736, three years after establishing the Georgia colony in Savannah, General James Edward Oglethorpe brought a group of soldiers and settlers, along with the Anglican ministers John and Charles Wesley, from England to St. Simons Island to build the fortified town of Frederica. Its primary role was to act as a buffer against the Spanish in Florida, protecting British settlements farther north, but Oglethorpe, a nobleman, idealist, and philanthropist, envisioned Georgia also as a place where poor people from the British Isles could succeed and prosper, and as a refuge for Protestants fleeing religious persecution from Catholics in Europe. Oglethorpe originally planned to settle the colony with inmates of English debtors' prisons—one of the general's closest friends had died in such a place—but so many other "deserving poor" and paying passengers applied that there was no room for imprisoned debtors. Mary Musgrove, the famed Creek-Scots woman who played a major role in the founding of Georgia, lived for a time at Frederica, as did the flamboyant and mysterious Christian

45

Fort Frederica was ideally situated on the western shore of St. Simons on the Frederica River.

Georgia's founder, General James Edward Oglethorpe, established the fortified town of Frederica in 1736. (From *The History of Castillo de San Marcos and Fort Matanzas from Contemporary Narratives and Letters* [Washington, D.C.: National Park Service, 1945])

Priber, who billed himself as the "Prime Minister of Paradise." Oglethorpe settled a group of German-speaking religious refugees on the eastern side of St. Simons. Life at Frederica proved to be very different for the colonists and Oglethorpe from what the general had imagined. Nonetheless, he succeeded in his mission to protect British settlements, defeating the Spanish in a famous conflict called the Battle of Bloody Marsh, fought on St. Simons in 1742. After the departure of Oglethorpe and the soldiers and settlers, St. Simons was abandoned for a time. The island probably served as a stop on the first Underground Railroad as escaped slaves from plantations in the Carolinas traveled by boat down the coast to better lives in Spanish Florida. During the American Revolution, the tiny Georgia navy fought British warships in the Frederica River in a battle colorfully nicknamed the " Debacle at Raccoon Gut." After the revolution, live oak timbers were cut on St. Simons to build the first ships of the U.S. Navy.

When Oglethorpe arrived on St. Simons, he believed the people he and the trustees had handpicked to come to Georgia would be able to pull themselves out of poverty by staying sober and working as farmers, artisans, and tradespeople. To help the colonists steer clear of temptation, internal conflict, and sloth, the leaders banned rum to discourage drunkenness, Catholics and Frenchmen to deter strife, and slavery to ensure the colonists employment. Colonists were barred from acquiring large tracts of land, a measure intended to forestall the establishment of large plantations; Oglethorpe and the trustees did not want Georgia to become another South Carolina, the neighboring slave colony ruled by wealthy aristocrats.

The leaders thought Georgia could produce commodities such as wine and silk to export cheaply to Great Britain; imported silk cost the British half a million pounds a year. Oglethorpe planted thousands of white mulberry trees on St. Simons to feed the silkworms, but there is no indication that silk was ever produced on the island. A community of Salzburgers—Lutheran religious refugees from Austria—settled near Savannah and produced thousands of pounds of silk over five or six decades after the founding of the colony, but the business was never a commercial success. Georgia silk was used to make a dress for the British queen, probably to publicize the fledgling industry. Late frosts, low wages, and inferior silkworms all contributed to the demise of colonial silk production, as did the later legalization of slavery, which made other enterprises more profitable. Although Georgia silk was said to be as fine as any produced in Italy or China, commercial silk was last exported from Savannah in 1790.

Although Oglethorpe planned for a group of the Salzburgers to settle on St. Simons, they declined to come: Frederica was a military colony, and their religion forbade them

The tabby remains
of the entry to the
soldiers' barracks at
Fort Frederica

to bear arms. The general sent them to Ebenezer, a town west of Savannah founded by
an earlier group of Salzburgers. Oglethorpe found another group of German-speaking
refugees willing to settle on St. Simons and fight, if necessary, in behalf of Great Britain.
They formed their community, German Village, opposite Frederica on the east side
of the island. Living conditions were probably slightly better there than at Frederica
because German Village was exposed to sea breezes, which helped keep the summer heat
and bugs at bay. The bulk of the island sheltered the village from the cold, northwest
winter winds that sweep across the marshes between St. Simons and the mainland.

Oglethorpe chose an ideal location for the fort. Ships had to round sharp river bends
as they neared the bluff where the fortified town was established. Enemy ships would
come in range of British guns before they could turn broadside and fire their own cannons. When the general and the first settlers and soldiers arrived on St. Simons, the
land on the bluff had already been cleared. The site was an old Indian field, probably
the former location of San Simón, the Spanish refugee settlement for non-missionized
Indians established in the late 1600s. The English speakers with Oglethorpe anglicized
the settlement's name to St. Simons and adopted it for the entire island. The British

Tabby

TABBY IS A unique and durable building material that evolved with the Spanish occupation of the southeastern coast in the 1500s. It was probably North America's first masonry, predating concrete made with Portland cement by centuries. There is no natural surface stone on the Georgia sea islands, and bricks in early America were expensive and hard to transport. The raw materials for tabby were freely available: dried oyster shells from old Indian mounds, fresh water from springs and rain-fed ponds, and salt-free sand from inland dunes or the banks of freshwater rivers. At Frederica, tabby makers burned bushels of oyster shells in log-cabin-like structures called ricks, some as big as boxcars, to create an ashy lime that hardened on contact with water. Sand and whole or crushed oyster shells were used as aggregate. The mixture, poured wet into wooden forms, dried into tabby, durable enough to withstand storms, fire, rot, termites, and even cannonballs. Although original tabby was skimmed with a lime topcoat to protect it from weathering and to give it a more refined, stone-like appearance, the topcoat wears off over time, leaving rough tabby walls in variegated shades of buff and gray that blend perfectly with the island environment of Spanish moss and foggy mornings. Old tabby is often colonized by resurrection ferns, colorful lichens, and other native plants.

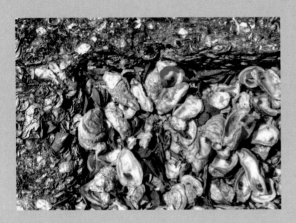

Tabby is a unique coastal building material made from oyster shells, sand, water, and shells burned to make lime.

The word *tabby* may derive from the Spanish term *tapia*, meaning a wall of pounded earth. Royal tapia contained small amounts of lime to harden the pounded earth. The Spanish refined the process in Florida, adding larger quantities of burned-shell lime. The British further adapted the process and anglicized the name to *tabby*. Tabby cats, with their light- and dark-gray-striped coats, are not named for the masonry, or vice versa, although the form boards used in old tabby construction do create a striped effect. Tabby cats are thought to be named for a centuries-old striped silk called *tabi* made in the Middle East.

general laid out the fortress in a star shape, with four bastions surrounded by a moat; dirt piled up as a rampart was topped with a palisade of cedar posts. The builders planted the rampart with turf in order to keep it from washing away in the island's semitropical downpours. The general described the moat as a "wet ditch," but tide gates leading to the river allowed it to be flooded. The moat and ramparts were soon expanded to encompass the entire town. Frederica's main fortifications and many of the colonists' houses were built of tabby, including the crenellated riverfront bastion and the two-story entrance to the soldiers' barracks. Both military structures still stand after more than 275 years.

At Frederica, Oglethorpe built his only house in America of tabby. He named it Orange Hall for the Seville orange trees planted on the property, which lay outside the walls of the fortified town. Since Oglethorpe was the first British governor of colonial

Georgia, some historians consider Orange Hall Georgia's first governor's mansion. But long before and even during Oglethorpe's tenure as the colony's governor (1732–43), the Spanish still claimed St. Simons as part of La Florida. The first Spanish governor's residence in St. Augustine predated Orange Hall by centuries. At any rate, Oglethorpe's tabby cottage was hardly a mansion. The egalitarian general ate the same plain food as his soldiers and slept by campfires with them, wrapped in his plaid wool kilt. Thomas Spalding, whose father later purchased Orange Hall, described the St. Simons house where he grew up as a modest cottage on an oak-shaded plot that included a garden and an orchard of oranges, figs, and grapes.

After building Frederica's fortifications, Oglethorpe spent most of his time establishing military outposts along the coast between St. Simons and Spanish Florida. He built forts on Georgia's Cumberland and Jekyll Islands and on Amelia Island on the northern Florida coast. He built a second fort on St. Simons, just east of where the island's lighthouse stands today. Fort St. Simons was made of earth piled up in a horseshoe shape, its parapet lined with barrels of prickly pears armed with sharp spines. To link Fort St. Simons to Fort Frederica, Oglethorpe built Military Road, also called King's Highway, although it hardly deserved the regal name. Just wide enough for two men to walk abreast, the road left Frederica, crossed the island, and ran south, skirting the marshes on the east side of St. Simons. The exact location of the eight-mile-long road is unknown, but some islanders say Demere Road south of the Bloody Marsh Monument roughly follows the same path.

Oglethorpe rushed to complete his coastal defenses because he knew a Spanish attack might come at any time. Although Spain and England were not at war in 1736 when Frederica was founded, relations between the two countries had been contentious for decades as both struggled for control of the New World. As the general prepared for war, he tried to keep the peace with his European neighbors to the south. When his friend and ally Tomochichi showed up at Frederica with his formidable war chief Hyllispilli and a group of Yamacraw warriors, Oglethorpe talked the chief out of attacking Indians in Florida to avenge an earlier attack by Florida Indians on the Yamacraw. Oglethorpe knew the British would be blamed if Tomochichi's British-affiliated warriors attacked Spanish-affiliated Indians.

The powder magazine at Fort Frederica, now a National Historic Monument managed by the National Park Service

Because of his military duties, Oglethorpe was often absent from St. Simons, where the colonists struggled to make a new life in a strange land. Conditions at Frederica were nearly intolerable in the first few years, especially for people accustomed to cooler

European climes. Until the settlers could build houses, they camped in primitive huts called booths, made of a pole framework thatched with palmetto fronds. Rattlesnakes coiled in the dense palmetto thickets where they harvested material for the thatch. They had to bathe in the brackish Frederica River early in the morning before the alligators were active. They fought an unending battle with deerflies, mosquitoes, and the ubiquitous sand gnats they called "merry-wings," which left them covered with red bites they grimly referred to as American chicken pox. Cattle ate their corn and trampled their gardens. Even their sheep were intractable, prompting a colonist to complain they were "not sheep but devils." Oglethorpe had advised building a pen for the animals before they arrived by boat, but the colonists thought the sheep could graze unfettered, as flocks did on the English commons. Instead, the sheep bolted into the woods "as wild as bucks" as soon as they were unloaded.

Added to the colonists' physical discomfort was the stress of living in a dangerous area. Frederica, the southernmost British fort in colonial America, was built on a stretch of coastal Georgia called the Debatable Land, which was claimed by both Spain and England. There were constant rumors at Frederica of an impending Spanish attack. Whenever a boat appeared on the horizon, the colonists stayed in an uproar until the ship was either identified as friendly or sailed out of sight.

Although harsh conditions and Spanish threats took their toll on Frederica's residents, contentious settlers created even more problems for their neighbors and for Oglethorpe, who disliked adjudicating civic disputes. The general, more accustomed to giving orders than arbitrating disagreements, complained he had more trouble with the eighty colonists at Frederica than he did with the entire Spanish Armada. Because of the troublemakers, some of the most productive settlers left town for good, including Samuel Davison, the constable and alehouse owner whose house shared a common wall with that of Thomas and Beatre Hawkins. Hawkins was Oglethorpe's regimental surgeon; his favored remedies included "barley liquor and an emulsion of Indian Corn." The ill-tempered Hawkins took advantage of his position as Frederica's magistrate, refusing to pay other colonists for goods and services. His neighbors took him to court, but he avoided paying debts even when judgments went against him. When Davison began enlarging his side of the domicile, Oglethorpe stopped construction for fear the regiment's only doctor would be upset. Davison, whose house was left exposed to the elements, was so angry that he moved his family into the stables until they could catch a boat for Carolina.

The remains of the Hawkins-Davison house, one of the British colonial houses in the fortified town of Frederica

Two young Anglican clerics, John and Charles Wesley, were among those who fled Frederica after being ill-treated by colonists. The Wesley brothers, who were born in Epworth, England, and educated at Oxford University, came to Georgia with Oglethorpe in 1736, eager to convert Indians to Christianity. They planned to impart religious doctrine and impose rigid discipline on the native people, much as the Spanish friars had done earlier. Although a number of historic illustrations show the Wesleys preaching to Indians, they never actually did. The trustees appointed John Wesley, the elder brother, as minister of the new Georgia colony in Savannah and sent Charles Wesley to St. Simons to be Oglethorpe's secretary, the secretary for Indian affairs, and Frederica's minister. Many of the colonists on the island were not religious, which certainly made Charles Wesley's job more difficult. But the pious, inflexible, newly ordained young minister, who had turned twenty-eight on the trip from England, created some of the problems himself. When he learned that a Frederica toddler had not been baptized by triune dunking, or total immersion three times in a row, he insisted the rite be repeated in the tidal Frederica River, still chilly in early spring. The mother refused, fearing her child

would be traumatized or even drowned, so Wesley kept after the father until he allowed the toddler to be dunked in the river three times. The enforced baptism did not endear Wesley to either parent.

At Frederica, Charles Wesley became the victim of two mean-spirited housewives, Beatre Hawkins and Anne Welch, who made his life miserable during his two-month tenure on the island in 1736. The women trumped up a confession, which they related to the young minister, claiming they had had sexual relations with an "important person" at Frederica. Charles Wesley assumed that the person was Oglethorpe, just as the women intended. Then the women went to Oglethorpe and accused Wesley of spreading vicious rumors that they had had sex with the general. Oglethorpe was outraged. He shunned Wesley, as did the other colonists after Mrs. Hawkins and Anne Welch spread the tale all over town. The washerwoman even refused to do the young minister's laundry.

Beatre Hawkins was the wife of Frederica's disagreeable doctor. Wesley first ran afoul of her on the trip from England when he informed his brother that the religious conversion she claimed was insincere. At Frederica, Wesley chastised Mrs. Hawkins for repeatedly beating her maid. She retaliated in a variety of spiteful ways, including having his bedroll and toiletries taken from his hut, forcing him to sleep on damp ground and to look unkempt and undignified, a serious problem for a minister. Mrs. Hawkins often sat up late around a campfire with a rowdy bunch of men. Since Frederica had no church, Charles delivered his five daily sermons either in a third-floor room of the storehouse or outside under the sheltering branches of a giant live oak. At Mrs. Hawkins's urging, the rowdies cursed and fired their weapons to disrupt the religious services. The use of firearms was banned on Sunday, but Dr. Hawkins, like his wife, had little respect for the law. One Sunday, he shot a rabbit. As he was being taken into custody for violating the firearm ban, Mrs. Hawkins broke a bottle over the custodian's head, almost killing the man. After Hawkins was stripped of his magistrate's position in 1743, he and his wife returned to England.

Lacking a church, the Wesleys often preached under a live oak tree.

After two months at Frederica, Charles Wesley abandoned hope of ever reaching the colonists and soldiers with his sermons and songs. After he returned to England, his brother came to St. Simons several times, in part because a Savannah woman whom John Wesley thought he loved was visiting on the island. Like his brother, John Wesley was harassed by Beatre Hawkins, who threatened to shoot him and tried to stab him with scissors. When he grabbed her wrists to restrain her, she attacked him with her teeth, shredding his clothes. On his fifth and final visit to Frederica, noting that he had "beaten the air in this unhappy place for 20 days," John left St. Simons with a parting comment: "It was not any apprehension of my own danger but with an utter despair of doing good there, which made me content with the thought of seeing it no more." Later, in England, the Wesley brothers made names for themselves. John Wesley led a movement that evolved into the Methodist Church. The Epworth by the Sea Methodist Conference Center on St. Simons is named for their birthplace in England. Charles Wesley, known as "a sweet singer," wrote the lyrics for more than six thousand hymns, including his most famous, "Hark, the Herald Angels Sing."

Like the Wesleys, about a third of the original 118 men, women, and children who came to Frederica fled during the first five years, discouraged by disputes, tired of tending crops, sheep, and cattle, weary of being plagued by insects, and sick of living in constant fear of enemy attack. Many of the colonists were London urbanites who had never lifted a shovel, much less tried to farm. Oglethorpe and the trustees had miscalculated the ability of colonists to grow enough food to support themselves in just a year or two. They had also overestimated the fertility of the sandy coastal soil. When the so-called Georgia Plan failed, Oglethorpe and the trustees blamed the colonists, believing they suffered from a lack of character that could best be remedied by more hard work.

The Salzburgers of Ebenezer and the settlers at German Village proved to be some of the Georgia colony's most industrious people. The Salzburgers were among some twenty thousand Protestants expelled from Austria in October 1731 by the Catholic archbishop of Salzburg, who gave Lutherans who owned no land just eight days to leave. Many froze to death while wandering in bitter cold and snow. A period illustration of Lutherans leaving Salzburg includes a reference to Matthew 24:20, "Pray that your flight does not take place in winter." The Lutherans who settled at German Village made a living by fishing and coaxing food crops to grow, supplying Frederica with fresh produce and seafood.

One of Frederica's most unusual residents arrived at the fortified town as a prisoner. He was also German, although he was accused of spying for the French. German-born Christian Gottlieb Priber was brought under guard to St. Simons in 1740 and imprisoned in the barracks to await interrogation by Oglethorpe, who had no idea what to make of him. Priber created a literary salon in his cell, where he entertained Frederica's intelligentsia, including a minister for whom he translated the Lord's Prayer and Bible verses into Cherokee. Described by Oglethorpe as "a very odd kind of man," Priber was a brilliant linguist who spoke a number of European and Indian languages. He had lived for a time among the Cherokee and, although he had a wife and children in Germany, married a chief's daughter and was adopted by her people. Priber outraged the British by informing his Indian friends that they were being cheated by English traders. He taught the Cherokee to use weights and measures, among other things, to make sure they were fairly treated. As a result, he was subsequently arrested on charges of being an Indian alienator and a French spy. Priber had two manuscripts in his possession when he was taken into custody. One was a dictionary, the first ever written in the Cherokee language. The other advocated the establishment of a utopian community called the Kingdom of Paradise, where Priber would serve as prime minister. In Priber's kingdom, people of all races would be welcome, including Indians from warring chiefdoms, criminals, debtors, slaves, and even Frenchmen. Priber's manuscript detailed the rights and privileges of Paradise residents, including the right of a woman to marry a different man every day. Children were to be reared by the entire community. Priber never realized his dream. He died in his prison cell on St. Simons and was probably buried somewhere on the island, although the location of his grave is unknown. Neither of his manuscripts has been found.

Another fascinating Frederica resident was a woman who played a major role in the founding of Georgia. Named Coosaponakeesa in the Creek language, and Mary Musgrove in English, she owned a substantial tabby house in the fortified town. The daughter of a Creek woman and an English trader from Charles Town, she served for a decade as Oglethorpe's translator and cultural guide. She interpreted for Oglethorpe and Tomochichi when the trustees were acquiring land for the Georgia colony. When Mary was nine, her mother died, and she was sent to school in Carolina in part to learn English. After her second husband's death, she was reported to be the wealthiest woman in Georgia. She owned trading posts and cow pens, or cattle ranches, in several strategic locations. Bilingual and grounded in both English and Creek cultures, she was able to make shrewd deals with British and Indian traders.

Her third husband, Thomas Bosomworth, urged her to actions that soured her relationship with the British. Bosomworth came to Georgia to seek his fortune. After sizing up his prospects, he returned to England to be ordained an Anglican minister and was appointed to serve as the colony's religious leader. Ignoring the wishes of the trustees, who wanted him in Savannah, Bosomworth moved to St. Simons, where, in the early 1740s, he briefly served as chaplain of Oglethorpe's regiment. When he married Mary Musgrove and became a wealthy man, Bosomworth gave up preaching in favor of fomenting discord. The renegade minister kept the Frederica colonists in a frenzy, convincing them an Indian massacre was imminent. He exploited his position as Mary's husband to acquire land and wealth from both the Indians and the British. He persuaded Mary's brother Malatche, chief of the Lower Creek, to have himself proclaimed emperor and to convey ownership of Ossabaw, St. Catherines, and Sapelo Islands to "Princess Mary." Mary and Malatche belonged to the high-ranking Wind Clan, which included the powerful Lower Creek chiefs, Old Brims and his successor, Chigelli, which may explain why the Indians granted Malatche's request. The transfer document awarding the islands to the Bosomworths was signed in January 1747, "on the fourth day of the Windy Moon." In return, Malatche was promised cloth, firearms, ammunition, and cattle. At Bosomworth's urging, Mary sued the British government, claiming she was owed for her work on behalf of Oglethorpe and the trustees. Courts in London awarded her some of the money she wanted as well as ownership of St. Catherines Island, where she and Bosomworth went to live. After Mary's death, Bosomworth remarried and sold part of the island to Button Gwinnett, one of three Georgia signers of the Declaration of Independence. Gwinnett built a tabby house on St. Catherines, but died from a dueling wound without ever paying for his island property. Bosomworth repossessed Gwinnett's holdings. Mary, Bosomworth, and his second wife are all buried on St. Catherines.

The ongoing tensions between Great Britain and Spain eventually exploded into war. Initially called the War of Jenkins' Ear, it started as a conflict over trade agreements in the Caribbean and was later subsumed into the War of the Austrian Secession. The War

Sunset over Bloody Marsh.

of Jenkins' Ear took its name from an incident in which a British merchant ship captained by Robert Jenkins was boarded in the Caribbean by Spanish coast guards searching for contraband. When they found it, they cut off Jenkins's ear and suggested he take it to Parliament as a warning to other British smugglers. Several years later, Jenkins took what he claimed was his mummified ear to Parliament, where it was used as propaganda by the faction advocating war with Spain.

War was declared in 1739. The following year, Oglethorpe attacked St. Augustine. His force included warships and British soldiers, Scots Highlanders from Darien, Georgia volunteers, and Indians. He mounted cannons on an island across the inlet from the Castillo de San Marco, a magnificent fortress built of Florida's coquina stone and tabby. Oglethorpe shelled the Castillo for thirty-eight days without ever breeching its thick walls; the soft coquina stone absorbed the blows. St. Augustine residents and troops, including escaped slaves who had trained as Spanish soldiers in Florida, all took refuge in the Castillo.

The First Underground Railroad

NORTH AMERICA'S first underground railroad ran south through Georgia, from slave colonies in the Carolinas to Spanish Florida, predating the more famous northbound Underground Railroad by a century or more. From the late 1600s until the mid-1700s, slaves escaped overland with the help of friendly Indians or down the Georgia coast in small boats, evading pursuers in the maze of tidal waterways west of the sea islands. Before British settlement, St. Simons and other sea islands probably served from time to time as railroad stops where the slaves could rest and find food and fresh water. After reaching safety in Florida, many escapees returned to Carolina to rescue friends and family members and to burn and raid British property. In 1693, Carlos II of Spain officially declared Florida a haven for escaped slaves, enraging Carolina planters and government officials, who were often one and the same, and aggravating relations between the two countries. Escaped slaves were among the Spanish troops who fought Oglethorpe's forces in St. Augustine and later on St. Simons. At the start of the War of Jenkins' Ear, Florida's governor authorized a fortified outpost north of the Castillo. Called Gracia Real de Santa Teresa de Mosé, it was the first sanctioned free-black settlement in what became the United States. It was headed by a black Spanish officer who escaped at age fourteen from a Carolina plantation. The site of Fort Mosé is now a park open to visitors.

With some exceptions, the British and Spanish held different views of Indians, Africans, and slavery. The British had no desire to integrate Indians or Africans into society or the military. They valued Indians primarily because they provided "vendable commodities," including slaves kidnapped from other chiefdoms. The British armed their Indian slave raiders, whose prime targets were women and children, and provided them with branding irons "to mark all skins, furrs [*sic*] and slaves."

The Catholic Church, by contrast, taught that slavery was an unnatural condition. Wealthier Spaniards often owned slaves, but most were treated as indentured servants. Many were paid for their labor, and all could sue abusive owners in court. Once free, former slaves, African and Indian, were expected to swear allegiance to the crown and take their place in Spanish society. Intermarriage was common. Able-bodied men were required to serve in the military. Religious conversion was compulsory, but most chose Catholicism over slavery.

Oglethorpe opposed slavery, but his stance was as much pragmatic as principled. When he attacked St. Augustine in 1740, he ordered his troops to return captured former slaves to British owners, who were to pay "a Sterling per head to the captors." During the attack, after Fort Mosé's soldiers and their families retreated to the stronger Castillo, Scots Highlanders and other British troops sent to occupy Fort Mosé were given orders to capture or kill any Spanish soldiers who ventured out in search of food. In a predawn raid, Spanish troops, including soldiers of Fort Mosé, attacked the outpost, catching the British soldiers sleeping. Sixty-eight British soldiers were killed and thirty-four taken prisoner. The British later claimed the Spanish committed atrocities: torturing, scalping, and beheading. They began calling the conflict the Battle of Bloody Moosa. Oglethorpe, ill and disheartened after his defeat, retreated to St. Simons and for months afterward sequestered himself at Orange Hall. He was harshly criticized by the British on both sides of the Atlantic because of the loss of so many men at St. Augustine.

Two years later, in 1742, the Spanish attacked St. Simons. Oglethorpe, with some 640 soldiers, immediately sent a message to the Carolina governor, asking for reinforcements. They never arrived. The governor, one of the general's critics, was reluctant to send soldiers for what might be a false alarm. Oglethorpe was a genius at military strategy. He had made ongoing efforts over the years to convince the Spanish that his troop strength on St. Simons was greater than it was. He once hosted Spanish military leaders at a reception in ornately decorated tents on the north end of Jekyll Island, a mile across the sound from south St. Simons. As the affair proceeded, British troops on St. Simons fired cannons in a display of military might, and mounted soldiers formed a military lineup in the dunes, arranging their seven horses, which were all they had, to make Oglethorpe's force seem much larger.

After the reception on Jekyll, Captain James Gascoigne (pronounced "gas-coin" on St. Simons) of the British warship *Hawk* invited the Spanish to supper on board. While they were dining, Tomochichi and other Yamacraw, dressed and painted for war, boarded the *Hawk* and complained to the visiting officials in threatening tones about attacks by Spanish-affiliated Indians. The Spanish returned to St. Augustine impressed by Oglethorpe's military strength as well as his hospitality.

The Spanish invasion of St. Simons began on July 5, 1742, in the heat of a southern summer. The armada of about fifty ships ran the guns of Fort St. Simons but suffered almost no damage because the inexperienced British soldiers manning the cannons were such poor shots. The Spanish fleet sailed into the Frederica River and landed some three thousand troops, including black soldiers from Fort Mosé, at Gascoigne Bluff. Oglethorpe spiked Fort St. Simons's cannons and withdrew his troops to Frederica, the stronger fortification, as the Spanish had done by retreating to the Castillo two years earlier when Oglethorpe attacked St. Augustine. The Spanish burned dozens of soldiers' houses on the island's south end and overran Fort St. Simons. They soon discovered Military Road but thought it was too narrow to be the main route to Frederica. On July 7, Don Manuel de Montiano, the governor of La Florida and commander of the Spanish troops, sent a scouting party up the road. The soldiers were engaged by a British patrol at Gully Hole Creek near Frederica. When the sounds of battle reached the fort, Oglethorpe and his Highlanders rushed to join the fight. In hand-to-hand combat, Oglethorpe captured two Spaniards himself. The Spanish retreated; twelve grenadiers from Havana were killed and ten captured. One Highlander died of heat exhaustion. Oglethorpe pursued the enemy south for about two miles to a point where Military Road crossed a stretch of high marsh. The general posted soldiers in the woods and returned to Frederica for reinforcements.

The Spanish leader, meanwhile, had sent reinforcements to protect his retreating troops. When the Spanish soldiers reached the marsh crossing, the British opened fire from the trees. The battle soon moved into the marsh. Except for the Highlanders, who stood their ground, the British soldiers were retreating in panic when Oglethorpe returned with more troops. By then the Spanish, who had run out of ammunition, were also in retreat.

The history-changing battles were, in reality, minor skirmishes. When the second battle ended, seven grenadiers lay dead in the marsh. The British later boasted that scores of Spanish soldiers had been killed and that the marshes ran red with blood, an obvious exaggeration. The conflict was first called the Battle of the Grenadiers but was later renamed the Battle of Bloody Marsh, which may have been coined by the British to counteract the image of the Battle of Bloody Mosé, where they had suffered such a staggering defeat. The Bloody Marsh National Historic Monument, in a small wooded park off Demere Road, commemorates the better known of the two conflicts, although the battle, whose actual site is unknown, may have been fought several miles farther north. There is a historic marker at the site of Gully Hole Creek.

The Spanish stayed on St. Simons another week, sending scout boats up the Frederica River and exchanging fire with Oglethorpe's troops. Again, Oglethorpe's military acumen paid off. Because of the fort's location, it was nearly impregnable from the river. Governor Montiano must have realized that an attack from the water was almost sure to fail. Oglethorpe, more worried the Spanish would launch another land assault, took

advantage of the fact that a French soldier among his troops had deserted to the Spanish during one of the previous battles on the island. The general had a letter written in French and sent to the deserter, ostensibly from a friend in Oglethorpe's regiment, urging him to tell the Spanish that Frederica was defenseless and that they should attack at once. The Spanish found the letter, as Oglethorpe intended, and put the deserter in irons as a spy. But Montiano was suspicious of the letter's contents, which also reported that two thousand British reinforcements were on the way. Oglethorpe's luck held. While the Spanish leader pondered his options, three British scout boats appeared on the horizon. South Carolina's governor had sent them only to assess Oglethorpe's request for reinforcements, but the Spanish thought they heralded the arrival of the troops mentioned in the letter. Montiano and his forces destroyed Fort St. Simons and retreated to St. Augustine.

Most of the conflicts in the War of Jenkins' Ear took place on other fronts. But the two minor battles fought on St. Simons in 1742 effectively ended Spain's two-century tenure in Georgia and established British dominance in the Southeast north of Florida. Although the treaty ending the war was not signed until 1748, the battles on St. Simons marked the last time the Spanish made a serious effort to claim the Debatable Land of coastal Georgia.

In addition, the battles on St. Simons marked the beginning of the end for Fort Frederica. Oglethorpe left for England in 1743, appointing Major William Horton to serve in his stead. Horton, a soldier-planter who built Georgia's first brewery, on Jekyll Island, and supplied Frederica with beer, was even worse as a civil manager than Oglethorpe. He not only took charge of the military but also seized Frederica's municipal seal and "appropriated to himself the authority of a prince like Louis XIV," one disgruntled colonist commented. After Oglethorpe's

Wild grapevines

Aerial view of coastal marshes

departure, soldiers at Frederica abused the Lutherans at German Village, whose names appear in historic records primarily because of the abuse. When Frederica's recorder, John Terry, tried to assist one of the victims, Colonel Horton helped persuade another colonist to accuse Terry of rape in order to discredit him. Terry was acquitted by a jury in Savannah.

Conditions at Frederica deteriorated. The settlers did little farming. The wife of a soldier opened a brothel in town. Drunken soldiers stole and broke into houses. There were incidents of rape, including one committed by the Reverend Thomas Bosomworth's brother, Abner Bosomworth, who was "discovered in the very posture of Perpetuating [*sic*] his abominable intention" on a Dutch girl. John Terry, the man falsely accused of rape at Horton's instigation, said of the fortified town: "Sodom and Gomorrah were more deserving of protection by the Almighty than Frederica."

Oglethorpe, who never returned to Georgia, disbanded the regiment in 1749 from England. When word of the disbanding reached St. Simons, the soldiers at Frederica

stayed drunk for three days. When they left, most Frederica residents followed. The settlers at German Village had already moved elsewhere. Neither Frederica nor German Village could survive without the soldiers, whose commerce supported them. Once again, St. Simons was left almost deserted, although a few of the original colonists stayed on the island.

A few years after Oglethorpe's departure for England, Georgia became a slave colony. Although Oglethorpe and the trustees had banned slavery, many Georgians, with the exception of the Ebenezer Salzburgers and the Highlanders in Darien, were unhappy about the ban. Oglethorpe and the trustees had opposed slavery in the fledgling colony for a number of practical reasons, including the fact that although the British needed armed settlers who would fight the Spanish, slaves were forbidden to bear arms. Georgians began smuggling Africans across the Savannah River from Carolina to work their farms and plantations. The trustees, aware they were fighting a losing battle, tried to formulate legislation that allowed slavery but limited its extent. The law was passed in 1750 and took effect in 1751, but the limits set by the trustees were widely ignored, especially by wealthy coastal planters from Carolina who had long wanted to expand into Georgia because their own lands were overworked and barren. Georgia's sea islands and coastal mainland were soon overrun by aristocratic planters from Carolina and the West Indies, who brought thousands of slaves along with them. Within a few years, Carolina planters dominated Georgia's colonial government and passed a proslavery statute to replace the one formulated by the trustees. During the next several decades, Georgia's slave population skyrocketed from fewer than five hundred to about eighteen thousand. Outsiders bought large tracts of land on St. Simons and in the adjacent Altamaha Delta, which offered rice-growing conditions similar to those in coastal South Carolina, where rice was rapidly becoming one of the economic mainstays of colonial America. Some of the newcomers and a handful of holdovers from Oglethorpe's day grew rice, indigo, and cotton on St. Simons before the start of the Revolutionary War, which delayed expansion of the island plantations into the giant estates many later became.

At the start of the revolution, all but one of Fort Frederica's cannons were sent to Fort Morris near Sunbury, about forty miles up the coast. Many St. Simons residents fled the island as well. Loyalists went to British East Florida or the British-held Bahamas; patriot families fled inland, knowing that British warships could easily attack the Georgia coast. Some Bahamian place-names may have migrated to coastal Georgia after the revolution by way of returning loyalists or slaves, or they may have been taken from Georgia

Early settlers at Frederica used palmetto fronds to thatch roofs on shelters they called booths. Rattlesnakes often make their homes in palmetto thickets.

to the Bahamas during the conflict. A marsh island on the Altamaha Delta is called Rockdedundy; a small island in the Exuma chain in the Bahamas is named Rocky Dundas.

A Revolutionary War battle between the British and the Americans was waged in the Frederica River just west of St. Simons on April 18, 1778, three years to the day after the first shots of the revolution were fired. Called the Frederica naval action by the Americans and the Debacle at Raccoon Gut by the British, it pitted three British warships based in East Florida against three smaller patriot boats, called row galleys, that made up the bulk of Georgia's navy. One of the British warships, the *Hinchinbrook*, had a record of seizing patriot ships and stealing precious cargoes of rice being shipped from Savannah. In one incident, the *Hinchinbrook* appropriated three hundred uniforms intended for patriot soldiers. After the start of the war, the Continental Congress authorized $2,000 for Georgia to build four row galleys in order "to secure the State's Rivers

against the predatory incursions of the Enemy." The row galleys, named the *Washington*, *Lee*, *Bulloch*, and *Congress*, were open, two-masted boats with sails, but their primary propulsion came from long oars, twenty to a side. Each oar was double-banked, or handled by two oarsmen, who rowed standing up. The galleys were pointed bow and stern, so they could move in either direction. The long, narrow, shallow-draft boats were fast and maneuverable in the protected brown-water tidal creeks and rivers but were not designed to sail in open water offshore. Their role was to stop ships from British East Florida from traveling through the Inland Passage between the sea islands and the mainland and attacking Sunbury, the southernmost American port, south of Savannah. The Georgia navy was asked also to help stop attacks by the British on American supply ships. Troops from Georgia had twice attempted to invade British East Florida at the request of the Continental Congress, but both efforts failed. They were planning a third attack when Colonel Samuel Elbert, commander of the Continental Army and

Navy forces in Georgia, learned that four British vessels had been sighted in the waters of St. Simons Sound. The British, anticipating another attack on Florida, had decided to make a preemptive strike in Georgia. The four British warships were the *Galatea*, the largest and best armed; the brigantine *Hinchinbrook*; the provincial sloop *Rebecca*; and the armed watering brig *Hatter*. The British commander deployed his ships around the island, left scouts at Fort Frederica, and settled down to wait through March and part of April for the counterattack.

Wars moved more slowly in those days than now. While the ships were at anchor, the British often went ashore on Jekyll and St. Simons to hunt and gather firewood. Onboard, the sailors passed the time mending sails and rigging and firing cannons. They careened (intentionally beached) the *Galatea* to scrape her hull and coat it with tallow. They cleaned the ship's interior with vinegar and fumigated it with smoke to prevent yellow fever and malaria. Many sailors had been sick with fever since leaving St. Augustine, and five of them died as they waited off St. Simons.

The British expedition was plagued with misfortune. The commander aboard the *Galatea* sent several small boats north on a scouting mission. When a storm drove them back, one boat capsized in St. Simons Sound and Lieutenant Alexander Ellis, commander of the *Hinchinbrook*, drowned. Lightning damaged the masts of the *Galatea*. The British ran short of food, requiring the men to go on half rations.

When the British commander learned that the row galleys had been relocated from Sunbury to Darien, he sent the *Hinchinbrook* and the *Rebecca* up the Frederica River along the western shore of St. Simons to ambush the patriot boats if they came south. The Frederica eels through the marshes of Glynn, touching high land at only three places: Gascoigne Bluff, Fort Frederica, and West Point/Pike's Bluff. Along its western shore and long stretches of its eastern side, the river is flanked by marsh.

Elbert, the patriot commander, marched 350 troops to Darien, where the row galleys were docked. The troops boarded three of the four boats, the *Washington, Lee*, and *Bulloch*, and headed south, along with a flatboat carrying weapons and artillerymen. They landed at Pike's Bluff, north of then-abandoned Fort Frederica. Elbert dispatched troops to Frederica, where they captured five British scouts. Before dawn, Elbert led his row galleys downriver to engage the enemy.

The British had set up a blockade, intending to ram and board the smaller row galleys. Conditions, however, favored the Americans, by accident or design. As the tide was

Island cedar

ebbing, the wind died, as it often does on outgoing tides. Dependent on sails, the British ships lay dead in the water. The patriots anchored their row galleys out of range of the British cannons and began shelling them with their larger guns. During the hours-long siege, the patriot barrage damaged the masts and rigging of the British ships and sank one of their longboats.

The British boarded the other longboats and began towing their ships toward St. Simons Sound, where they hoped to catch a breeze. The row galleys followed, continuing the bombardment. All three British ships ran aground at Raccoon Gut, one of thousands of small rivulets that branch into the marshes from larger waterways. Navigation charts today do not show the location of Raccoon Gut, but it was probably near the southern end of the Frederica River.

Now desperate, the British tried to lighten the watering brig *Hatter* by pumping out her fresh water. They deployed anchors in an attempt to haul the ships into deeper water. Realizing that the large vessels would move off the bottom only when the tide lifted them hours later, the British boarded the two remaining longboats, which were so overcrowded that they were forced to leave a few sailors behind on the *Hinchinbrook* as the rest rowed out to the *Galatea*.

The naturalist William Bartram explored St. Simons in 1774.

The patriots swarmed over the captured ships, taking prisoner the abandoned men on the *Hinchinbrook* and recovering the three hundred patriot uniforms captured earlier by the British. Elbert wrote to his commanding officer, informing him of the victory: "You must imagine what my feelings were to see our three little men of War going on to the attack of these three Vessels, who have spread Terror on our Coast . . . What is extraordinary, we have not one man hurt."

Before departing for Florida, the *Galatea* took seven unidentified people from St. Simons onboard, possibly slaves left behind when their owners fled, or loyalists, or both. Elbert was decorated for his leadership in the battle, achieved the rank of general in the Continental Army, and served as an early governor of the new state of Georgia.

The Frederica naval action, while of little importance in the Revolutionary War overall, revived the Americans' morale, especially in Georgia. It temporarily plugged an invasion route, the Inland Passage—now part of the Intracoastal Waterway—between British Florida and Georgia. The action also delayed the British capture of Georgia for eight more months. With the loss of the *Rebecca* and the *Hinchinbrook*, the *Galatea* became the only British warship left in British Florida, which reduced the number of attacks on American ships. In April 2005, on the 227th anniversary of the battle, a historic marker commemorating the victory of the Georgia navy was unveiled at Fort Frederica.

In the decades following the Revolutionary War, live oak timbers were cut on St. Simons and shipped to Boston, where they were used to build the first warships of the U.S. Navy, including the famous USS *Constitution*, nicknamed "Old Ironsides." The ship's sternpost was cut at Cannon's Point plantation on north St. Simons, named for one of Oglethorpe's colonists, Daniel Cannon, a carpenter who manned a lookout there. The natural curves of the giant live oaks permitted the builders to carve rounded sections from single blocks of wood, which made them stronger than pieced-together sections. For more than one hundred years, the stump of the famous tree was shown off to Cannon's Point visitors as the remnant of "Constitution Oak," even though John Couper, the planter who bought Cannon's Point after the war, had gone to British Florida with his loyalist employers during the revolution. The stump was displayed at the International Cotton Exposition in Atlanta in 1895 but was never returned to the island. During the War of 1812, Old Ironsides won all its battles against British warships. It was said that cannonballs bounced off of its tough live oak hull. After more than two centuries, Old Ironsides is still on the water, docked at the Charlestown Navy Yard in Boston and open for public tours. It is the world's oldest commissioned warship afloat today.

Live oak timbers cut on St. Simons were used to build the first ships of the U.S. Navy, including the famed USS *Constitution*, nicknamed "Old Ironsides." (Photo courtesy of the U.S. Navy)

A Revolutionary War battle fought in 1778 in the Frederica River pitted three row galleys of Georgia's navy against three British warships. Called the Frederica naval action by the patriots and the Debacle at Raccoon Gut by the British, the battle was won by Georgia's tiny navy.

Planters on the Points

TWO OF THE REGION'S most successful planters represent the extremes of the type of men who developed the fourteen large plantations on St. Simons after the Revolutionary War. Scottish-born John Couper and Irish-born Major Pierce Butler were described by the historian Malcolm Bell Jr. as being "as different as cotton from rice." Where Major Butler was serious, stiff, and formal, Couper was outgoing, mischievous, and charming. Couper lived on St. Simons year-round and managed his own properties; Butler resided in a Philadelphia mansion and hired managers to run his Georgia plantations. Couper was born to a middle-class Scots family and came to America as a teenager—"for the good of my native land," as he jokingly put it. He was working in Savannah when the revolution began and, as mentioned previously, retreated to British Florida with his loyalist employers. He did not buy property on St. Simons until after the war.

Major Butler was the third son of an Irish nobleman and so was unlikely to inherit land, title, or wealth. His father bought him a commission in the British Army when he was eleven, and by the time he was fourteen, he was fighting with the British against the French in North America. The major set out to marry well, and he did. His wife was Mary "Polly" Middleton, the daughter of a wealthy Charleston planter and slave trader. Through her, Major Butler inherited valuable property and slaves in South Carolina; he later bought land on St. Simons before the Revolution. He fought with the patriots during the war.

By 1800, Major Butler and Couper had each purchased thousands of acres on St. Simons, including the entire north end. That area, situated on two broad points, was aptly described by a planter's daughter as "a swallow-tail to the island." Viewed upside down on a map, St. Simons does resemble a fat-bellied, swallow-tailed wading bird with the long plume called East Beach sweeping back from its head.

Couper owned the easternmost section, Cannon's Point; Major Butler owned the western point, which he called Hampton, although many older islanders still call the property Butler's Point. Major Butler's plantations were run by a series of managers, who often resorted to harsh punishments that included flogging slaves with a lash and chaining them in iron ankle cuffs. Perhaps because of his early military training, Major Butler expected his plantations to be run with regimental efficiency. Unlike the slaves on Couper's plantations, Major Butler's were not permitted to leave his properties to

Portraits of John Couper of Cannon's Point Plantation and
Major Pierce Butler of Hampton Plantation. The two plantations
were situated on two points on the north end of St. Simons.
(Left, Courtesy of the Coastal Georgia Historical Society; right,
National Archives)

visit friends and relatives or even to attend church with other island
slaves. The major feared they would be spoiled by contact with slaves
from plantations whose owners were not as strict. Butler's properties
operated as a self-contained unit, with almost everything they needed
being grown, built, caught, gathered, hunted, or crafted by the slaves.

By contrast, Couper's slaves were permitted to visit other plantations, attend church, and enjoy far more freedom than the Butler
slaves. Couper was lighthearted, Butler was rigid, and the attitudes of
the two planters no doubt trickled down to the slave quarters.

Butler and Couper did have a few things in common. Both were
civic minded. Butler served several terms as the first U.S. senator
from South Carolina, and Couper represented Glynn County at
Georgia's constitutional convention. Couper sold the federal government four acres of land on south St. Simons for $1 so that the island's
first lighthouse could be built. Like all the island planters, Couper
and Major Butler were known for their hospitality. At Cannon's
Point, the Couper family's dining table always accommodated a
few guests and sometimes as many as twenty. A favorite island story
illustrates how comfortable visitors felt at Couper's estate. He and his wife, Rebecca,
invited a newlywed couple to honeymoon at Cannon's Point. The young people settled
in until after the birth of their second child.

Major Butler, whose wife died before the revolution, often invited guests to his
St. Simons plantation when he was not in residence. In 1804, Vice President Aaron
Burr took refuge at Hampton following a duel in New York in which Burr killed former U.S. treasury secretary Alexander Hamilton. Burr and Butler had served together
in the U.S. Senate and were political allies, even if not friends. Burr, who was running
for president against Thomas Jefferson at the time, was happy to flee to remote
St. Simons to escape public opprobrium as well as murder charges.

Couper and Major Butler had something else in common: they both became very
rich, at least for a time, growing rice and Sea Island cotton.

CHAPTER III　Antebellum Time

[1751–1861]

WHEN GEORGIA legalized slavery in 1750, outsiders eyed the larger sea islands and coastal rivers of the colony as virgin territory begging to be exploited. By the 1760s, an elite group of planters from South Carolina and the West Indies owned most of the best agricultural land in coastal Georgia. The Revolutionary War interrupted plantation development on St. Simons, but after the war, planters raced to prepare the island and its environs to grow a variety of profitable crops. By the early 1800s, thousands of slaves were not only raising cotton, corn, and sugarcane on island plantations but also developing the unique Gullah Geechee culture, which survives today on some of the sea islands and more remote pockets of the coastal mainland. The labor of island slaves was organized according to the task system developed by the coastal planters, which was more liberal than the gang system common to inland plantations.

The historian Mart A. Stewart describes the rapid growth of slavery on the islands thus: "Within a few years . . . planters and their slaves molded the lands of Georgia's coastal plain that had proved useless to the first colonists into formidable units of production."

One of the most profitable crops grown on St. Simons was cotton, but it was not the same upland cotton grown in the Georgia interior and other parts of the South. Many people considered the cotton grown on the sea islands the finest in the world.

Known in the Caribbean as Anguilla cotton, long-staple black-seed cotton became adapted so well to St. Simons and other semitropical sea islands of the southeastern coast that it came to be called Sea Island cotton. It made the islands famous and many of the planters rich. It was grown only in the sandy soil and salt-air environment within thirty miles of the ocean; the finest of all grew on the sea islands in sight of the Atlantic. The first Sea Island cotton grown in North America was probably produced by James Spalding on St. Simons. Spalding emigrated from Scotland in 1760 and opened a warehouse at Frederica with a partner, where they stored goods for trading posts the two men operated in Florida. Spalding purchased land on the south end of St. Simons and established a plantation he called Orange Grove, perhaps in tribute to Orange Hall, Oglethorpe's tabby house near Frederica, which Spalding bought when he first came to the island. A friend sent Spalding packets of seeds for long-staple cotton from the Bahamas, and he planted them in the spring of 1787 on the banks of a small rice field. Although the plants grew well and blossomed, they yielded no cotton the first year. The second year, when the plants ratooned, or spread from the roots, the bolls opened and Spalding's slaves harvested the first Sea Island cotton crop. Experts say Sea Island cotton is stronger and silkier than any other variety, ideal for making delicate lace and fine cloth with a lustrous sheen. It is still grown and valued today for the same qualities.

Sea Island cotton was harder to pick and process than upland or short-staple cotton. On St. Simons, a top field hand could pick about one hundred pounds of the long-staple cotton a day; upland slaves were expected to pick twice that much short-staple cotton. To boost production, sea island planters staged weekly picking competitions; slaves won prizes of rice and molasses. Sea Island cotton also had to be gently ginned, using special rollers to remove its tiny seeds. After it passed through the cotton engine, or gin, the cotton had to be moted by hand. Moting was the tedious process of hand-picking dirt particles, broken seeds, and stained fibers from the lint. The task was often done by women and children, whose small hands were better suited for the work. After the cotton was moted, it was packed into 300- to 400-pound bags; bales of upland cotton, which could stand rougher treatment, often weighed 1,000 pounds or more. Major Butler was so proud of the Sea Island cotton produced on his plantations that he had each bag stamped with his initials before shipping it to market in Liverpool.

Anna Matilda Page King, the owner and manager of Retreat Plantation (Estates of George Alexander Heard and Jean Keller Heard)

Thomas Butler King, the husband of Anna King, was an early American statesman who preferred nation building to planting the Sea Island cotton for which Retreat became famous. (Estates of George Alexander Heard and Jean Keller Heard)

Some of the best Sea Island cotton was grown by a woman: Anna Matilda Page King, who owned and operated one of the largest plantations on St. Simons. In 1824, three years after she married Thomas Butler King of Massachusetts, she inherited Retreat Plantation and fifty slaves from her father. The giant plantation, on property owned earlier by James Spalding and his son, Thomas, sprawled over more than two thousand acres on the south end of St. Simons, stretching west from the lighthouse almost to Gascoigne Bluff. It encompassed the land now occupied by the Sea Island Golf Club and the surrounding subdivisions, as well as most of McKinnon Airport. Retreat's relatively modest main house, built by the Spaldings, as well as a four-story wooden cotton barn, a two-story tabby slave hospital, and a number of other outbuildings, commanded stunning views of St. Simons Sound and Jekyll Island. Golfers who play the Seaside Course at the Sea Island Golf Club and visitors to Sea Island's posh Lodge on the club's grounds enjoy the same views today.

Anna's husband, Thomas Butler King, liked the notion of being a planter more than he liked growing Sea Island cotton, the crop that won fame for Retreat on both sides of the Atlantic. Plantation management was left in Anna King's capable hands for years at a time while her husband went off to serve as a state senator (1832–37) and a U.S. congressman (1839–42, 1845–50). President Zachary Taylor made King his special agent in the new state of California, and President Millard Fillmore appointed him the first collector of the Port of San Francisco. King spent a great deal of time promoting grand projects of benefit to the country and to Georgia, including the first transcontinental railroad and the Brunswick-Altamaha barge canal. He also served as a lobbyist for the Southern Pacific Railroad Company. As a consequence, King was rarely in residence at Retreat.

Anna Page King did not marry until she was twenty-six, considered late for a woman of her era. An only child, she learned plantation management from her father, Major William Page, a South Carolinian who came to St. Simons as one of the early managers of Major Butler's north-end plantations. Major Page later bought Orange Grove Plantation from Thomas Spalding and renamed it Retreat. Spalding, who purchased most of Sapelo Island, grew Georgia's first sugarcane there as an experiment in 1806. Within a few years, sugarcane had become the third most valuable crop for the coastal planters.

During her husband's long absences, Anna King took charge of hundreds of horses, hogs, cattle, mules, chickens, and an ox. She kept the plantation's financial records, exported the crops, distributed food and clothing, and directed the house servants.

THRESHING MILL.

MAIN FLOOD GATES.

DITCHING.

A RICE FIELD.

REAPING.

FLOOD GATE.

THE RICE BIRD.

THE RICE FLOODED.

An artist's representation of aspects of antebellum rice culture. St. Simons planters used slave labor to dike wetlands on the Altamaha Delta and grow huge crops of rice there. (Courtesy of the Coastal Georgia Historical Society)

She cultivated and experimented with seeds, developing a strain of especially fine Sea Island cotton and overseeing its planting. The fact that Retreat's fields fronted St. Simons Sound may have contributed to the quality of the crop. Among her other duties, Anna King planned and supervised the construction of plantation buildings and reared ten children to adulthood, with scant help from her absentee spouse.

Like Anna King of Retreat, the Coupers at Cannon's Point were noted for the quality of their Sea Island cotton. They experimented as well with Persian date palms, oranges, lemons, figs, peaches, mulberries, apricots, nectarines, plums, European grapes, and a variety of other trees, flowers, and shrubs. James Hamilton, for whom Couper's son was named, traveled the world and often sent plants and seeds to the Coupers for their experiments. Hamilton and John Couper grew up together in Scotland and came together to America. They remained close friends for the remainder of their lives. Hamilton's eponymous plantation was on the southwest side of St. Simons on Gascoigne Bluff; it included the present-day site of the Epworth by the Sea Methodist Center as well as an oak-shaded county park and a marina on the Frederica River. An astute businessman, Hamilton became one of the island's most successful planters. He spent part of the year on St. Simons and traveled the rest of the time. Before the Civil War, Hamilton sold his plantation to his namesake, James Hamilton Couper, and moved to Philadelphia, where he lived in a style befitting one of the first millionaires in the United States.

The Coupers often wrote about their horticultural experiments in journals of the day. They became such well-known agriculturists that President Thomas Jefferson asked John Couper to try to grow olive trees on St. Simons. Jefferson arranged for the American consul in France to ship the trees across the Atlantic, but did not offer to pay for them. Couper delayed the shipment for more than a decade because of the cost of the trees, but he eventually ordered them, grew them to maturity, and pressed high-quality oil from the olives.

John Couper's son, James Hamilton Couper, a brilliant man and a highly respected planter, was nothing like his genial father in personality. He was so staid and proper that his father took to calling him "the old gentleman." James Couper was part owner and manager of Hopeton, Altama, and Elizafield plantations, three successful rice planta-tions on the Altamaha Delta, which fans across five miles as the giant river meets the incoming push of the Atlantic near the coast. After extensive modifications with slave labor, the delta provided some of the best rice-growing territory in coastal Georgia. Along with South Carolina, Georgia produced nine-tenths of the nation's rice crop before the Civil War.

Rice was the first big money crop for Georgia planters, and coastal Georgia was well suited for growing it. The extreme tides of the Georgia Bight influence the rise and fall of water levels in the Altamaha and other coastal rivers for as far as thirty miles inland. The Altamaha's outflow is powerful enough to push a freshwater layer, or wedge, on top of the heavier saltwater that floods upriver twice daily on the incoming tide. Rice planters exploited this characteristic. They timed the spring planting to coincide with the full-moon tides of March, when the freshwater wedge rose to the level of flood-gates installed at either end of the diked rice fields that spread across the delta. As soon as the rice was in the ground, the gates were opened in order to flood the fields

James Hamilton Couper, son of John Couper (Courtesy of the Coastal Georgia Historical Society)

The chimney from the steam-powered rice mill on Butler's Island still stands on the Altamaha Delta off U.S. Highway 17 between Darien and Brunswick. (Photo by Jingle Davis)

with fresh water and thereby protect the seeds from voracious ricebirds—migratory bobolinks—until the crop sprouted. When the fields needed draining, the floodgates were opened on the outgoing tide. The ricebirds appeared again in fall to eat the ripening grain but were often eaten instead by planters, who considered the fat, rice-fed bobolinks a delicacy.

The rice was alternately flooded and drained during the summer growing season, according to the needs of the crop. The process was complex, requiring expert knowledge and judgment. Rice cultivation was harder than growing cotton, sugarcane, or corn and required different skills. The coastal planters valued slaves imported from the rice coast of Africa (the area of West Africa from modern Senegal to Liberia) because they already knew how to grow rice in tidal areas. After Major Butler sold his inherited South Carolina properties, he moved his experienced rice slaves to coastal Georgia and hired Roswell King Sr. of Connecticut in 1802 to manage his plantations. King came to the task with no agricultural experience; according to the historian Mart A. Stewart, he barely knew rice from grass when he first arrived on the island. Not long after King took over the job, Major Butler promoted Sambo, a favorite slave brought from South Carolina, to the position of head driver over all his delta fields, because of his rice-growing expertise. Anxious to establish his authority, the inexperienced King resented Sambo's knowledge as well as his influence over the other slaves. King's weekly letters to Major Butler were a litany of complaints about Sambo: he was arrogant, impudent, disrespectful, and lazy; he whipped slaves while he was drunk; and, worst of all, he unlocked a storage building so that other slaves could steal corn. Major Butler eventually gave in to King's complaints and sold Sambo, whose fate is unknown.

The brutal labor of clearing the delta, diking the fields, and growing the rice fell to the slaves, who cleared the swampy delta islands of hardwood trees and brush, along with hundreds of giant bald cypresses, relatives of the ancient sequoias of the West Coast and just as magnificent. Some of the trees were more than a thousand years old. In the rice fields, slaves labored in mud up to their ankles or higher. They were plagued by heat, humidity, insects, poisonous snakes, and alligators. They died of fevers, injuries, infections, heat exhaustion, dysentery, snakebite, cholera, and other ailments, including overwork.

Once the delta land was cleared, slaves dug the mucky earth, shovelful by shovelful, and wheeled it in barrows to build miles of dikes to create the rice fields, a process that took years. With floods called freshets rolling downriver, and storm tides surging in from

Reduced-size replica of a rice fanner made by the late Allen Green of Sapelo Island, a descendant of slaves whose beautifully woven sweetgrass baskets are prized by collectors, including the Smithsonian Institution. Similar baskets are still made on the rice coast of Africa. (Photo by Jingle Davis)

the Atlantic, the dikes and floodgates required constant maintenance. Dikes were usually planted with grasses and shrubs to prevent erosion, but on Butler's Island, sour orange trees topped the dikes. Visitors often commented on the fragrance of the blossoms and admired the trees laden with ripe fruit.

Slaves hand-dug deep canals through the delta so that flatboats loaded with rice could transport it to mills in Darien and on some of the larger rice plantations. After more than 150 years, most of the canals are still navigable. The seventy-five-foot-tall brick chimney of the steam-powered rice mill from the 1850s still stands on Butler's Island off U.S. Highway 17 between Brunswick and Darien, as does the plantation house, now occupied by staff from the Georgia Department of Natural Resources, the agency that manages the delta.

On the mainland across from St. Simons, a rice plantation called Hofwyl is now a state historic site, open to the public. Visitors to Hofwyl see exhibits that detail the growing and processing of rice crops. Before mechanized rice mills were built, and even afterward, slaves pounded rice by hand in large wooden mortars with long pestles to loosen the hulls, then cleaned it in handwoven fanners: large, flat, circular baskets made in an African style from indigenous coastal materials. Gullah Geechee people in the historic Hog Hammock community on Sapelo Island still make museum-quality baskets of sweetgrass, also called purple muhly grass (*Muhlenbergia filipes*), and saw palmetto (*Serenoa repens*). Slaves used the flat rice fanners to toss the pounded grain in the air so that the wind could blow away the lighter chaff. Whenever the slaves were fanning rice, they wanted a stiff breeze, so they called or whistled for Tony, the wind, just as they did on the rice coast of Africa: "Blow, Tony, blow—Blow, Tony, blow."

When Cannon's Point and Hampton were hit by a powerful hurricane in 1804, Vice President Aaron Burr, who was staying at Hampton, happened to be visiting the Coupers on the eastern point. In letters to his daughter, Theodosia, Burr described his experience of the storm. Two Butler slaves had rowed Burr down Jones Creek from Hampton to Cannon's Point to spend the day with the convivial Couper family. When they tried to return to Hampton that evening, rising wind drove them back. Burr spent the night with the Coupers in their well-built house, set high on a sturdy tabby foundation. The slave oarsmen probably weathered the storm in the quarters on the Couper plantation.

"In the morning the wind was still higher," Burr wrote to his daughter.

The planter John Couper of Cannon's Point used tabby to build slave cabins, outbuildings, and the foundation of his antebellum home.

More than six hundred acres of Cannon's Point will be preserved by the St. Simons Land Trust and opened to the public for tours and recreation. The land, which includes one of the largest maritime forests on the Georgia coast, includes the historic remains of Late Archaic shell rings and other prehistoric Indian settlements as well as ruins from the island's antebellum period.

It continued to rise, and by noon blew a gale from the North, which together with the swelling of the water became alarming. From twelve to three [o'clock] several of the outhouses had been destroyed, most of the trees about the house were blown down. The house in which we were shook and rocked so much that Mr. C. began to express his apprehensions for our safety. Before three [o'clock], part of the piazza was carried away, two or three of the windows bursted in. The house was inundated with water, and presently one of the chimneys fell. Mr. C. then commanded a retreat to a storehouse about fifty yards off, and we decamped men, women and children.

When the wind died shortly afterward, the slaves rowed Burr back to Hampton, but just before they reached Butler's house, the hurricane-force winds rose again, this time blowing out of the southeast. They had crossed between the two points while the eye of the storm was passing over the north end of the island. Burr and the Coupers survived, but many slaves were drowned, including nineteen owned by Butler, sixteen of them on low-lying Butler's Island. The hurricane left many island houses and buildings damaged or destroyed and devastated the delta's entire rice crop.

Slaves dug the mile-long Rifle Cut by hand as a shortcut for flatboats carrying rice to mills and markets. The cut is so straight a rifle bullet could pass straight through.

Overseeing the repair of Hampton fell to Roswell King Sr.—Major Butler being, as usual, away—who stayed on as manager until 1819, after which his son, Roswell King Jr., took over management of the Butler properties. In spite of the similarity of the names, Major Pierce Butler, Thomas Butler King, and the Roswell Kings were not related. Under the management of the Roswell Kings, Major Butler's slaves grew hundreds of acres of Sea Island cotton at Hampton and on two marsh impoundments on the west end of Little St. Simons, called Experiment and Five Pound Tree, the latter so named because the bulk of the six-hundred-acre marshy area supported only five main impoundments, or fields. Slaves were often sent to isolated Five Pound as punishment. Butler slaves grew sugarcane and corn on impounded land, but the primary crop on Butler's delta property was rice. Over a period of years, his slaves, working with nothing more than hand tools, muscles, and courage, diked seven hundred acres of low-lying land on the Altamaha Delta for rice cultivation. After more than two centuries, the old dikes and slave-dug canals still define the delta, although the impoundments were opened permanently years ago to curtail mosquito breeding in still water.

King Sr. is credited with making Butler's plantations a financial success, but he accomplished it at the expense of the slaves, according to the late historian Malcolm Bell Jr. Like his employer, King Sr. believed he was humane in his treatment of the slaves and professed to prefer the carrot to the stick. But Butler slaves were regularly subjected to floggings and other severe punishments. It seems surprising now that King, along with the other island planters, often expressed the belief that their "people," as they called the slaves, were not only happy but also grateful to their owners. They were shocked and furious when 138 of Major Butler's happy people, 238 of James Hamilton's, and 60 of John Couper's fled to the British when St. Simons was invaded during the War of 1812.

In writing to Butler of the exodus, King Sr. commented, "I can never git over the Baseness of your ungrateful Negroes." The island planters were convinced the slaves would not have left their owners had they not been tricked by British military men, who allegedly told them lies to persuade them to leave. The planters in turn warned their slaves that if they joined the British, they would be resold in the West Indies, an area notorious for slave mistreatment. A number of Butler slaves who fled to the British were sent to Nova Scotia, where many of their descendants still bear the Butler name. Other slaves who escaped were settled in England or English territories.

Major Butler held King Sr. responsible for the loss of his slaves, although King tried his best to get them back. King and Butler also disagreed over plantation management

and the fact that King was spending more and more time attending to his own business affairs in Darien, which included ownership of a sawmill and the directorship of a bank. Butler fired King, who later moved inland and founded the mill town of Roswell, fifteen miles north of Atlanta in Cobb County, leaving his son, Roswell Jr., in charge of the Butler holdings.

Two distinct cultures evolved on the St. Simons plantations: that of the planters and that of the slaves. Planters and their families were well-educated, well-traveled, well-connected people known for elaborate entertaining and hospitality, progressive agricultural practices, and public service. Planters on St. Simons sent their sons to boarding schools and to universities such as Oxford, Yale, and Princeton; their daughters attended academies for young ladies in Savannah or Charleston. The children of island planters often married the offspring of other island planters, cementing relationships and consolidating family lands and fortunes.

Most of the St. Simons planters lived graciously but not ostentatiously in houses raised high off the ground on brick or tabby foundations. Tall, floor-length windows welcomed sea breezes, and louvered wooden shutters blocked the hot southern sun from

John Couper's house at Cannon's Point
(Courtesy of the Coastal Georgia
Historical Society)

spacious verandas. The houses of the island planters resembled the plantation houses of the West Indies more than the white-columned Tara-like mansions of upcountry Georgia. British planters from the Tropics who migrated to South Carolina and, later, to St. Simons brought the airy, West Indies–style houses to the sea islands.

The well-educated island planters stocked their libraries with classics as well as books and periodicals on agriculture, geology, architecture, history, science, medicine, music, conchology, languages, astronomy, navigation, and a wealth of other topics. The library of the Couper family was reported by the *Atlanta Constitution* in 1888 to be "the most valuable and complete library in the south."

All island planters were famous for their hospitality, but none could rival that of John Couper. The Coupers' house at Cannon's Point was always filled with visitors, who were treated to picnic excursions to the beach, horseback and carriage rides through the woods, weeklong house parties, musicales, and a variety of other entertainments. Rowing regattas staged by Couper and other island planters attracted competitors from Charleston, Savannah, and even farther away. The regattas pitted the slave oarsmen of coastal plantations against one another and prompted spirited betting by both planters and slaves.

Gourmet Dining at Cannon's Point

GUESTS AT Cannon's Point raved about the gourmet meals prepared by Couper's master chef Sans Foix, who was skilled in the art of French cooking. Sans Foix was a free black man trained by Cupidon, the French chef of the Marquis de Montalet. The marquis, who owned part of Sapelo Island, was among the French noblemen and women who left France during the revolution to save their necks from the guillotine. The late historian Bessie Lewis of Pine Harbor captures the flavor of the Sans Foix kitchen and his culinary genius:

> In the great kitchen he was in supreme command, with two or three lesser helpers to do his bidding. The pots and kettles suspended on the cranes and hooks in the big fireplace—there were no stoves—held savory stews and vegetables. In the tin "kitchens" placed in front of the fire whole quarters of meat would be roasting, to be basted at just the right moment. Broilers would be used over the red hot hickory or myrtle coals, and bake ovens with lids for coals on top held delicious cakes. The long handled toasters and waffle and wafer irons stood beside the fireplace, ready for use in their turn. Often corn wafers baked for dinner were kept in rows laid on either side of the chimney to keep them hot and crisp, and a good child could run in and be given a hot buttered wafer to sustain him until the serving of the meal.

Meals were accompanied by a variety of fine wines, Champagne, Sauternes, claret, and other spirited beverages. The Coupers often served orange shrub, a popular island drink made with chips from sour Seville oranges grown on St. Simons, steeped for two weeks in brandy and sweetened with sugar made from cane grown on the island.

When John and Rebecca Couper's thirty-three-year-old son James Hamilton Couper married sixteen-year-old Caroline Wylly of The Village, a plantation that occupied the same property as the old German Village of

Oglethorpe's day, the guests were served a buffet feast. The ceremony was held in 1827 on Christmas night.

Again, Bessie Lewis captures the atmosphere: "At eleven o'clock the guests went in to supper in the drawing room, with an overflow table on the piazza. Never was a meal more truthfully called a 'bounteous repast.' There were cold roast and boiled turkey, stuffed hams, oyster pies, patties of shrimp and crab, syllabub and the punch bowl twice filled. All this with breads and cakes of every description gave the tables good cause to groan."

Syllabub, similar to eggnog but without the eggs, was a traditional English dessert drink popular on St. Simons. It was made of sweetened rich milk or cream curdled with alcohol. A charming recipe of 1871 from *The Household Book of Practical Receipts*, by Mrs. George W. M. Reynolds, gives the following instructions for syllabub: "Put into a large bowl one pound of powdered sugar, and pour on it the juice (strained) of four lemons; stir well and then add one quart of port wine, one quart of sherry and one pint of brandy; grate in two nutmegs and place the bowl under the cow and milk it full."

Couper taught a young slave named Johnny to play the fiddle. During the wedding reception, Johnny stood on the lawn, playing for the guests. Johnny also played the bagpipes, and when Christ Church Frederica was considering the purchase of a new organ, the fun-loving Scotsman sent Johnny to play bagpipes for the congregation, saying he hoped they would prefer the music of his beloved pipes to traditional organ music. Couper was probably joking; at any rate, the congregants opted for the organ.

John Couper sold the federal government four acres of land on south St. Simons for the first lighthouse. The builder, James Gould of New England, used tabby blocks and bricks harvested from the ruins of Fort Frederica. The lighthouse opened in 1811. (Courtesy of the Coastal Georgia Historical Society)

After John Couper sold the government the land for the first lighthouse, James Gould of Massachusetts was hired as the builder. Gould had come to the island in the late 1700s to survey the live oak timbers for the first ships of the U.S. Navy. He built the octagonal lighthouse tower of tabby blocks cut from ruins at Fort Frederica, and then finished the final dozen feet with the "best northward brick," also salvaged from the fort. Gould was hired as the first keeper when the light was activated in 1811. The tower was eighty-five feet high, counting the ten-foot-tall iron lantern where oil lamps were suspended on chains. Some of Gould's descendants still live on St. Simons, and Gould's Inlet, flanked by Sea Island's south beach and the tip of East Beach, is named for the family. The present tower was designed and built in the late 1800s by the celebrated Georgia architect Charles Cluskey of Savannah, who assisted in renovating the U.S. Capitol. Construction of the new lighthouse took about a decade. Cluskey and several of his workers died of malaria a year before it was finished. In those days, lowland around the lighthouse was pocked with stagnant ponds where disease-carrying mosquitoes bred.

Malaria was once endemic on St. Simons and the rest of the southern coast. White people did not stay on the low-lying delta rice plantations during the hot rainy season, which stretched from mid-May until first frost in fall. Warm weather brought swarms of mosquitoes that spread malaria, yellow fever, and other mosquito-borne ailments. Instead, most of the island planters and their families retreated to houses in the North or to the pine barrens inland, where the resinous scent of stately, longleaf pines protected them from fevers, or so they thought. Longleaf pine, also called heart pine and yellow pine, once covered a wide swath of Georgia's coastal plain from the Piedmont to the coast. At one time, as many as sixty million acres of longleaf pine forest stretched from Virginia southwest to Texas. Called the pine barrens by early settlers, the longleaf forests were far from barren, although they grew in poor, sandy soil. Longleaf forests were the mainstay of a complex ecosystem that sheltered hundreds of species of animals and plants, many of which have now gone extinct. A number of surviving pine barrens species are threatened or endangered, including red-cockaded woodpeckers and indigo snakes.

Georgia longleafs were valued as ship's masts because they grew tall and true, prompting the once-popular phrase "straight as a Georgia pine." Their heartwood is as dense and strong as red oak and is naturally resistant to pests and rot. It is also beautiful. Heart pine lumber is streaked in colors ranging from pale yellow to glowing amber to golden brown to rich red, all in a single board. Experts say the pine barrens were the rain forests

of the southern United States. The Baxley-born naturalist writer and longleaf pine advocate Janisse Ray says the pines sing when the wind catches them just right.

In antebellum times, people believed malaria and other mosquito-borne diseases were caused by miasmas, or damp, noxious air that wafted up from swamps and other lowlands. Malaria derives its name from the Italian mala aria, which translates as "bad air." The Coupers were among the few planter families that stayed year-round on St. Simons; their land was high enough and sited so that ocean breezes blew the bad air—and the mosquitoes—away. Not until the late 1800s did scientists discover that mosquitoes were the disease carriers for malaria. Many people continued to blame swamp miasmas well into the twentieth century.

Malaria was one of the reasons that rice planters on St. Simons preferred to purchase slaves who came from the rice coast of West Africa. The Africans not only were experienced at growing rice in tidal areas but were also said to be immune to malaria, which they were not. On rice plantations, slave mortality was appallingly high. Two-thirds of

the Africans who worked the rice fields died before the age of sixteen. Some slaves who inherited the recessive sickle-cell trait from one parent acquired partial immunity to the disease. Those who inherited the recessive trait from both parents developed full-blown sickle-cell disease. Slaves with the disease suffered bouts of severe pain and strokes and died young; their red blood cells, which carry oxygen through the body, were deformed, crescent shaped rather than plate shaped. Today sickle cell disease is still common in the coastal South, but modern medical treatments can reduce pain and extend the life spans of sufferers.

The culture of the island planters was, at least on the surface, charming, admirable, and often romanticized by white people of later generations. It could not have existed, however, without the other culture that evolved on St. Simons during antebellum times: that of the thousands of slaves who made the plantations possible as well as profitable. The slaves were thrown forcibly into the cultural gumbo of early America. With roots

A brick chimney marks the remains of the
home at Retreat Plantation.

Wealthy island planters, including Anna King of Retreat, built
slave hospitals on their property. Now home to the Sea Island Golf
Club, Retreat Plantation on the south end of St. Simons was one
of the most prosperous on the island.

stretching back to scores of African regions and tribes, and lacking a common language, they created a unique creolized culture called Gullah or Geechee or Gullah Geechee, which survives today, especially in rural parts of coastal Georgia and South Carolina. The Gullah Geechee language is the only known English-based creole in the United States. It was widely spoken on St. Simons until well after public schools were integrated in the 1960s. Even now, Gullah Geechee babies on the sea islands often learn words and phrases of the lilting language in songs and folktales from their parents and grandparents. The isolation of the sea islands helped the Gullah Geechee people to preserve more of their African heritage—language, religious beliefs, food, music, storytelling, basket weaving, net building, and other traditions—than any other African American community in the United States. The Gullah Geechee culture continues to inform and influence life on St. Simons today. Many descendants of island slaves still make their homes on the island, as do the descendants of some of the planters.

Slaves on St. Simons lived in crowded frame or tabby cabins with dirt or plank floors and small unglazed windows shuttered at night to keep out cold in winter, insects in

Old photograph of a slave cabin on Gascoigne Bluff (Courtesy of the Coastal Georgia Historical Society)

summer. Two families often shared a double pen, or duplex cabin, their living quarters separated by a central chimney. The cabins were sparsely furnished with handmade items or plantation castoffs. Slaves had no books; if they did, they hid them because it was against the law for slaves to read or write. The wives of coastal planters sometimes defied the law and taught favored slaves to read, write, and do basic arithmetic, tutoring one or two slaves along with their own children before the white youngsters went off to school. At that point, the slave children's schooling usually ended.

The plantation workday began when the head driver blew the conch before dawn to wake the other slaves. The conch horn was made from a large whelk shell whose knob was broken off to provide a mouthpiece. The deep, husky bellow of the conch, audible over long distances, is akin to that of a foghorn. Although large whelks are increasingly hard to find on St. Simons beaches, island children still make conch horns and learn to blow them.

Starting early to avoid the heat of the day, slaves labored on a task system. Unlike work gangs on inland plantations, who labored from dawn to dusk, coastal slaves were assigned specific plots of land, called tasks. A slave who could complete a whole task

The remains of the slave hospital at Retreat Plantation. The tabby ruins were stabilized in recent years by the Sea Island Company.

in a day was considered a full hand; one who completed half a task was a half hand, and so on. Young people were usually classified as quarter hands. The task system was considered more enlightened than the gang system, because task slaves who completed their work early were usually allowed, for the remainder of the day, to fish, hunt, build boats, weave baskets, and knit fishing nets. In addition to their owners' vegetable gardens, slaves tended their own small plots, where they grew peas, corn, peppers, benne (sesame), sweet potatoes, okra, and other produce. They raised chickens and ducks in the clean-swept yards of the slave quarters and kept hogs in fenced pens, fattening them up for slaughter by letting them forage for acorns in the woods. Although the planters and plantation managers wanted their slaves to be dependent on them, archaeological studies indicate that slaves on St. Simons provided as much as 60 percent of their own food. The slaves earned a little money to buy tobacco, clothing, and other items by selling surplus eggs, chickens, seafood, game, and produce, as well as handmade items, to their owners or to residents and merchants in nearby Darien. Experts say the task system, which gave the slaves time on their own to pursue their crafts, enjoy music and stories, and play games helped preserve the Gullah Geechee culture.

The Sapelo Island memoirist Cornelia Bailey says slaves often grew food plants that had been brought from Africa to the sea islands by slave traders because newly imported slaves refused to eat unfamiliar European food. Others say the captives, who were often held for months in camps on the African coast before boarding slave ships, hoarded seeds and plants and smuggled them aboard. However they reached America, food of African origin is still popular on the sea islands. Islanders use okra to thicken gumbo (in Gullah Geechee, *okra* means "gumbo"); they eat black-eyed peas (or red peas) and rice to celebrate the New Year; and they plant benne for good luck. Gungercake, now called gingerbread, was first made with gunger, or ginger, roots native to Africa. Muslim slaves on Sapelo Island made sweet rice cakes called *saraka* and passed the tradition down to present generations. On slave ships, captives chewed the nuts of kola trees to satisfy hunger and thirst and to settle upset stomachs. Kola nuts, native to western Sudan, later became an important ingredient in drinks such as Coca-Cola.

On island plantations, slaves were encouraged to marry as long as they married people on their home plantations. Marrying someone from abroad, or from a different plantation, was known as having a broad wife or husband, and the practice was forbidden by many planters, in part because they feared that separated spouses would slip off for visits and neglect their work. There was another reason. Babies born into slavery became the property of their mothers' owners, so planters preferred their male slaves to father children for the benefit of their own plantations. Except on Sundays, the slaves' day off, young children stayed home with elderly slave women while their parents worked. Nursing babies accompanied their mothers to the planters' houses or to the fields. Babies were left close by in the shade, and their mothers took breaks to feed them. Infant mortality was high on southern plantations, in part because midwives made a practice of spreading spiderwebs on newly cut umbilical cords to stanch bleeding. When gathered from stables, the spiderwebs swarmed with tetanus germs. Newborns treated with tainted webs died of lockjaw, a death so common that people called it the nine-day fits.

In recent years, scholars have discovered that St. Simons and neighboring Sapelo Island had a higher concentration of Islamic slaves than any other part of the antebellum South. Many Muslim slaves had been educated as children in Africa and could read the Qur'an and write in Arabic. David S. Williams, the Miegs Professor of Religion at the University of Georgia, estimates that at least 20 percent of the slaves brought to New World colonies were Muslims with enough training in Arabic and Islamic traditions that they were able to keep aspects of their faith alive. Wealthy island planters handpicked

Left-handed and right-handed whelks from St. Simons beach

Slaves planted an avenue of live oaks leading to the plantation house at Retreat.

Muslims as slaves because they believed them to be more intelligent and of better character. They gave them responsible jobs as drivers, skilled laborers, and house servants. Salih Bilali, a trusted Muslim driver on the Couper plantations, managed more than five hundred slaves for months at a time when his owners were away. John Couper's son, James Hamilton Couper, described Bilali as "a strict Mahometan who abstains from spiritous liquors, and keeps the various fasts, particularly that of the Rhamadam." Salih Bilali was not related to another Muslim man of stature named Mohammed Bilali on Sapelo Island, although the two became friends after they were brought to the neighboring Georgia sea islands. Over generations, many of the Islamic customs and beliefs were replaced by those of Christianity, the faith of the planters.

The story of Major Butler's slave Morris, told since antebellum times on the island, illustrates the size of the emotional chasm between planters and slaves. Morris, the head driver on Little St. Simons, saved more than a hundred of his fellow slaves from drowning in the hurricane of 1804, the same storm witnessed by Aaron Burr. The slaves, working under Morris's supervision on the small island, panicked and ran for the boats, hoping to cross the Hampton River to larger St. Simons before the storm reached its full fury. Using his authority and his driver's whip, Morris forced the terrified people to take shelter in the only structure on Little St. Simons, the hurricane house, where they rode out the blow in safety. Many other coastal slaves, especially those on low-lying rice plantations, died in the hurricane.

Major Butler would have suffered a huge financial loss if one hundred or more of his slaves had drowned. To show his gratitude, he presented Morris with an engraved silver cup and offered him his freedom. Since Major Butler's offer, which he no doubt considered generous, did not extend to Morris's wife and children, Morris opted to remain a slave in order to stay with his family.

The famed British actress Fanny Kemble married Major Butler's grandson, Pierce Mease (pronounced "Mays") Butler, who inherited the island plantations with his brother, John. Kemble visited St. Simons for a few months during the winter and spring of 1838–39 with her husband and their two young daughters. The sexual exploitation of slave women by white men was one of many grim realities of slavery that shocked her most.

Frances Anne "Fannie" Kemble, born into a family of distinguished actors, wanted to be a writer. During her lifetime, she published journals, plays, essays, and poems that won critical acclaim. But when desperate family finances prompted her to pursue an acting career in her late teens, she was a natural from the moment she stepped on stage. As Juliet in Shakespeare's play, she packed theatres in Europe and the United States. Later in life, overweight and matronly, she continued to captivate audiences with her dramatic

Gullah or Geechee?

NORTH OF THE Savannah River, the people usually call themselves Gullah; in Georgia around the Ogeechee River and farther south, *Gullah* becomes *Geechee*, although the two terms are used interchangeably or in combination. Well into the twentieth century, the Gullah Geechee language was considered substandard, but it is recognized and valued today as North America's only English-based creole, similar to Krio, which is spoken in Sierra Leone. The African American linguist Lorenzo Dow Turner, the godfather of Gullah Geechee studies, began work on the culture in 1929 and discovered some four thousand words in the creole that have roots in West African languages: Mandinka, Wolof, Fula, Mende, Vai, Yoruba, Igbo, Kongo, and others.

The word *Gullah* may derive from *Angola* or from the Gola tribe of the Sierra Leone–Liberia border, or from *Gallinas* or *Galo*, other names for the Vai people of West Africa. *Geechee* may come from the Kissi tribe (pronounced "geezee"), although many scholars and coastal Georgians believe the name derives from the Ogeechee River south of Savannah. The U.S. Supreme Court justice Clarence Thomas is Gullah Geechee and grew up speaking the creole in the tiny, rural Pinpoint community, which was settled near Savannah by former Ossabaw Island slaves after the Civil War. Justice Thomas has said that because he was teased about his speech when he was growing up, he is still reluctant to speak in public.

readings. The American-born novelist Henry James considered her one of the most fascinating women he had ever met.

When Pierce Mease Butler saw the young Kemble perform on tour in America, he courted her until she married him. The union was stormy at best. Kemble, passionate, outspoken, and temperamental, was a woman ahead of her time. She thought men and women should be equal partners in marriage, not a view popular with her husband or most other men of the era. In addition, Mease Butler had a well-deserved reputation as a playboy and gambler, which he maintained after their marriage and the birth of their daughters, Frances ("Fan") and Sarah ("Sally"). Kemble left her husband on several occasions, but returned for the sake of the girls. Her journal suggests she loved him, at least some of the time. Mease Butler's most heated arguments with Kemble came over the issue of slavery. Two years after they married, Mease Butler needed to hire a new manager for the Georgia plantations, and Kemble was determined to go south with him to see for herself the system that financed their lavish lifestyle. Mease Butler, who often

The British actress Fanny Kemble captivated audiences on both sides of the Atlantic. She married Pierce Mease Butler, who inherited Hampton and Butler's Island plantations from his grandfather, Major Pierce Butler. Kemble wrote about the months she spent on the plantations, praising the area's beauty but reporting the poor treatment of the slaves in a journal published during the Civil War. (Courtesy of the Coastal Georgia Historical Society)

boasted of how well his slaves were treated and how much they loved him, thought a firsthand tour might soften or even change his wife's abolitionist sentiments. The couple came to Georgia with their daughters in December, after the end of the fever season.

Kemble was captivated by the lush beauty of St. Simons, describing it in great detail in her journal. She was appalled, however, by the realities of slavery. She listened to complaints from slaves, observed their grim lives, and tried to improve conditions for them. She may have done more harm than good. Slaves were punished for talking to her, and Mease Butler soon forbade her to bring their complaints to him.

Possibly because she knew about or suspected her husband's philandering, or perhaps simply because she related more easily to women, Kemble focused her attention on the female slaves. In one entry, the twenty-three-year-old actress showed her naivete by asking a married slave woman why she had submitted to the advances of the white overseer. The woman explained she had no choice: "We do anything to get our poor flesh some rest from de whip."

Beyond the degradation of rape, there could be horrifying consequences for slave women whose owners forced themselves upon them. Julia Maxwell King, the wife of Roswell King Jr., had two slave women on St. Simons "strung up and lashed" for bearing children fathered by her husband, even though the slaves had no choice in the matter. Julia King personally supervised the initial whipping and then sent the women, Scylla and Judy, to the desolate stretch of impounded marsh on Little St. Simons called Five Pound Tree, ordering the driver to flog the women daily for a week.

Shortly before the Civil War, Mease Butler was responsible for the largest single sale of human beings ever conducted in the United States. The sale occurred in 1859, well after Kemble and her husband divorced. Mease Butler consigned more than 436 slaves to be auctioned in Savannah in order to raise money to pay his debts, many incurred by gambling on the stock market. He specified that the slaves were to be sold in nuclear-family groups, but the two-day auction is still referred to as the "weeping time" by Gullah Geechees on St. Simons because so many people were wrenched away from grandparents, aunts, uncles, grown siblings, cousins, sweethearts, and lifelong friends, as well as from the only home many had ever known. Mease Butler made more than $300,000 from the sale, enough to satisfy his creditors and treat himself to a European trip.

When Fanny Kemble's now-famous *Journal of a Residence on a Georgia Plantation* was published during the Civil War, it became an overnight best seller in England and the northern United States, but was reviled in the South. Resentment of Kemble was

Spanish moss

long-lived, especially on St. Simons, where much of the abuse she reported occurred. Although the journal has long been credited with—or blamed for—dissuading Great Britain from supporting the Confederate war effort, England had already become disenchanted with the southern cause by the time it was published in 1863.

The respected Glynn County historian Margaret Davis Cate pointed out several of Kemble's errors in what has been described as a "scathing critique" of the journal in an article in the *Georgia Historical Quarterly* of March 1960. Cate is said to have written the article to discourage the publisher John A. Scott from issuing a modern edition of the journal; she feared it would inflame passions at a time when southern schools, restaurants, and other public places were on the verge of being integrated. Scott was not persuaded; he published a new edition in 1961, and Kemble's journal is still in print.

Anna Matilda King of Retreat Plantation was also a prolific writer. Over a period of forty-two years, she wrote more than a thousand letters to her husband and other relatives and friends, describing her life at Retreat and elsewhere on St. Simons. Anna King often wrote with pride and pleasure about her private gardens, where she planted only fragrant flowers and shrubs, including almost a hundred varieties of roses. She called flowers without scents "plants without souls." When her gardens were in full bloom in spring, sailors claimed they could smell their perfume a dozen miles out to sea. Anna King wrote also about her husband's financial failures. Thomas King declared bankruptcy when the cotton economy collapsed in the 1830s; he lost all the property he had purchased adjacent to Retreat, along with a number of slaves he owned. Because Major William Page's will made it clear that Retreat Plantation and the slaves Anne King inherited belonged only to his daughter, her property was exempt from the bankruptcy. Page, an astute man, may have suspected that his daughter's entrepreneurial husband might overextend himself and suffer financial reversals.

In her letters, Anna King makes it clear that she missed her husband and wanted him with her. She lived at Retreat until her death in 1859. Thomas Butler King died in 1864 and is buried at Christ Church alongside his wife. Many of the King descendents, and descendants of their former slaves, still live on St. Simons, including the family of Neptune Small, a slave at Retreat who helped plant the picturesque avenue of live oaks that still stands at the entrance to the Sea Island Golf Club.

The Christ Church congregation was founded in 1736 by John and Charles Wesley. The ministers held services for colonists and soldiers under live oak trees and in a storage building they called a "chapel." Island planters officially organized Christ Church in 1807 on one hundred acres of Frederica commons granted by the Georgia Legislature. The grant included three lots in the town of Frederica that the church could rent out for income. The church was the second Episcopal congregation to be formed in Georgia and the third established in the United States. Until the first church building was erected in 1820, with funds donated by planters, congregants met in the pastor's house. The first church, a small square building painted white with green shutters and topped by a belfry, was surrounded by the live oak trees under whose branches the Wesleys had preached to the Frederica colonists and soldiers almost a century earlier. Christ Church soon became the social center for planters and their families on St. Simons.

Caroline Couper Lovell, the great-granddaughter of John Couper, wrote that congregants began arriving at 9 a.m. for the service that would begin two hours later. The

Christ Episcopal Church, Frederica, is one of the island's best-known historic sites. The original congregants were organized by Charles Wesley, the Anglican minister whose brother, John, founded the Methodist Church.

women gathered to talk while the men sat on benches in the shade, sharing news of crops and politics and reading mail delivered to the churchyard by Frederica's postmaster. Children romped over the grounds, though strictly admonished to stay clean at least until after church. When the little church needed repairs, a beehive filled with honey was discovered in the belfry. The congregants harvested the honey and sold it for money to repair the church. For a while afterward, Christ Church was nicknamed the Beehive Church, and the women's missionary society was called the Busy Bees.

Susie Baker King Taylor

THE REMARKABLE Susie Baker was just fourteen years old when she opened one of the South's first sanctioned schools for liberated slaves during the Civil War. Baker later published her autobiography, describing her time on St. Simons as well as her work later as a nurse, cook, and laundress in a black Union regiment. Her narrative is the only known document written by a black woman who served in the Union army; it is also one of the few memoirs of the Civil War written from an African American perspective.

Born in August 1848 in coastal Georgia on the Isle of Wight plantation of Valentin Grest, Baker was a favorite of the plantation's mistress, sleeping on the foot of the Grest bed whenever the master was away. Planters' wives often made pets of slave children, taking them on trips, giving them toys and sweets, and treating them as they might a cute puppy. As the child grew older, he or she was usually replaced by a younger child, while the former pet was sent to work in the master's house or in the fields. The Grests may have been especially fond of Baker. When she was seven, they sent her and her younger brother to Savannah to live with their grandmother, Dolly Reed, a free woman, who enrolled them in an underground school. A number of underground schools operated in the coastal city before the Civil War. They were called bucket schools because the students hid their books in buckets or concealed them in other ways. Teachers at the schools took enormous risks; some who were caught had their thumbs cut off. One Savannah teacher was whipped in public after his bucket school was discovered. Baker learned to read and write from Mary Woodhouse, a free black woman who instructed twenty-five to thirty slave children in her house with the help of her daughter Mary Jane.

"We went every day about nine o'clock, with our books wrapped in paper to prevent the police or white persons from seeing them," Baker remembered. The students entered and left the house one by one so that nobody would suspect the widow of running the school. Baker spent about two years at the Woodhouse school, then transferred to a school run by a free woman who later became Georgia's first black nun. Baker was tutored also by a white Catholic playmate, Katie O'Connor, who attended a Savannah convent school. O'Connor told Baker: "If I would promise not to tell her

Susie Baker King Taylor was one of about six hundred liberated but not yet officially freed slaves held in a Union refugee camp on St. Simons during the Civil War. Educated in underground schools in Savannah, she opened one of the first sanctioned schools for black children and adults in the South. (Courtesy of the University of Georgia Press)

father, she would give me some lessons. On my promise not to do so and getting her mother's consent, she gave me lessons about four months, every evening. At the end of this time, she was put into the convent permanently, and I have never seen her since."

Because she was literate, Baker forged passes for her grandmother and other blacks in Savannah, who were required to have them to go out at night. Black residents gathered for clandestine political meetings by using passes written by Baker. Her grandmother was arrested for attending a political meeting and for singing hymns branded as treasonous because they contained such lines as "We shall all be free." Valentin Grest intervened and Reed was released, but Baker was sent back to the Grest plantation in Liberty County. In April 1862, while Union cannons were firing on Fort Pulaski east of Savannah, Baker, then fourteen, heard the cannon fire from the neighboring county. "I remember what a roar and din the guns made," she wrote later. "They jarred the earth for miles."

Two days after Union forces captured the fort and blockaded the port of Savannah, Baker left the Grest plantation with her uncle and a number of other children. They traveled by boat to St. Catherines Island, where they remained under Union protection for about two weeks. In mid-April, Baker and about thirty others were taken aboard a gunboat bound for St. Simons.

CHAPTER IV   A Time for Civil War

DURING THE CIVIL WAR, liberated but not yet officially freed slaves followed northern soldiers en masse. They needed food, shelter, and protection, something the Union army was not prepared to provide while fighting a war. The federal government aimed to solve the problem by setting up contraband camps around the South; southern slaves were called contraband because they were legally considered property until President Lincoln signed the Emancipation Proclamation in early 1863. (The status of slaves in areas not in rebellion, such as Delaware or Washington, D.C., was not affected by the proclamation.) The government established two refugee camps on St. Simons: one at Retreat Plantation, overlooking St. Simons Sound, and the other at Gascoigne Bluff, on the Frederica River. A northern sailor on a blockading ship depicted one of the contrabands, a lovely young woman, in an ivory carving brought back to St. Simons by a circuitous route more than a century after the work was done. Some contrabands held at camps on St. Simons, including Susie Baker, later joined the Union army, but at least two slaves who had been owned by island planters aided their former owners during the war. A controversial Union regiment of free blacks organized in Boston under a young white commander was stationed

at Hampton Plantation on St. Simons in 1863. Their poignant story was portrayed in the popular film *Glory* (1989). During the last days of the war, former sea island slaves were granted land on the southeastern coast by General Tecumseh Sherman, but following Lincoln's assassination, most of the property was returned to its former white owners. Only a few planters came back to St. Simons after the war to try to make their old plantations profitable.

During the early days of the war, white occupants of St. Simons and the other sea islands fled to the mainland at the behest of General Robert E. Lee, who said he would be unable to protect them or their property from the Union navy. Most St. Simons planters and their families sought safety inland, many in Wayne County, about forty-five miles away, taking many of their slaves along with them. Some slaves, especially elderly ones, were left behind on the island, and others probably hid in the woods or marshes during the exodus and returned to their old quarters after the Union takeover of St. Simons. For most of the war, Union ships blockaded about thirty-five hundred miles of southern coastline from New Orleans to Virginia, along with a stretch of the Mississippi River. The so-called Anaconda Plan was devised by Winfield Scott, general in chief of the U.S. Army, to cut off southern commercial shipping and divide Confederate forces by encircling much of the South with the snake-like blockade.

Susie Baker was among the freed slaves assigned to the contraband camp on Gascoigne Bluff, which she called Gaston Bluff. She had been at the camp only a few days when a white Union officer asked the teenager to open a school for contraband children. She agreed on the condition that books would be provided. For the remainder of her time on the island, Baker taught about forty children during the day and a similar number of adults at night, "all of them so eager to learn to read, to read above anything else."

St. Simons, under the control of the Union for most of the war, was raided several times by Confederate soldiers who slipped onto the island to commit acts of sabotage, including burning the coaling wharf at Gascoigne Bluff or kidnapping contrabands, and to spy on northern forces, most of whom were aboard the Union ships offshore. Baker said people in the camps were terrified of being captured by Confederate soldiers, who would put them to work digging ditches, moving heavy equipment, and otherwise laboring for the southern cause. Male contrabands on the island were left to guard the camps, armed with a scant handful of cast-off weapons.

"The rebels, knowing this, could steal by them [the contrabands] under cover of the night and getting on the island would capture any [black] persons venturing out alone

Gascoigne Bluff, one of the island's most historic locales. Gascoigne is pronounced "gas-coin" by longtime islanders.

and carry them to the mainland. Several of the men disappeared, and as they were never heard from we came to the conclusion they had been carried off in this way," Baker wrote. On one such island raid, Confederate soldiers chased two contrabands. Afterward, ninety others from the camps combed the island looking for the southerners. The Confederates killed two of the searchers and wounded a third, who died later. One of the men killed was the uncle of Susie Baker's future husband, Edward King of Darien. Baker and King had met when he worked as a carpenter in Savannah; by either coincidence or design, both ended up at the St. Simons camp. After the contrabands were killed, Union troops, including three hundred marines from the blockading boats, then joined the search and found the Confederates' boat, trapping them on the island. The Confederate raiders escaped by enlisting the help of a former St. Simons slave, Henry Capers, who had been left behind "by his old master, Mr. Hazzard, as he was too old to carry away," Baker wrote.

In her autobiography, she described a number of settlements on St. Simons, "just like little villages," where she and the other contrabands went "on business, to call, or only for a walk." The settlements were probably slave quarters occupied by Gullah Geechees who had not evacuated to the mainland with their owners; the "business" Baker referred to may have involved the purchase of eggs, fresh vegetables, seafood, or other items from the residents. Capers, who lived in one of the settlements, hid the Confederates in the loft of his cabin. Union troops searched the place but overlooked the loft. That night, Capers gave the Confederates his boat so that they could escape to the mainland. The Union commander who later learned of Capers's aiding of the enemy banished him to the mainland as punishment.

Capers's actions were not unusual. Many slaves and freedmen fought for the Confederacy, hid their owners' valuables from Union forces, and accompanied their owners to war as body servants, even after emancipation. As for the Confederate soldiers whom Capers helped, he had probably known them all their lives. Captain Miles Hazzard, whose family had owned him and who led several guerrilla missions to St. Simons during the Union occupation, may have been among the raiders Capers assisted.

The story of Neptune Small is one of St. Simons's most famous tales, often told to illustrate the affection felt by slaves for their owners. Born on Retreat Plantation about the same time as one of the Kings' sons, Henry Lord "Lordy" King, Small was reared as a privileged playmate and future body servant for several of the King brothers. He was

Neptune Small, a slave who accompanied two of his owners' sons when they joined the Confederate army during the Civil War. When the elder son was killed, Small brought his body back to Georgia. He was rewarded by the King family with land on St. Simons now occupied by Neptune Park. (Courtesy of the Coastal Georgia Historical Society)

tutored along with the King sons by Anna King; he slept on the floor beside Lordy's bed; and he fished, hunted, and rode horseback with the King boys. When Lordy King enlisted in the Confederate Army in 1861, Small was sent along as his body servant and cook, a common practice at the time. Most officers were accompanied to war by menservants. After months of combat, King was killed at the Battle of Fredericksburg (December 11–15, 1862). When King did not return to camp for supper, Small searched the dark, bloody battlefield and found his young owner's body, which he shepherded home to Georgia—not an easy task in the war-torn South. Because the family had fled to the mainland with other island planters, King was initially buried in Savannah. His body was later moved to the family plot at Christ Church Cemetery.

After Lordy King was killed, the family said Small volunteered to return to the battlefront to serve a second son, Richard Cuyler "Tip" King. Small stayed with Tip until the Confederate surrender, then returned with him to St. Simons. Small worked for the King family after the war, which included caring for Lordy King's grave until Small's own death in 1907. Small chose his own postwar surname, perhaps because of his small stature. In gratitude for his service, the Kings granted Small a plot of land on the island, where he built a house and reared his family. Part of the property later became Glynn County–owned Neptune Park by the pier. Small's house was in an oceanfront grove of live oaks where the park's picnic tables are now located. Glynn County officials purchased the Neptune Park property over the objections of his family, according to his descendants, many of whom still live on St. Simons. Small was buried at the Retreat Plantation slave cemetery, now part of the Sea Island Golf Course, where other members of his family are interred. A tabby monument with a bronze plaque marks his grave.

In June 1862, rumors swept through the contraband camps at Retreat and Gascoigne Bluff that a war settlement was pending. "Those [African Americans] who were on the Union side would remain free and those in bondage were to work three days for their masters and three for themselves. It was a gloomy time for us all," Susie Baker remembered. There were rumors that all freed slaves would be sent to Africa. Before the war, President Lincoln had endorsed a program sponsored by the American Colonization Society to settle freed slaves in the African nation of Liberia; he decried slavery but did not then contemplate emancipation. Lincoln drafted the Emancipation Proclamation in the summer of 1862 but waited until Union forces won a major battle before proclaiming it; the defeat of Lee's forces at Antietam that September provided him the occasion he sought.

For the duration of the war, Union blockade ships cruised the waters east of St. Simons, anchored in the sound, and took on fuel at the Gascoigne Bluff coaling wharf. Union sailors and marines often came ashore on the island, probably in search of fresh water, food, and firewood, or just to stretch their legs. In January 1863, sailors from the gunboat *Ethan Allen* raided Retreat Plantation, taking, along with other spoils of war, a mantel clock from the house. The clock traveled aboard the *Ethan Allen* when the gunboat returned to Boston. In 1930, the clock was sold at a Massachusetts estate auction. The antiques dealer who repaired it found pasted on the back of the dial a note that read: "This clock was taken from the Thomas Butler King Plantation on St. Simons Island, Ga., by members of the crew of the United States gunboat *Ethan Allen.*"

When the dealer learned that descendants of the King family still lived on St. Simons, he arranged to have the clock returned. It was presented to King family members in May 1930, sixty-seven years after the clock went missing. The well-publicized ceremony, attended by legislators from both states and a number of other dignitaries, was held in Retreat Plantation's old tabby slave hospital, at the time a clubhouse for caddies at the Sea Island Golf Club. The historic clock was displayed at the players' clubhouse until the structure burned in 1935 and the clock was destroyed.

A Union seaman serving on one of the blockading ships was intrigued by a young woman assigned to the Retreat Plantation contraband camp. Her name was Nora August. What little is known about her is inscribed on the base of the scrimshaw bust carved in ivory by the seaman. It is likely he was a whaler who learned the art of scrimshaw on a New England whaling ship. Whalers were at sea for months, even years, at a time, and the sailors occupied themselves by carving elaborate scenes, portraits, inscriptions, and busts from ivory tusks and whale bones. Little is known about the unknown artist. He may have been a member of the New England Antislavery Society; the society's emblem of a chained black man, kneeling and raising his hands in supplication, is carved into the base of the bust, along with the society's motto: "Am I not a man and a brother?"

According to the inscription on the bust, Nora August was twenty-three at the time the carving was done. She had been purchased in St. Augustine in April 1860, but the inscription does not offer any information about who bought or sold her; it is unlikely she was ever a slave on St. Simons. She was probably liberated by Union forces in Florida and brought to St. Simons to the contraband camp.

The year the war ended, the unknown scrimshander presented the ivory carving to "the Nurses of Darien in the Year of Our Lord, 1865," as the inscription reads. For many

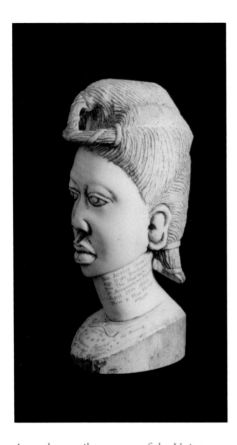

A northern sailor on one of the Union ships blockading the southern coast during the Civil War carved an ivory bust of a slave named Nora August, one of the contrabands held in a camp at Retreat Plantation on St. Simons. More than a century later, the carving was purchased by the former owner of the Sea Island Company and brought back to the island. (Courtesy of Sea Island Company)

years, it was assumed that the Darien referred to was the small coastal town near St. Simons. But Darien, Georgia, had been burned to the ground by Union troops in 1863 and was still in ruins in 1865. It is more likely the artist presented the bust to the nurses at Fitch's Home for Soldiers and Their Children in Darien, Connecticut. The scrimshander was probably a patient at the home, which was founded by the wealthy New England businessman Benjamin Fitch in 1863 as the first institution in the United States for disabled Civil War veterans and war orphans. It evolved into a network of similar facilities in other states and inspired the formation of the Veterans Administration, known today as the U.S. Department of Veterans Affairs. In 1920, the bust of Nora August turned up at a retirement home in a suburb of London, England. It remained there until the retirement home closed in 1975. The ivory carving was purchased by a California man, who offered it for auction in 1979. The late Alfred W. Jones Sr., a founding father of the Sea Island Company, heard of the carving and bought it. Jones thought it fitting for the bust carved at Retreat Plantation more than a century earlier to come back home. For years, the scrimshaw was displayed in the clubhouse of the Sea Island Golf Club, which now occupies the grounds of Retreat. It was featured in an exhibition, *Before Freedom Came*, in 1992 at the Museum of the Confederacy in Richmond, Virginia, which included documents, art, memorabilia, and other items from American slave life. A photograph of the ivory bust, the highlight of the exhibition, was featured on the program cover. The carving is now at Sea Island's archives on St. Simons, according to Bill Jones III, grandson of the company founder.

In October 1862, Nora August and the other contrabands on St. Simons were relocated to camps in South Carolina and Florida. Nora August was probably returned to Florida; Susie Baker and Edward King were sent to Beaufort, South Carolina. They arrived just as the First South Carolina Volunteers, a contraband force, joined the Thirty-Third Regiment, United States Colored Infantry, which was organized by General David Hunter, an avid abolitionist and the Union commander of the Department of the South. Edward King was inducted as a sergeant. Susie King, who had turned fifteen a few months earlier, noted that she and King were married by then. They were assigned to Company E, along with other contrabands from St. Simons, many of whom were related to Baker or King. The black soldiers were first outfitted in red coats and pants; they objected, saying the enemy could see them a mile away, and the uniforms were changed. Susie King was enrolled in the regiment as a laundress. She, along with other soldiers' family members, traveled with the troops to campaigns in South Carolina,

Slave Names

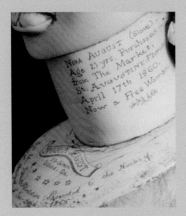

All that is known about Nora August, including her name, is carved into the ivory scrimshaw bust. (Courtesy of Sea Island Company)

SLAVES DID NOT usually have surnames. They were often referred to by the names of their owners, as in *Butler's Jim* or *Couper's Sally*. After the war, many former slaves adopted their owners' surnames, in part because the names were already familiar in their communities. *Butler's Jim* became *Jim Butler; Couper's Sally* became *Sally Couper*. Slaves were given second names when two slaves on a plantation had the same name. The second name was often related to the job the slave did or to some other identifying characteristic. One of two Toms on the same plantation might be called Crab Tom because his job was catching blue crabs. Ebo Sam would have been one of the Ebo, or Igbo, people brought from the Bay of Biafra area in Africa.

Another naming tradition was directly linked to the Gullah Geechees' African roots. In Ghana, the Ivory Coast, and other parts of West Africa, children are still named for the day of the week or month they are born, their birth order, and other significant information. Cudjo, Cusie, Cuffy, and their variants translate as Monday, Tuesday, and Friday. The name of former secretary general of the United Nations Kofi Atta Annan, who was born in Ghana, indicates he was born on Friday (Kofi or Cuffy) and was a twin (Atta). African naming traditions were often rendered in English. A slave named January was probably born in that month. Nora August may have received her second name at birth, or she may have chosen August as a surname after emancipation.

Georgia, and Florida, washing and cooking for them, but after she showed a talent for nursing, her primary job became caring for the sick and wounded.

In February 1863, smallpox broke out in camp. Susie King had been vaccinated against the disease, but she believed the sassafras tea she always drank before tending patients was equally responsible for keeping her healthy. Once after a battle, a number of badly wounded soldiers who were unable to eat solid food begged her for soup. None was available, so she made a soft custard for the invalids, improvising with a few cans of condensed milk and turtle eggs gathered from the beach. While she was visiting wounded soldiers from her regiment at the Beaufort hospital for black troops, Susie King met the famed Civil War nurse Clara Barton. "Miss Barton was always very cordial to me, and I honored her for her devotion and care of those men," she wrote. Barton had first declined to nurse black troops but soon moved past her bias and cared for all the wounded.

For more than a year, King and the other soldiers of the Thirty-Third Regiment received no pay. While they could depend on the army commissary for food and supplies,

The First African Baptist Church, built in 1869, is the oldest surviving church building on St. Simons. Its congregation was organized by island slaves before the Civil War.

their wives and children traveling with them received nothing. The women survived by doing washing for officers on the gunboats and by baking cakes and pies to sell to "the boys in camp." Although a number of Union officers lobbied the government to award full pay to the contraband soldiers, they were not paid until 1864, a year and a half after they joined the Union army. Susie King and the other black women who washed and cooked for the troops and nursed the injured were never paid for their work. The Kings were later assigned to an army camp in coastal South Carolina "named for our hero Colonel Shaw."

Susie King referred to Colonel Robert Gould Shaw, the son of ardent New England abolitionists. He was recruited to command the Fifty-Fourth Massachusetts, the first all-black regiment in the Union army. It was composed of northern black men who were free before the war, unlike the contrabands recruited in the South from the ranks

Oysters grow on muddy marsh banks in the intertidal zone between high and low tides.

Colonel Robert Gould Shaw of Boston, who led the first regiment of black soldiers in the Union army, was based, along with his soldiers, at Hampton Plantation on St. Simons during the Civil War. He wrote about the island's beauty as well as his opposition to burning the small town of Darien, fifteen miles north of St. Simons. (Courtesy of the Library of Congress Prints and Photographs Division)

of newly liberated slaves. When Shaw's soldiers marched out of Boston with great fanfare in 1862, the well-known poet-pacifist John Greenleaf Whittier watched the parade with other notables of the day. Whittier said the twenty-five-year-old Shaw, uniformed and mounted on his ebony horse, "looked as beautiful and awful as an angel of God come down to lead the host of freedom to victory." It was a prophetic statement; a Union officer later ordered Shaw to act as God's instrument on a mission the young colonel bitterly opposed.

Shaw was a member of one of the wealthiest families in the United States. As a teenager in 1853, he traveled with his family to Europe and met Fanny Kemble. During the Shaws' meeting in Italy with Kemble, the renowned actress "held the family spellbound" with horror stories of slavery at Hampton and on Butler's Island.

Shaw was no doubt astonished to be sent to the same plantation that Kemble had described to him and his family a decade earlier in Europe. When Shaw and his men arrived in June 1863, St. Simons was occupied by the Second Regiment, South Carolina Volunteer Infantry (African Descent), organized by General Hunter and led by Colonel James Montgomery. Shaw and the Fifty-Fourth Massachusetts set up camp at Hampton, with Shaw occupying the former house of Butler's overseer. He reported that elderly Butler slaves still on the property remembered Kemble with great affection. They also professed to have fond feelings for their former master, Pierce Mease Butler, Shaw noted.

Colonel Montgomery and General Hunter had little sympathy for slave owners, especially wealthy ones. Montgomery had cooperated on occasion with the notorious white abolitionist John Brown, who seized a federal arsenal in Harper's Ferry, West Virginia, in order to arm slaves for a major revolt. Like Hunter, Montgomery believed extreme measures were justified against anyone who owned slaves. It may have been Montgomery and his troops who damaged Christ Church and graves in the church cemetery during their tenure on St. Simons. Captain Miles Hazzard, the Confederate soldier who led raids on the island during the war, discovered his parents' graves had been disturbed by the Union troops. He left a note for Montgomery posted on a stick outside the cemetery: "Beside these graves I swear by Heaven to avenge their desecration. If it is honorable for you to disturb the dead, I shall consider it an honor and make it my ambition to disturb your living." No graves in Christ Church cemetery were bothered after that.

Montgomery was especially hostile to planters who owned large tracts of land and hundreds of slaves. Soon after Shaw's regiment settled at Hampton, he and his soldiers accompanied Montgomery's troops to Darien, which, like St. Simons, was home to a

number of wealthy planters. Before the war, Darien was Georgia's second most important port. Tons of cotton, rice, turpentine, and timber were loaded at docks on the Darien River, the northern branch of the giant Altamaha, and shipped to markets around the world. The Fifty-Fourth Massachusetts and the Second South Carolina boarded a gunboat and three transports for the fifteen-mile trip from St. Simons to Darien, which Montgomery believed was a rendezvous point for Confederate blockade-runners. By the time Montgomery and Shaw arrived, the town had been heavily shelled and residents had fled inland or to the Ridge, a settlement a few miles north of Darien on an ancient dune ridge overlooking the marshes, hammocks, and waterways between the mainland and Sapelo Island. Many of the delta rice planters and their families routinely moved to the Ridge in warmer weather to escape malaria and other lowland fevers.

Montgomery ordered the soldiers to raid Darien for anything useful to the troops. Useful items that later turned up in regimental tents included rosewood and black walnut furniture, pianos, luxurious carpets, oil paintings, sets of china, books, and looking glasses. The soldiers also confiscated lumber and "droves" of sheep and cows.

When Montgomery told Shaw to burn Darien to the ground, Shaw objected, in part because the Union soldiers had met no Confederate resistance, and the young soldier saw no reason for the action. Shaw wrote later that Montgomery told him why he wanted Darien destroyed: "The reasons he gave me . . . were that the Southerners must be made to feel that this was a real war, and that they were to be swept away by the hand of God like the Jews of old." In a letter to his mother, Shaw said he did not like the idea of becoming God's instrument and found it "revolting to wreak our vengeance on the innocent and defenseless women and children" whose houses would be destroyed.

Shaw also feared that burning Darien would turn public opinion against his soldiers. Black troops were controversial in both the North and the South. Even in liberal Boston, a hotbed of the antislavery movement, Shaw's soldiers had been harassed and ridiculed before leaving the city. When white soldiers pillaged and burned, the destruction was written off as a routine act of war. If black soldiers did the same, Shaw believed it would fan the flames of racism, which indeed it did, even decades after the Civil War. Shaw followed Montgomery's orders, however, and had his troops torch the town. Montgomery himself set fire to the last of the buildings. The blaze engulfed about eighty houses, three churches, a school, the courthouse and jail, several mills, and a number of stores and warehouses loaded with rice, resin, and turpentine. The flames and black smoke from the burning naval stores were visible as far away as St. Simons. As Shaw had feared, newspapers around the country condemned the actions of the Fifty-Fourth, and some people in coastal Georgia, especially in McIntosh County and Darien, still resent the burning.

Shaw protested up the chain of command. He wrote to his mother too, expressing shame for his part in the destruction. After the war, Sarah Shaw raised money to help rebuild one of the Darien churches burned by her son's regiment and wrote letters to government officials, trying to set the record straight regarding her son's role in the incident. When the Fifty-Fourth returned to St. Simons, a dispirited Shaw stepped up training for his men. He wanted his troops to be well trained and above reproach. He also wanted them to show courage in battle. During the Civil War, white soldiers often broke and ran when they first encountered the enemy. The widespread assumption was that black soldiers would refuse to fight at all. Shaw knew that if his soldiers fled under fire, black troops would be stereotyped as cowards.

Perhaps because of his own youth and insecurity as a leader, Shaw became a martinet, drilling his troops in the island's summer swelter and imposing severe penalties for

minor infractions. Soldiers were punished for such things as firing weapons without supervision and for being a nuisance in camp. Shaw rousted his men long before dawn every day and drilled them for hours, and then drilled them again in the afternoon. He conducted daily inspections of troops and equipment. He reviewed the entire regiment in formal dress parade every evening. Taps at 9:30 p.m. did not need to be enforced; the exhausted soldiers were happy to fall into bed.

In his free time, Shaw enjoyed the lush beauty of St. Simons—the old oaks, gleaming beaches, and expanses of green marsh. He explored abandoned plantations, including Cannon's Point and Retreat. His soldiers killed two alligators in camp at Hampton and learned to be wary of other island wildlife. One of Shaw's officers commented, "To tell the honest truth, our boys out on picket look sharper for snakes than they do for rebels."

The Fifty-Fourth Massachusetts ate well, supplementing its rations with cattle left behind by the island planters and sea turtle eggs they dug from the beach. They bathed in the brackish Hampton River and rinsed in warm summer rains. Shaw augmented the furnishings of the overseer's house with spoils of war from looted houses in Darien. He wrote letters and studied military tactics.

The Attack on Fort Wagner, South Carolina. Colonel Shaw and many of his men were killed in the attack and buried in a mass grave. (Courtesy of the Library of Congress Prints and Photographs Division)

On June 25, 1863, Shaw and the Fifty-Fourth traveled with Montgomery's Second to South Carolina to join the attack on Charleston, the only southern port city not under Union control. In July, Shaw and the black soldiers of the Fifty-Fourth Massachusetts exhibited extraordinary courage in the assault on Fort Wagner, a Confederate battery on Morris Island, near Charleston. Shaw led the charge and was killed along with a number of his men. The Confederate commander returned the bodies of Union officers who led white troops but, intending an insult, buried Shaw in a mass grave with his black soldiers. There were Union proposals to retrieve Shaw's body, but his father, a Union officer, announced that he was proud to have his son interred along with his troops. Robert Gould Shaw was twenty-six when he died. He was subsequently hailed as a hero, not only for his bravery in battle but also for his courage as a leader in the fight for full pay for black troops.

After the Civil War, Susie Baker King and her husband moved to Savannah, where King died in a work-related accident shortly before their only child, a son, was born. Susie King started a private school but was put out of business by free public schools that soon opened in the city. She took a series of domestic jobs, then left her son with her mother and traveled to Boston with a wealthy family as their maid and cook. After marrying Russell M. Taylor of Boston, she devoted the remainder of her life to the organization she helped found: the women's auxiliary of the Grand Army of the Republic. She later served as the organization's president. Susie Taylor made only a few trips back to the South. One was in 1888, when she visited her dying Grandmother Reed in Savannah, the free woman who had arranged to educate Baker and her younger brother. A decade later, Susie Taylor traveled to Louisiana to nurse her son, who had fallen ill while traveling with a theatre troupe. She never mentions her son's name in her memoir. She wanted to take him to Boston, where good medical treatment was available for black people, but because of Jim Crow laws, she was not permitted to book a sleeping berth for him on the segregated train. She stayed in Shreveport and nursed her son until he died; he was just thirty. Susie Baker King Taylor died in Boston in 1912. Her first-person account of her life and times provides a unique and valuable portrait of conditions in coastal Georgia before and during the Civil War from the perspective of a literate slave and a free woman.

In January 1865, word of a field order issued by General Sherman blazed through the black community of the southeastern coast even faster than Sherman's troops had burned through Georgia. Sherman had just completed his fiery march to the sea when President Lincoln directed him to meet in Savannah with Secretary of War Edwin M. Stanton and twenty black ministers to discuss issues of emancipation. Four days later, a few months before Lee surrendered to Grant, Sherman issued Special Field Order No. 15. To Sherman, a racist and reluctant liberator, the order was a pragmatic way to deal with the tens of thousands of black refugees he had long considered a hindrance to his troops. The order, vilified by every southern landowner whose property was affected and by many others besides, provided for the Union to confiscate a thirty-mile-wide strip of the coast from Charleston to Jacksonville, including St. Simons and the other sea islands. The order banned most white people from the area and called for the redistribution of about four hundred thousand acres of land to the freedmen and their families who had worked the coastal plantations as slaves. The land was to be divided into plots of up to forty acres, and the army was to provide each head of household with a mule to pull a plow, which some say led to the expression "forty acres and a mule."

Lincoln appointed the inspector general of the United States to make sure the order was enforced. In March, the president established the Bureau of Refugees, Freedmen, and Abandoned Lands, which soon became known as the Freedmen's Bureau, to help with the effort. Lincoln was assassinated on April 14, 1865, a week after the Confederate surrender at Appomattox Courthouse, Virginia. Vice President Andrew Johnson, a southerner, took over the presidency; he rescinded Sherman's field order that same autumn, returning much of the coastal land to its former white owners. By that time, however, some forty thousand freedmen had been awarded plots and were already raising crops on property they had every reason to believe was theirs. A number of the Gullah Geechee people formerly owned by St. Simons planters came back to the island to reunite with family members and loved ones, to claim land the government promised them, or to return to the place that had been home. Most likely, their reasons were a combination of all three.

Few planters came back to St. Simons, either because they had other sources of income or because they realized it would be difficult, probably impossible, to make their plantations profitable without slave labor. Well educated and well connected, most island planters who needed employment found it elsewhere, although Reconstruction was a difficult time for everyone in the southern states.

Frances "Fan" Butler Leigh and her father, Pierce Mease Butler, did come back to the island in 1866 to try to revive their rice plantations on the Altamaha Delta and their cotton plantations on St. Simons. Fan's father and his brother John had become the second-largest slave owners in Georgia when they inherited land and slaves from their grandfather, Major Pierce Butler. John never took an active interest in the plantations, which Mease Butler ran in absentia, as his grandfather always had. According to the terms of Major Butler's will, Pierce and John had to change their surnames from Mease to Butler in order to claim their inheritance, since Major Butler had no sons to carry on the family name. The major had been one of the wealthiest planters in a region that, before the Civil War, was considered one of the five wealthiest in the world. Fan was the daughter of Mease Butler and the English actress Fanny Kemble. Kemble and Butler lived apart for decades before they finally divorced. Fan spent most of that time with her father.

During the decade following the Civil War, Fan helped her father manage the plantations on St. Simons and Butler's Island, running them alone after his death. She kept a journal, much as her famous mother had done during her time in coastal Georgia. Although Fan shared her mother's appreciation for the natural beauty of St. Simons—some of her

Fanny Kemble's Writer Grandson

FAN BUTLER'S ELDER SISTER, Sarah "Sally" Butler Wister, was an abolitionist like her mother. Sally's son, Owen Wister, followed in the footsteps of his famous grandmother, Fanny Kemble, and became a writer. When Wister went to Europe to study music, Kemble arranged for him to perform for the famous composer Franz Liszt, who proclaimed the young man "a profound talent." Wister's musical ambitions were thwarted when his father ordered him home to find a real job. He worked at the Union Safe Deposit Vault, a job that soured him on the banking industry and bankers for life. A year later, he entered Harvard Law School.

After being diagnosed with neurasthenia, a vague illness then described as exhaustion of the central nervous system's energy reserves by urban stress, Wister began spending time out west. During visits to Wyoming and other western states, he kept journals that he later mined for short stories, plays, and novels. Frederick Remington, the iconic artist of the American West, illustrated some of his fiction. Wister's best-known work was the popular novel *The Virginian*, published in 1902. The book introduced characters that became standard fare in westerns for decades to come: the hero with the fast draw and high morals, the prim schoolmarm, the black-hearted villain. The leading character's laconic line "When you call me that, smile" was widely quoted. Cecil B. DeMille's career was launched when he produced the first cinematic version of the novel, a silent film in 1914. The Western Writers of America presents an annual award for lifetime contributions to the field of western literature. The award is named for Wister.

descriptions of the island are just as lyrical as Kemble's—she saw slavery, emancipation, and the Gullah Geechees from her father's perspective. That outlook put her at odds with her mother, and for the rest of Fanny Kemble's life, the relationship between her and her daughter Fan was strained.

Fan published her observations of St. Simons in 1883, two decades after the publication of her mother's famous journal, at least in part to refute Kemble's negative portrayals of slavery and slave owners, including Fan's beloved father.

When she and her father arrived on St. Simons, Fan Butler was delighted to find so many of their former slaves living on the property. She contended that they were there because they were devoted to their former owners. Fan said many had been offered up-country jobs after the war but had chosen instead to return to the Butler fold: "They not only refused good wages, but in many cases spent all they had to get back, a fact that speaks louder than words as to their feeling for their old master and former treatment."

Historical accounts indicate that neither Major Pierce Butler nor his grandson, Fan's father, were among the island's more enlightened slave owners. Floggings and other severe punishments were common in Major Butler's day. Fanny Kemble talked to a number of enslaved women and reported that many were coerced to submit to sexual advances from at least two of Butler's overseers, Roswell King and his son, who both fathered children by slave women. There are allegations that Fan Butler's own father, reputed to be a Don Juan, exploited his female slaves, too. When Fan traveled with her father from Philadelphia to the Georgia plantations, hoping to return them to prewar productivity, a number of Gullah Geechees were squatting on the island. A few families had been given or sold land by their former owners, but many former slaves simply moved into the old quarters where they had lived before the war. Many from St. Simons and the other sea islands settled on the mainland, buying cheap land and forming small communities in the pine barrens, where they scratched out a living farming and raising livestock. Any Gullah Geechees who managed to achieve independence after the war were anathema to Fan Butler, who remarked that whenever they found another means of earning a living, they lost interest in working for her.

Quite a few former Butler slaves, including those auctioned en masse in Savannah in 1859, returned to Butler's Island and St. Simons after the war. After Fan Butler and her father contracted with them to work the rice and cotton fields, the Butlers relocated in early May as usual to Hampton, the plantation on north St. Simons. At Hampton, Fan was disturbed to find the Gullah Geechees had been "under the influence" of northern troops during the war. In addition to Colonel Robert Gould Shaw, the Fifty-Fourth Massachusetts, and the black contraband soldiers who served under Montgomery, the island had been visited regularly by Union sailors and marines stationed on blockade ships. The northerners, Fan said, had "filled the poor people's minds with all sorts of vain hopes and ideas . . . that their former masters would not be allowed to return, and the land was theirs, a thing many of them believed, and they had planted both corn and cotton to a considerable extent."

Fan was certainly aware of Sherman's highly publicized Special Field Order No. 15. It was disingenuous of her to claim the "vain hopes and ideas" of the Gullah Geechees were based on misinformation or lies. Indeed, some planters whose land had already

A branch of the Altamaha River, which spreads across a five-mile-wide delta as it nears the Atlantic north of St. Simons.

St. Cyprian's Episcopal Church in Darien,
built after the Civil War by former slaves

been awarded to former slaves were required to purchase it back, including the St. Simons planter Horace Bunch Gould of Black Banks, the son of the man who built the island's first lighthouse. Former slaves on Butler's Island and Hampton would have been aware of that. Gullah Geechees on the island probably hoped the Butlers, like many other planters, would never return to St. Simons.

Fan's father told the Gullah Geechees they could keep the crops they had already planted, "but that they must put in twenty acres for him, for which he would give them food and clothing, and another year, when he hoped to put in several hundred acres, they should share the crop," his daughter wrote. It was already late in the year for planting. Her father's demand that the former slaves plant crops for him was, Fan said, "more to establish his right to the place than from any real good we expect to do this year." Her comment indicates she knew her father's claim to the land might be shaky.

Like many other white southerners, Fan Butler was enraged that former slaves were given the vote, especially when an officer at the Freedmen's Bureau told her she had to allow them four days to go to the polls. Referring to other coastal planters, Fan wrote: "I think most of the gentlemen felt as I did, that the negroes voting at all was such a wicked farce that it only deserved our contempt." She ignored the governmental directive and told her Butler's Island employees they could not vote until they finished work. They defied her and traveled to Darien, where they cast ballots for the first time in their lives. Fan later noted that the errant voters all returned to the rice plantation ahead of schedule and completed their tasks in record time. She was gratified, however, that only a few of her Hampton employees voted. Hampton was on the extreme north end of St. Simons; polling places were on the south end, a twenty-four-mile round trip. "Their ardour about voting was considerably cooled by the fact that they had twelve miles to walk to the polls . . . So only a few out of the whole number went, and we had no trouble about it," she reported.

Fan Butler had rigid ideas about how the former slaves who became her employees should behave. When some of the Gullah Geechee men failed to tip their hats in passing or addressed her as "Miss Fanny" instead of "Missus," the female equivalent of the prewar term "Massa," she threatened to run them off the property. She might have reacted in similar fashion had white employees she considered inferior failed to salute her as she thought proper because of the rigid class distinctions of the time. When black women who worked for her wanted to stop wearing traditional slave head coverings, Fan barred them from her house, commenting that they looked "too ugly" unless their "black wooly heads" were covered. Her racism was not reserved for blacks. She was repelled by the appearance of the Chinese workers hired by a neighboring planter, commenting that the Asians were even uglier than the Gullah Geechees. Through it all, however, Fan continued to profess great affection for her family's former slaves and to insist they cared for her and her father. When an old house servant put a washbasin, water, and towels on Fan's father's grave because he had always called for those items first thing in the morning, she was moved to tears. "No wonder I loved them," she wrote.

Like many other wealthy, upper-class people of the time, the Butlers had a well-developed sense of noblesse oblige, considering it their duty to care for people who were less fortunate. They probably also feared their reputations would suffer if they treated their former slaves too badly. Shortly after the Butlers returned to St. Simons, Mease Butler made arrangements to feed and clothe former slaves who were too old or ill to work. The support would last for the rest of their lives. He also provided three years' worth of support for young children. Fan reopened the plantation's slave hospital and helped care for patients herself with the help of Gullah Geechee nurses and a book of popular remedies of the time. She dedicated a room in the hospital as a school for black children and paid for their tutors. During the war, the Gullah Geechees had used a hospital room as a church. Fan allowed them to continue the practice.

After her father's death from malaria in 1867—he unwisely stayed on Butler's Island through the summer—Fan ran the plantations herself, with assistance from white overseers. Most of them, she concluded, were either incompetent or cheats; at any rate, none ever achieved the results she wanted. In 1871, she married an English minister doing missionary work in America. The Reverend James Leigh helped his wife with plantation management and also preached the Gospel up and down the coast. In Darien, he raised funds to build a black Episcopal church, which he named St. Cyprian's in honor of a martyred African bishop, and Fan Leigh provided funds for an adjacent school. In spite of their efforts, the Leighs failed to make the family plantations profitable without slave labor. They turned the property over to an agent and left for England.

Gullah Geechee Music

MUSIC HAS ALWAYS BEEN an integral part of the Gullah Geechee culture. The slaves brought African rhythms and harmonies to coastal Georgia that have since inspired countless musicians and musical forms. On St. Simons and the Altamaha Delta, the slaves sang when they were ditching, diking, planting, hoeing and harvesting crops, threshing rice, cleaning and baling cotton, rowing boats, and loading ships. African drums were banned by most planters, so the slaves used stout sticks and pounded on the floor to beat out rhythms. The songs not only defined the pace of the task at hand but also helped the hard workday pass. Slave oarsmen on St. Simons paced their strokes to the rhythm of their songs, each song unique to its plantation. When a rowboat passed at night, islanders who heard the oarsmen singing could tell which plantation the boat came from.

Lydia Parrish, who lived on St. Simons with her well-known artist husband, Maxfield Parrish, in the early 1900s, spent almost twenty-five years doing research for her book, *Slave Songs of the Georgia Sea Islands* (1942). Parrish describes the counterclockwise dance called a shout, in which the dancers never cross their legs or allow their heels to leave the floor and circle faster and faster as the dance goes on. The Gullah Geechee scholar Lorenzo Dow Turner said the word *shout* in this context was probably derived from the West African Arabic word *saut*, a sort of Islamic dance done to exhaustion. The shout is believed to be the oldest surviving African American performance tradition in North America.

Not long after she came to St. Simons, Parrish organized the group that later became the Georgia Sea Island Singers. Group members have changed over time, but the current members continue to perform Gullah Geechee songs and shouts at venues all over the world. The late Bessie Jones, a well-known member of the first Georgia Sea Island Singers, often accompanied the songs with claps, changing from bass to treble claps by cupping her hands in different ways. The musicologist Alan Lomax, who spent time on St. Simons with the writer and folklorist Zora Neale Hurston in the 1930s, said the Gullah Geechee people produced "a large body of noble and touching songs probably unmatched for singability and worldwide popularity. They came from a people generally regarded in that period as ignorant, uncouth, and hopelessly miserable. A good many [songs] were created on St. Simons Island by the ancestors of [the

Georgia Sea Island Singers] and are still sung there beneath the moss-hung live oaks." Lomax returned to the island during a southern tour in 1959–60 and recorded the Singers. The two compilations he made are volumes 12 and 13 of *Southern Journey: An Alan Lomax Collection*.

Gullah Geechees who worked at sawmills on St. Simons in the late 1800s and early 1900s invented songs to suit their labor. Some featured sly lyrics intended to communicate messages to their employers. "Pay Me My Money Down," a favorite with the dock laborers, warned stevedores to pay the workers or go to jail. Versions of the song were later recorded by the Kingston Trio, Pete Seeger, and Bruce Springsteen. The laborers made up songs about well-known national events also, including the battle of the Alamo.

Some of the Gullah Geechees' best-known songs originated in coastal Georgia. Some experts believe the spiritual "Michael Row the Boat Ashore" originated on Sapelo Island. The Gullah Geechee phrase "come by here," which in the rapid-fire creole sounds like *kumbaya*, was first documented in 1926 in coastal Georgia. Robert Winslow Gordon, a Harvard-educated, out-of-work English professor and folklore collector, captured the song on a hand-cranked recording cylinder when he and his family lived in Darien from 1925 until 1929. Gordon identified the singer as a black man named H. Wylie, who sang in the key of A. Gordon wrote "Darien" on the cylinder, which may indicate that Wylie lived there. Gordon traveled the Georgia coast, recording Gullah Geechee music wherever he found it. The St. Simons causeway had opened just before he moved to coastal Georgia, and he recorded songs on the island.

In 1928, Gordon established the Archive of American Folk Song at the Library of Congress and served as its first director. His original recording of Wylie singing "Come By Here," or "Kumbaya," as it is now known, is preserved in the archive. During the 1960s, "Kumbaya" became a protest song, although it was rarely sung as originally intended. More recently, the word *kumbaya* has been used to ridicule liberal idealism. H. Wylie's version of "Kumbaya," recorded at a time of Jim Crow laws and lynchings in the Deep South, was a religious song that told of black people who were weighed down by trouble and despair and were asking God to "come by here" and help them.

CHAPTER V

A Move toward Modern Time

AWMILLS SAVED St. Simons after the Civil War. The few white families who remained on the island lived in greatly reduced circumstances; scores of black islanders were destitute. Conditions were so desperate that to keep the residents from starving, the federal government sent ships to the beach with cargoes of donated food. Everyone planted vegetable gardens and a few acres of money crops: corn, cotton, and sugarcane. They harvested figs, peaches, and sour oranges from overgrown orchards and gathered nuts and wild grapes from the woods. They hunted game and dug sea turtle eggs on the beach. Chickens pecked around the verandas of run-down plantation houses and the ramshackle porches of old slave cabins. Pigs rooted in the woods; cattle foraged in the savannas. Gullah Geechees had long called the tidal waterways and marshes around the island "God's Pantry." The pantry helped feed many islanders during the decade following the war. A vibrant community grew up around the sawmills on Gascoigne Bluff, where ships and crews from all over the world docked to take on cargoes of Georgia yellow pine. Most of the timber was cut from the vast pine barrens of the southeastern mainland and rafted down the Altamaha River to the lumber mills in Darien and on St. Simons. When an epidemic of yellow fever swept the southern

lowlands, the island's mill superintendent and his family and friends fled upriver on a mill tugboat to catch a train inland and escape the deadly disease. People on St. Simons were spared the epidemic, but hundreds of people in Brunswick and Savannah died of yellow fever. In later years, the mill boats that carried passengers and cargo to and from St. Simons began bringing visitors from the mainland to enjoy the lively mill community. Soon ferryboats were making scheduled runs between Brunswick and the new pier on the island's south end. Developers built hotels on the island, and people from all over Georgia caught the ferries to enjoy the island's white-sand beaches and historic attractions. Some built cottages near the lighthouse and spent summers on the island. The short-lived Spanish-American War (1898) prompted the government to build two cannon batteries on the south end of St. Simons to defend against the Spanish navy. A Scottish shipping magnate later built a millionaire's mansion on property that embraced the east battery. The island's causeway opened in 1924, allowing visitors to drive to St. Simons and neighboring Sea Island.

The first sawmill was built on Gascoigne Bluff in 1874 by the Brunswick businessman Urbanus Dart Sr. and his sons. The Dart mill employed nine men and earned its moment of fame by sawing most of the timber used in construction of the Brooklyn Bridge. The mill was successful, but modest in scope compared to the giant sawmill that was opened on the bluff two years later by Dodge, Meigs & Company of New York. The big mill was later joined by a planing mill and a cypress mill owned by the same company.

Norman W. Dodge, the son of the New York merchant prince and philanthropist William E. Dodge, and Titus B. Meigs, another wealthy New Yorker, bought Hamilton Plantation on Gascoigne Bluff for their mill operations. Anson Phelps Green Dodge Sr., the brother of Norman W. Dodge, served as superintendent. White residents of the region, including a few once-wealthy scions of island planters, found jobs as bookkeepers, supervisors, foremen, and supply clerks at the mills' offices. About three hundred Gullah Geechee men, many from St. Simons, Brunswick, and Darien, and others from as far away as Savannah, Macon, and South Carolina, hired on as planers, engineers, sawyers, log turners, carpenters, yard workers, stevedores, watchmen, cooks, and bricklayers. One black man served as

Water from the Aquifer

BEFORE COASTAL PULP MILLS and other mainland industries tapped into the aquifer, many houses on St. Simons had artesian wells with sufficient pressure to provide water for second- and third-story bathrooms. That ended in the mid–twentieth century when giant industrial wells in Glynn County were pumping more water every day than metropolitan Atlanta. The big wells not only reduced pressure in the freshwater layers of the aquifer but also allowed pressurized saltwater layers to rise up and contaminate low-pressure cones of fresh water around the well pipes. Several wells in Brunswick had to be abandoned because of saltwater contamination. Mainland industries now treat and recycle a great deal of water, reducing the risk to the aquifer of salt intrusion and helping conserve its enormous—but not infinite—supply of fresh, pure water.

If drawn from the upper layers of the aquifer, artesian water smells like rotten eggs because of the high sulfur content. Locals who drank and bathed in sulfurous well water said it acted as a natural insecticide, helping repel mosquitoes and sand gnats. Artesian water is rich in minerals and natural fluoride too. Even so, in the days when most island households had private wells, visitors often brought jugs of drinking water with them because they hated the smell and taste of sulfur water.

On St. Simons, some of the summer cottages built in the early 1900s on the eroding shore north of the lighthouse were washed away by storm tides. An artesian well left behind on the beach poured its fresh water into the Atlantic for decades. Until it was capped by the county in recent years, the well's outflow was popular with sea- and shorebirds, which came to drink, and with islanders who dabbled their feet in the chilly artesian water to cool off on hot days.

the mill's barber. Women worked as house servants for mill executives or as nurses in the mill hospital. A Brunswick newspaper of the time estimated that a thousand people, black and white, depended on the mills for income. In 1885, black mill workers were paid $1 for an eleven-and-a-half-hour workday. It was a decent salary for black people, and it was paid as promised at a time when blacks had little recourse against employers who failed to pay them at all.

The giant Upper Mill was a model of new technology and efficiency. The huge saws screamed through 125,000 board feet of lumber a day. The mill burned its own sawdust for power. It boasted the first electric lights on St. Simons and the first telephone and telegraph lines. The mills owned the only ice cream freezer in Glynn County and sometimes loaned it out to Brunswick and other ice-cream-deprived communities. The mills had their own post office. Mail was carried to and from the island by rowboat in the early years, and during stormy weather it was common for islanders to hear that the mail carrier's boat had overturned in the sound. Mill workers drilled the island's first deep well, 437 feet down into the vast freshwater reservoir called the Floridan aquifer. The well's six-inch pipe had enough natural artesian pressure to shoot a gusher thirty-eight feet into the air.

Water from the well was stored in high tanks and gravity-fed to various parts of the operation and to offices and houses occupied by mill officials. A slab pit burned bark around the clock, so there was always a danger of fire in the wooden buildings. With so much water stored in the tanks, the workers stood ready to battle blazes, although Rose Cottage, the elegant house built by Anson Dodge Sr. on the bluff, burned to the ground in 1884 in spite of all the stored water.

In time, four mills, including Dart's, which was bought by Dodge, Meigs, stood shoulder to shoulder on the mile-long bluff. Old plantation buildings were pressed into service for mill operations. Workers stayed at the plantation's main house and at Ivy Cottage, the new boardinghouse. Hamilton Plantation's two-story tabby cotton barn served as the general store and commissary. Today, walls of the cotton barn still stand, incorporated into the dining hall at Epworth by the Sea, the Methodist conference center founded on the upper bluff in 1950. Other plantation buildings are still in use at Epworth.

Gullah Geechees settled in three St. Simons neighborhoods in the postwar decades: South End / Harlem, near the lighthouse; Harrington, out Frederica Road; and Jewtown, on Demere Road near the sawmills of Gascoigne Bluff. Jewtown was originally called Levisonton; it was founded by two Jewish brothers, Sig and Robert Levison of Brunswick, who opened a store in the community to compete with the mill store and commissary. Residents soon changed Levisonton to Jewtown, the name it is called by islanders today, with cheerful disregard for political correctness. Gullah Geechees from all three communities worked at the mills; others had seasonal jobs on neighboring Jekyll Island while the northern millionaires were in residence.

Tabby slave cabins on Gascoigne Bluff were turned into mill offices, including one for Dr. Massey, nicknamed "the pill doctor" by Gullah Geechees. Hamilton Plantation's private wharf, where tons of Sea Island cotton had been loaded for shipment, was refurbished as Steamboat Landing, a public dock. The Frederica River was deep enough at the dock for ships drawing twenty feet of water. Cargo and passenger boats traveling the inland waterway stopped daily at Steamboat Landing, picking up or dropping off timber buyers, visitors, and mill employees. Turkeys were a chief coastal export, and St. Simons was headquarters for the trade. The boats hauled island turkeys to mainland markets.

Norman W. Dodge built St. James Union Church on Gascoigne Bluff in 1880, sparing no expense. In colonial times, St. Simons was part of St. James Parish, which may have

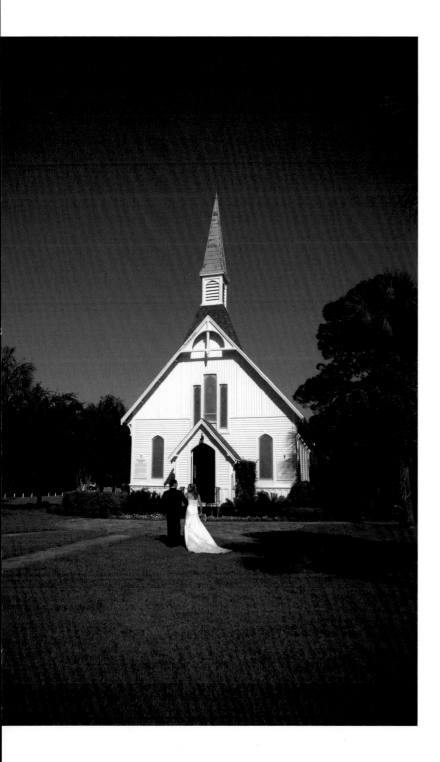

suggested part of the church's name. The different denominations that united there prompted the "Union" appellation. Until the church bell was installed, congregants were called to worship by someone striking a broken saw blade like a gong. Dodge commissioned tall art-glass windows for the church; one is attributed to Louis Comfort Tiffany. The oldest window depicts the Confession of St. Peter. Ministers were brought over from the mainland to preach on Sunday afternoons. St. James Union Church, now Lovely Lane Chapel, is the second-oldest church building on St. Simons. The First African Baptist Church on Frederica Road, built just after the Civil War, is the oldest.

In 1911, a few years after the mills closed, St. James Union Church was deconsecrated. The stained-glass windows and altar were moved to Christ Church for safekeeping. The building served as a recreation center until 1949, when the upper bluff was purchased by the United Methodist Church as a conference center. At Epworth by the Sea, the Methodists restored the mill church, reinstalling the altar and the English art-glass windows. It was reconsecrated and named Lovely Lane Chapel, after the church in Baltimore where attendees at the Christmas Conference of 1784 organized the first Methodist Episcopal Church in the United States. Over time, the Methodist Episcopal Church became the United Methodist Church.

Abby Fuller Graham, daughter of the mill superintendent Warren A. Fuller of Massachusetts, compiled a scrapbook of mill days on the island. Graham, who in the 1930s founded the first public library on St. Simons, wrote accounts of the period, too. During St. James Union's first Christmas, congregants erected a holly tree "covered with green leaves and red

Abandoned after the sawmills closed in the early 1800s, St. James Union Church was later restored by Epworth by the Sea, the Methodist conference center on Gascoigne Bluff, and renamed Lovely Lane Chapel. The picturesque chapel is a popular venue for island weddings, christenings, and other special events.

berries." The tree's candles were lit, and Kris Kringle appeared, looking like "a funny old clown." Santa Claus arrived in a hat and coat white with snow, a mixture of cotton and flour. Described as "a fat fellow with a long, mossy beard," Santa Claus wished everyone Merry Christmas in "a funny language"—German—and bore a strong resemblance to the Austrian captain of a ship then docked at Steamboat Landing.

Santa Claus helped distribute gifts. Each child received a picture book, an orange, an apple, a string of popcorn, and a bag of candy. Everyone sang Charles Wesley's "Hark the Herald Angels Sing." Nowadays, island children receive stockings from Santa Claus, who arrives via boat at the village pier, weather permitting.

During the late 1800s and early 1900s, steam- and sail-powered timber schooners from New England, Europe, and South America, as many as twenty at a time, anchored in the Frederica River, waiting their turn to load lumber at Steamboat Landing. Stevedores bossed the loading operations and hired their own crews. Black sawmill workers from St. Simons formed their own labor union, one of the country's first. Before the ships took on lumber, they dumped their ballast stones in the marsh along the Frederica's banks. Across from the Methodist center are small marsh islands whose trees and shrubs grow on ballast-stone foundations. Foreign seeds hitchhiked to Georgia on the stones, and some survived, including the salt-tolerant tamarisk, or salt cedar, *Tamarix gallica*. Tamarisk bears small flowers along slender stalks, resembling feathery pink plumes.

A thriving mill community grew up on Gascoigne Bluff. Oyster-shell walkways led past beds of colorful flowers. A grove of pine and cedar trees screened industrial sectors from residential ones, as did the tall picket fences bordering the roads. The community's centerpiece was Rose Cottage, built near Steamboat Landing by Anson Dodge Sr. Charismatic Dodge Sr. came to St. Simons for a time to run the family mills, but it was his son, Anson Dodge Jr., who left his indelible mark on the island. Rose Cottage was designed in the modern style and built of "the finest and most beautiful Georgia curly pine," hand-selected from the millions of board feet processed at the mills. As befitted its name, Rose Cottage was surrounded by hundreds of varieties of roses in a riot of colors. A pomegranate hedge along one side of the cottage, along with the chinaberry, palm, and banana trees, gave the place a tropical feel. Honeysuckle arbors added their sweet perfume to the salty air. Rose Cottage was the pride of St. Simons until it burned down; the fire was blamed on a faulty chimney flue. Everyone escaped without harm, although the teacher boarding at the cottage lost all her clothes and $50 in cash.

Urbanus Dart Jr., called Barney, whose father had built the island's first sawmill, built and launched a workboat to carry employees and supplies back and forth to the mainland. Brunswick residents soon discovered the charms of riding the *Ruby*, named for Captain Dart's daughter, over to the island to enjoy all the activity at the mill town. Foreign timber-ship captains often brought wives and children on their long voyages, and the bluff, where many different languages, including Gullah Geechee, were spoken, took on a cosmopolitan air. Music was the universal language. Sailors strolled around while playing tunes on harmonicas, accordions, and Jew's harps, trading tunes with islanders. The mill owners staged boat races in the Frederica River to entertain residents, visitors, and sawmill workers. Ever-hospitable island families opened their homes to people from the ships and the mainland.

The St. Simons sawmills were still in their infancy when Georgia suffered the worst yellow fever epidemic in the history of the southeastern coast. More than half the population of Brunswick was stricken, and residents were in danger of starving because the quarantined city could not get supplies. The mayor and the chairman pro tem of the board of health issued a desperate plea for help in the *Darien Timber Gazette*, in September 1876, begging outsiders to send "good nurses, groceries, etc." Warren Fuller, then manager of the mills, knew the epidemic could easily jump across the marshes and tidal waterways to St. Simons. He, his family, and a few friends boarded a small mill tugboat, the *Hamilton*, with plans to travel up the Altamaha River to Doctortown, near Jesup, and catch a train to the inland city of Macon, out of fever range. There were twenty-seven people on board: thirteen men, six women, and eight children, including a two-month-old baby. They carried provisions for two days. As they steamed up the Altamaha, the tugboat's pilot repeatedly ran aground in the river's tricky shoalwaters. It sometimes took all day for the men to push the tugboat back to deeper water. When the refugees ran out of food, they hailed a stranger on the riverbank, who led them miles through the woods to his cabin. When the man's wife learned the travelers were from the fever-ridden coast, she made it clear they were "as welcome as a nest of rattlesnakes," Fuller wrote in a letter to his family. Two refugees from the *Hamilton* were sent to buy food; they returned with four chickens, a pound of coffee, and a little flour. The chickens went into a pot, and the flour was used to make batter cakes. When the tugboat finally reached Doctortown, then just a sawmill and outbuildings, the mill owner fed the weary travelers, put them up for the night, then drove them in a wagon pulled by his mule team to catch the train. The epidemic spared St. Simons, but Brunswick lost 112 citizens to yellow fever.

The St. Simons sawmills prospered because the vast white pine forests of the northeast and Canada were gone, decimated by northern timber companies. Timber barons looking south for a fresh source of trees struck gold in the yellow pine forests of Georgia. A group of New Yorkers, including William Dodge, formed the Georgia Land and Lumber Company and purchased five hundred square miles of Georgia longleaf pine, most in the vee between the Ocmulgee and Oconee Rivers. The two rivers merge at the point of the vee to form the Altamaha, the largest watershed in Georgia and the third-largest river that empties into the Atlantic on the Eastern Seaboard.

The Georgia Land and Lumber Company tract was ideally situated for a major timbering operation. Overhead tramways and railroad spurs were built to join the nearby Macon and Brunswick Railroad, a land link to the continent. Logs were floated down the Ocmulgee, Oconee, and Ohoopee Rivers to the Altamaha, the riverine superhighway that runs 137 miles through southeastern Georgia to the Atlantic. The company built logging camps in the woods, many occupied by Georgia dirt farmers who plowed, planted, and harvested crops in summer and fall and cut timber and rafted logs in winter and early spring, when the rivers ran high enough for the log rafts to clear sandbars and snags.

The company made such an enormous investment in Reconstruction-ravaged Georgia that when William Dodge asked the state legislature to carve out a new county in the company-owned tract and name it for him, the legislators were happy to comply. Eastman, the county seat, was named for another company executive, William Pitt Eastman, and smaller communities bear the names of other company officials.

Once the logs reached the Altamaha, they were jammed together into rafts at least sixty feet long, confined and shaped by perimeter log booms. The rafts were held together by a few pins, nails, and sapling crosspieces. Each raft contained about fifty logs and was built with a pointed bow for fending off the riverbank and other obstructions. Each had long oars fore and aft, called sweeps, for steering; a crude shelter, where the three-man crew huddled in bad weather; and a pile of sand, where the cook built his fires. Standard raft rations were lard, bacon, cornmeal, syrup, coffee, and chewing tobacco, supplemented with fish and game caught or shot by the crew. Animals fleeing the flooded river swamps or trying to cross the river—rabbits, squirrels, deer, snakes, and even panthers and bears—sometimes climbed aboard the silent, slow-moving rafts. The game often showed up later on the raftsmen's tin dinner plates.

The cumbersome rafts were difficult to steer and sometimes broke apart when they hit underwater obstructions. When the perimeter booms separated, the logs scattered in the strong current. Some spun out of sight into the flooded, low-hanging trees and thickets of the river swamps; others were swept downriver. It was almost impossible to reassemble a raft on the river. The disgusted rafters swam to shore and walked back to the lumber

Tabby warehouses once lined the bluff on the Darien River, the northern branch of the giant Altamaha River as it spreads to meet the sea.

camps to repeat the process. The loss of a raft was a huge financial blow. Timber scavengers, however, cheered the breakup of every raft. The scavengers prowled the riverbanks, making their living by salvaging wayward logs. Some sunken logs are being salvaged from river bottoms today by companies that specialize in antique hardwood.

When they reached Darien, the rowdy raft hands fortified themselves in the town's bars and saloons for the long trip home. Some visited houses of ill repute, which scandalized Darien's churchgoing citizens. Until the timber could be milled, the rafts were gathered in a giant log boom just upriver from town. The rafts were packed together so tightly in the boom that people could walk on top of them for a mile or more. A number of sawmills on the bluff in Darien and on outlying islands were operated by the Hilton Timber and Lumber Company, which merged in 1888 with Dodge, Miegs of St. Simons. The Hilton-Dodge Lumber Company, which listed assets of $1 million, was for a time the world's largest producer of longleaf pine and other types of lumber. For years the towboats *Iris* and *Passport* pulled timber rafts destined for the St. Simons mills across the Altamaha Delta, navigating slave-dug passages through the delta marshes and the twisting tidal waterways between Darien and the island.

One of the ferries that operated between Brunswick and St. Simons in the late 1800s and early 1900s, bringing day-trippers and overnight vacationers to the island (Courtesy of the Coastal Georgia Historical Society)

Ultimately, the St. Simons sawmills fell victim to their own success. By the late 1800s, the bulk of Georgia's longleaf pine forests were gone. The last mill at Gascoigne Bluff shut down in 1903 and was dismantled a few years later.

After the mills closed, most white islanders left St. Simons in search of jobs on the mainland. The handful who stayed were far outnumbered by the island's Gullah Geechee residents. Some of the latter had acquired land on the island and constructed houses, perhaps using scrap lumber from the mills. Others lived in old slave cabins, built shacks of tin and tarpaper, or stayed in rented houses or concrete-block duplexes. Until the building boom of the late twentieth century elevated the price of all island land, the three Gullah Geechee neighborhoods remained the poorest on St. Simons. Although black islanders had been officially liberated since 1865, with the adoption of the Thirteenth Amendment, they were a long way from equality. Entrenched attitudes about race were among the few things on St. Simons that stayed the same after the Civil War. It would take almost a century, and the civil rights movement of the 1960s, before black islanders would even begin to enjoy the full rights and benefits of citizenship.

The closing of the mills might have devastated the economy of St. Simons had it not been for tourism, the island industry that grew up with the sawmills. People from all over Georgia had developed a taste for St. Simons after riding over on mill boats to spend the day. Soon, a fleet of ferries, including the *Seagate* and the side-wheeler *City of Brunswick*, were carrying a stream of summer visitors from inland Georgia to St. Simons. The ferries operated from the late 1800s until the causeway opened in 1924.

One of the regular visitors to the island was Bess Alice Norris, who was a little girl when she first rode the ferry from Brunswick to St. Simons with her parents and three older brothers. The ferry docked at the new pier, built in 1887, the same year Bess was born. The Norris family lived in Macon, in Middle Georgia. Along with a number of other vacationers, they traveled to Brunswick on one of the excursion trains that brought visitors to the coastal city to catch a ferry to the island. Although Bess never learned to swim, she was excited to wear her new bathing costume—navy blue trimmed in white, with a sailor collar and a knee-length skirt—and splash for the first time in the ocean while her brothers cavorted with other teenage boys in deeper water around the pier, admiring the teenage girls. At lunchtime, Bess's parents spread a blanket in the shade of live oaks for a picnic lunch of fried chicken, pickled peaches, and sweet tea. Later the Norrises promenaded on the pier with other vacationers, the men wearing straw boaters and summer suits, and the women dressed in airy pastel or white dresses, their delicate complexions protected by broad-brimmed hats.

Swimmers on St. Simons beach wearing typical Victorian bathing costumes (Antique postcard courtesy of Freddie Pilgrim)

Some of the visitors, many of them wealthy people from Atlanta, headed to the new, three-story Hotel St. Simons, several miles up the beach from the pier. The hotel was a large, rambling structure that could accommodate three hundred guests in a main building and twenty adjacent cottages. It stood amid the sand dunes in the present-day location of county-owned Massengale Park, with a green lawn sloping down to the beach. The same hoteliers owned the Oglethorpe Hotel, an upscale winter resort in Brunswick that catered to wealthy visitors, including the millionaire members of the exclusive Jekyll Island Club. In summer, when the Oglethorpe's business waned and dust sheets covered the furnishings at the Jekyll millionaires' club, the hoteliers ferried furniture, linens, cooking equipment, table settings, and employees from the Oglethorpe to the Hotel St. Simons. In autumn, the process was reversed.

People staying at the Hotel St. Simons in the early years rode from the pier in a carriage drawn by two mules. Later they caught a mule-drawn trolley that ran on rails laid along one leg of the pier. The mules were replaced by a steam-engine-pulled tram called the Florida Limited and then by a motorized trolley. Rails ran along a beachfront street called Railroad Avenue, most of which now lies beneath the Atlantic Ocean. Island entrepreneurs offered horse-and-buggy tours to the ruins of Fort Frederica, abandoned

The three-hundred-room Hotel St. Simons was located on the site of county-owned Massengale Park. Owners of the popular summer resort also owned the Oglethorpe Hotel in Brunswick, a wintertime stopover for millionaire members of the Jekyll Island Club. The owners moved furniture, tableware, linens, and employees back and forth between the two hotels, according to the season. (Courtesy of the Coastal Georgia Historical Society)

Jekyll Island Club

JEKYLL ISLAND, St. Simons's neighbor to the south, is now a state park, open to everyone, but in 1886, a group of northern millionaires belonged to one of the world's most exclusive clubs there. Rockefellers, Pulitzers, Cranes, Vanderbilts, Goodyears, Macys, and other tycoons of industry spent winters on the island until the beginning of World War II. The millionaires purchased Jekyll from the DuBignon family for $125,000.

Members of the Jekyll Island Club, who together controlled one-sixth of the nation's wealth, spared no expense on their winter playground. They imported pheasants, white deer, and other exotic game to hunt; they built a golf course, tennis courts (outdoor and indoor), a swimming pool, and Sans Souci, one of the first condominiums in the United States. In the "splendid isolation" of the island, the millionaires and their guests played croquet, rode horseback, shot skeet, and bowled on the lawn of the Jekyll Island Club, which resembled a fairy-tale castle. The millionaires all dined at the clubhouse on meals prepared by gourmet chefs, since their elaborate cottages had been built deliberately without kitchens. Gullah Geechees from St. Simons and Brunswick often worked on Jekyll when the millionaires were in residence, taking care of the cottages and the clubhouse, grooming the grounds, cleaning the stables, and looking after the horses, along with providing dozens of other services demanded by the wealthy club members.

At the start of World War II, when German submarines were targeting ships off the Georgia coast, the millionaires abandoned Jekyll, leaving their cottages stocked with expensive furnishings, antiques, art, and other items of value.

The centerpiece of the Jekyll Island Club is now a beautifully renovated luxury hotel on state-owned Jekyll Island.

After World War II, the millionaires discovered new winter playgrounds and never reopened the Jekyll Island Club. The state bought Jekyll in the late 1940s. Former Georgia governor Melvin Thompson approved the purchase of the island for just $675,000. Herman Talmadge, who challenged Thompson for the governorship, always called Jekyll "Thompson's white elephant." Before the state takeover, many items from the millionaires' cottages found their way into the houses of area residents. In 1951, after the creation of the Jekyll Island Authority, state convicts were sent to the island to prepare it for public use before the opening of the Jekyll causeway in late 1954. The prisoners built the perimeter road and installed drainage and landscaping for planned motels and neighborhoods. There were constant rumors on St. Simons that a convict had escaped by swimming across the sound and hiding out on the larger island.

plantations, and other sites of interest. Islanders sold homegrown produce, baked goods, and handcrafted items such as cast nets and palmetto baskets. Ferries brought ice packed in sawdust; Gullah Geechee men cleaned off the giant blocks, loaded them into carts pulled by horses, oxen, or mules, and delivered the ice to hotels and private cottages on the island.

The vacationers sparked a south-end building boom. A giant wooden waterslide went up by the pier, along with a two-story dance pavilion and bathhouse. Two hotels, the Bellevue and the Jekyll View, opened in the pier section, along with a post office to replace the one at the mills. Two rows of summer cottages, most with no heat, electricity, or indoor plumbing, were built in the shadow of the lighthouse. The majority of the owners hailed from Waycross, about sixty-five miles inland; the cottages were collectively called the Waycross Colony. Women, children, and grandparents, with the help of cooks and handymen hired on St. Simons, spent entire summers at the Waycross Colony, bringing horses, cows, pigs, chickens, and other necessities of life over on the ferries. Working husbands commuted on weekends by train to Brunswick, then by ferry to St. Simons.

Every summer, the Georgia militia set up tents on the Parade Grounds, now Neptune Park, bringing men and equipment to the island by barge. The soldiers often drilled on the beach near the pier, providing a fine show for the tourists. Over the years, thousands

People from Waycross built a cluster of summer cottages in the shadow of the lighthouse. (Courtesy of the Coastal Georgia Historical Society)

Beach erosion is a natural process on all sandy sea islands. Rates of erosion can be accelerated by human activities.

of Georgia militiamen trained on the island, going home with happy memories of St. Simons and stories to tell their friends and families. Men training at the militia encampment were delighted to have the company of young ladies from the Waycross Colony, hotel guests, people who lived on the island, and visitors who came over for day trips. St. Simons became such a popular vacation spot that people all over Georgia began calling it simply "The Island."

Everyone loved the pier section. To the east lay the open ocean, stretching thousands of miles to North Africa; to the west, a band of blue-gray defined the trees of the mainland. In St. Simons Sound, pods of bottlenose dolphins thrilled visitors with easy rolls and exuberant tail slaps. Jekyll Island now lies about a mile south of St. Simons across the sound. Old-timers always said the islands were closer together once, close enough for people to shout back and forth from their beaches. Erosion, caused by natural forces and ongoing channel dredging, continues to whittle away the beaches of both sea islands.

The pier, redesigned, repaired, and rebuilt a number of times since 1887, has long been a favorite island destination, offering views of ocean sunrises and spectacular sunsets of fall and winter over the mainland. In summer the pier's railings are always crowded

The St. Simons Hotel greeted visitors at the end of the pier. (Courtesy of the Coastal Georgia Historical Society)

with fishermen and crabbers. In earlier days, teenagers dared one another to dive off one end of the pier while fishermen were landing large sharks on the other end. The largest sharks were once hung by their tails from pier railings and butchered for their jaws, but the bloody practice has fallen out of favor, to the relief of many islanders. Years ago, a shrimper who accidentally caught a shark in his net in St. Andrews Sound, south of Jekyll, docked at the pier to offload the giant fish, which islanders claimed was a tiger shark twenty feet long.

Teenagers carved their names or initials and those of their sweethearts on the seats and backs of the pier's wooden benches. During a hurricane in the mid-1940s, the end of the pier, which then had a roof, broke loose and floated down the sound, bobbing along like a little house. At the end of the Victorian era, bands played and people danced on summer nights at the pier pavilion. One evening, a young man named Hunter Hopkins was escorted from the pier pavilion by police because he and his dancing partner, a woman visiting from New York, were doing a racy dance—the fox-trot. Years later, an elderly Hopkins talked about that night to a writer who recorded his brush with the law.

Bess Norris often told stories of her St. Simons visits to the same writer, her granddaughter. On that first trip, Bess's fair skin was pink and tender by the time the ferry

Robert Sengstacke Abbott, born on St. Simons to former island slaves, became the island's first black millionaire. Abbott graduated from law school and, in the early 1900s, founded the *Chicago Defender*, which became the most successful black-owned newspaper in the United States. Abbott urged southern blacks to migrate north to escape Jim Crow laws and lynchings. He dedicated this monument to his father and two aunts in the 1930s.

whistle announced the boat's departure for the mainland. En route to Brunswick, the ferry broke down. With the boat dead in the water, the passengers sweltered while the engine was being repaired. Bess was sunburned, hot, and thirsty. She cried for water, but nobody had anything for her to drink. Another passenger came to the rescue. He had bought a small watermelon from one of the vendors on the island. With his pocketknife, he cut the melon into cubes, giving one to each of the passengers. Bess recalled, more than half a century later, how refreshing that small cube of warm watermelon tasted.

Such memories were made every summer on St. Simons as people from all over Georgia and beyond came to introduce their children to the Atlantic Ocean, enjoy the cool sea breezes in the days before air-conditioning, fish, crab, swim, beachcomb, sightsee, and socialize on a beautiful island. Although many people were attracted to St. Simons, few people settled there year-round in pre-causeway days. After the sawmills closed, there were few paying jobs on the island. At summer's end, tourist-related seasonal work vanished along with the visitors. The island hotels were closed and shuttered for the winter, and the pier section rolled up its sidewalks. Self-sufficient islanders went back to farming, fishing, and fashioning handmade items to use or to sell to tourists the following summer.

Many older islanders claim that relations between blacks and whites on St. Simons between the Civil War and the civil rights movement were better than they were in many parts of the Deep South. No lynchings were ever reported on the island, nor did the Ku Klux Klan rally on St. Simons; nonetheless, the island was segregated well into the 1960s and beyond. It was not until the end of the twentieth century that African Americans began to enjoy the same benefits as white island residents.

Before the civil rights movement, many black islanders found a semblance of equality only by moving to the North, including one who may have been the first black man born on St. Simons to become a millionaire after the Civil War. Robert Sengstacke Abbott, born in Frederica to former island slaves, graduated from law school and in 1905 founded the *Chicago Defender* with an investment of $25. The publication grew to become the largest and most influential black-owned newspaper in the United States and made Abbott a wealthy man. He and his newspaper crusaded against racism, encouraged southern blacks to move to the North, and promoted talented black entertainers.

From the 1930s through much of the 1960s, the *Chicago Defender* advertised performers on the Chitlin' Circuit, a route traveled by now-storied black musicians who played around the United States in barns, juke joints, segregated theatres, private clubs, and dance halls. It was called the Chitlin' Circuit because the clubs, including several on St. Simons, served soul food, including chitlins, or pork intestines, along with barbecue, fried fish, and pickled pigs' feet. Some of the clubs sold ten-dollar pint bottles of moonshine out the back doors to island teens, who hung around listening to the exciting new music until somebody ran them off.

Rock 'n' roll got its start on the circuit with some of the all-time greats, including three born in Georgia: Little Richard, James Brown, and Otis Redding. Fats Domino rode the circuit, as did B. B. "Blues Boy" King, Ray Charles, the Supremes, the Temptations, and many others. Brunswick-born Chick Morrison, who played drums with Cab Calloway and other big-time entertainers, performed on St. Simons at such places as Club 400, the LaQuartz Club, and the Melody Inn. In his book *The Chitlin' Circuit and the Road to Rock 'n' Roll*, Preston Lauterbach calls the circuit "a major force in American musical history." He notes that civil rights organizers later took advantage of the circuit's social networks to spread the word about planned activities, potential problems, and other information valuable to people in the movement.

Through his father, Robert Abbott was a direct descendant of Salih Bilali, the Muslim slave owned by the Coupers of Cannon's Point, on north St. Simons. After his father's death, Abbott's mother took him to Savannah, her hometown, where she married John H. H. Sengstacke, a German-reared immigrant and outspoken Congregationalist minister with the American Missionary Association. His views inspired his stepson to fight for equality. The *Defender*'s slogan was "American race prejudice must be destroyed."

To publicize his cause, Abbott used many of the same yellow-journalism tactics employed by well-known white publishers of the time, including William Randolph Hearst and Joseph Pulitzer. Abbott wrote editorials urging black southerners to migrate to northern states for better educations, jobs, and voting rights, and to escape segregation, Jim Crow laws, lynchings, and other violence. An estimated six million blacks moved north, many to Chicago, where southern musicians such as Muddy Waters made intimate nightclubs in the midwestern city a mecca for blues fans. White southerners, concerned that their cheap labor was heading north, began arresting groups of

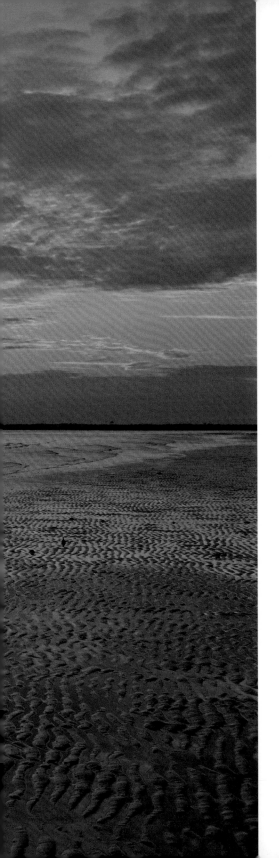

blacks boarding northbound trains. If a black family began selling or giving away possessions, they were likely to be jailed on trumped-up charges.

Abbott printed stories in bold red ink of lynchings and other atrocities committed against black people in the southern states. At the time of the *Defender*'s crusade, there was a lynching in the Deep South every four days. A number of southern cities outlawed the newspaper and imposed penalties on anyone caught reading or distributing it. Since many circulation methods used by white newspaper owners were off-limits to Abbott, especially in the South, the *Defender* was distributed around the country by an underground (and aboveground) railroad of black Pullman porters, Negro-league baseball players, and entertainers.

On a visit back to St. Simons, Abbott had a white granite obelisk installed near his birthplace to honor two of his aunts and his father, Thomas Abbott. The obelisk now stands near the entrance of the Fort Frederica National Monument.

The island's first twentieth-century resident millionaire was F. D. M. Strachan, whose father founded Strachan Shipping Company, now an international corporation. In 1910, Strachan built an estate he called Beachlawn on a large tract of waterfront property near the pier. Beachlawn's centerpiece was a graceful, 7,500-square-foot mansion with broad verandas overlooking St. Simons Sound and Jekyll Island. Locals said Strachan built his mansion in full view of Jekyll after being turned down for membership in the exclusive Jekyll Island Club, which limited membership to one hundred of the world's wealthiest families. When Beachlawn blazed with lights during parties on winter nights, islanders said Strachan was letting club members across the sound know that rich people were entertaining in fine style on St. Simons too.

For decades, the Strachan estate was the pride of the pier section and the King City subdivision, which was developed by Mallery King, a scion of Retreat Plantation, on part of the old plantation property. The Strachan estate had an artesian-fed cistern capped with a gazebo roof. Neighborhood children scaled the estate's fence at night, crept up the cistern's ladder, and swam in the deep dark cold water. Near the front gates, a gnarled persimmon tree produced tempting globes of orange fruit that clung to the branches long after the tree lost its leaves in fall. Out trick-or-treating one Halloween, children scaled the fence—keeping an eye out for the estate's caretaker—picked a few firm persimmons, and retreated back over the fence to eat them. The fruit was unripe, and instead of the treat they expected, the children got mouthfuls of astringent, tongue-shriveling alum. Not even Halloween candy could take away the awful taste.

After Strachan's death in 1966, the estate passed through several owners before being sold to a development company, which offered the mansion for $1 to anyone who would move it off the property. A South Carolina developer bought it, intending to use it as the clubhouse at Haig Point Plantation, a private, upscale golf resort on Daufuskie Island, South Carolina. In a nationally publicized adventure in house moving, the historic house was pushed to Beachlawn's bulkhead and, on an extreme high tide, loaded onto a barge for the 110-mile trip up the Intracoastal Waterway. Thousands turned out to watch the move. Paul deVere, a South Carolina freelance writer, rode along on the voyage, taking notes and waving to people on docks and passing boats from his rocking chair on the mansion's veranda. The estate's old carriage house, restored as a private house, is the only original building still standing on the property. The rest of the land was developed with single-family houses.

A beachfront house on the old estate property still holds the remains of a military battery built in 1898 to defend St. Simons during the Spanish-American War. The site has eroded, but a broken tabby wall, visible from the low-tide beach in front of a private house in the Butler Mews subdivision, marks the landward side of the battery's location. America's involvement in the war lasted less than a year, but powerful people on the Georgia coast helped persuade the federal government to build defenses on St. Simons, Jekyll, and Little Cumberland Islands to protect the area from an attack. The millionaire members of the Jekyll Island Club, as well as other residents of coastal Georgia, were terrified of the Spanish Caribbean Squadron, according to Hans Neuhauser of Athens, an expert on Georgia's coastal defenses for the war.

The war began because Cuba wanted independence from Spain. The United States sent the battleship *Maine* to Havana harbor in order to show support for the freedom fighters but otherwise tried to stay out of the war. In mid-February, the *Maine* exploded and sank, killing 268 Americans. It was later determined that the explosion was caused by a faulty boiler on the *Maine*, but American newspapers, including the *Savannah Morning News*, the *Brunswick Times*, and the *Brunswick Call*, published inflammatory articles and editorials claiming that the Spanish were responsible for blowing up the battleship and warning that the U.S. coast was vulnerable to attack from the sea. In early March, a delegation representing the Jekyll Island Club traveled to Washington to ask President William McKinley and his cabinet to fortify their winter resort. A Brunswick newspaper reported that the millionaires were afraid their beautiful cottages on Jekyll would be

damaged. Days later, a flotilla left Spain under the command of Admiral Pascual Cervera, its destination unknown, prompting more inflammatory news articles. Panicked citizens from Texas to Maine began clamoring for coastal defenses.

In late April, Spain and the United States declared war on each other. One of the famed ironclad monitors, the naval ship *Passaic*, had been mothballed in Brunswick since the Civil War. The old ship was towed to Port Royal, South Carolina, for repairs, with the intention of returning her to patrol the waters off Brunswick, St. Simons, and Jekyll.

Several temporary batteries were built on the Georgia coast, including two on the south end of St. Simons, two on Jekyll Island, and one on the north end of Little Cumberland. Officials said the sites were chosen to guard the Brunswick port; they were also positioned to protect the millionaires' cottages on the west side of Jekyll.

Work began on St. Simons's west battery on April 16, 1898, probably in the vicinity of the Sea Island Golf Club on property that, at the time, was still owned by the Kings of Retreat Plantation. The battery, built of wooden planks covered with sand, was mounted with four twelve-pound Napoleon cannons. The east battery was closer to the pier, on property also owned by the Kings. Construction was done by fifty black workers, perhaps Gullah Geechees from the island who knew the art of working with tabby. The east battery included a low tabby wall that stood just in front of three Civil War–era ten-inch Rodman guns brought in by tugboat from Savannah. Army troops stationed on St. Simons at a temporary site called Camp Barker near the lighthouse manned both batteries.

In late May, the Spanish squadron was blockaded in the harbor of Santiago, Cuba, and when the fleet attempted to escape, it was destroyed by the U.S. Navy. In July, Colonel Teddy Roosevelt led his famous charge up Cuba's San Juan Hill. The batteries on St. Simons were vacated by August 1, 1898, less than four months after they were built. Soldiers manning the installations never fired a cannon at an enemy ship; the dreaded Spanish never came closer to St. Simons than Cuba. Spain's military commander in Cuba surrendered on July 17, an armistice was signed in mid-August, and a formal peace treaty followed in December.

The Napoleon guns of the west battery were sent to the Augusta Arsenal after the war. The three Rodman guns of the east battery guarded St. Simons Sound until 1908, when they were sold for scrap. The ironclad *Passaic*, which had been

A low tabby wall that served as part of the east battery, which was built to defend the area during the Spanish-American War, now helps protect a modern beachfront home on the old Strachan estate from the Atlantic.

Soldiers were bivouacked in tents in Neptune Park during the Spanish-American War in 1898. Two batteries were built on the island's south end to defend against the dreaded Spanish Caribbean Squadron, which never came closer to St. Simons than Cuba. (Courtesy of the Coastal Georgia Historical Society)

repaired and deployed to patrol the Gulf of Mexico, never returned to Brunswick. The historic monitor was sold in 1899, probably for scrap. Both the east and west batteries on St. Simons suffered from the major hurricane that hit the Georgia coast in October 1898. It was the second major hurricane of the season to affect St. Simons. A shore survey done in 1900 shows that the waterline temporarily moved landward of the east battery's tabby wall. The broken wall is the only part of either battery that survives today.

The peace treaty with Spain awarded possession of Puerto Rico, Guantanamo Bay, and Guam to the United States and allowed the country to purchase the Philippines for $20 million. Cuba gained its freedom from Spain, and the United States became established as a world power. And although U.S. Secretary of State John Hay called the conflict "a splendid little war," that view may have been a little rosy. The Philippine War

of Independence, fought in 1899–1902 against the United States as a direct response to the Spanish-American War, resulted in upward of 250,000 deaths, nearly all of them civilians.

The only casualty of war on St. Simons was the Hotel St. Simons, which shut down briefly during the conflict and burned to the ground in 1898. Rebuilt, it burned again. Later, the Bellevue and Jekyll View hotels in the pier section were destroyed by fire. In pre-fire-department days on St. Simons, many of the island's historic wooden structures burned and were never rebuilt.

Island dog with muddy paws

A St. Simons Saint

Anna Alexander, born to former St. Simons slaves in about 1865, was later named the first black Episcopal deaconess in the United States. Alexander founded the Good Shepherd Episcopal Church and parochial school in the tiny Pennick community north of Brunswick. In addition to teaching at other parochial schools in Darien and Brunswick, she was employed at Camp Reese, an Episcopal camp on St. Simons, where she received permission to bring some of her black students in the 1930s. (Courtesy of the Episcopal Diocese of Georgia)

ISLAND-BORN ANNA ALEXANDER, whose parents were slaves on St. Simons, was consecrated as the first black Episcopal deaconess in the United States in 1907. In 1999, the Episcopal Diocese of Georgia named her a saint. Alexander devoted her life to the Good Shepherd Episcopal Church, which she founded in Pennick in northern Glynn County, as well as to parochial schools in Darien, Pennick, and Brunswick. She walked for miles between the schools to teach her classes, always dressed in a deaconess's habit: a black dress with a spotless white collar and cuffs, a shoulder-length black veil, and a large silver cross on a chain around her neck. She worked at a white Episcopal church camp on St. Simons and received permission to bring some of her black students to the retreat, according to Jan Saltzgaber, a retired history professor and Episcopal deacon who now lives on the island and has researched Alexander's life.

Anna Ellison Butler Alexander was born to Aleck and Daphne, newly freed slaves at Hampton, the Sea Island cotton plantation then owned by Pierce Mease Butler. Daphne was the daughter of the slave Minda (or Minta) and Butler's white overseer, Roswell King Jr. Aleck was taught to read by the British actress Fanny Kemble, Butler's wife, during the months she spent on St. Simons in 1838–39. The couple took the surname Alexander after emancipation.

In September 1884, Anna Alexander founded the Good Shepherd Episcopal Church in tiny Pennick, one of the mainland communities settled in the pine barrens by former sea island slaves. Congregants first met in a brush arbor, then in abandoned shacks. She built the church and one-room school next door in 1902 with her own hands, according to members of her congregation. Gullah Geechees in Pennick were not tenant farmers; they owned the land they worked. The area was home to poor white farmers as well. Anna Alexander taught them all, black and white, young and old. She later expanded the Pennick school to two rooms and added a second-story loft, where she lived until her death in 1947. Although she did not want a marker on her grave, the large granite cross in front of the church marks her burial place. Her remains were moved after the small cemetery where she was first buried was all but lost in the woods.

Alexander's former students still remember her as a small slender woman who was often too busy to smile. They describe her as a strict but loving teacher who insisted that Pennick children learn to read and write, even though many of their adult relatives could not. One

The Good Shepherd Episcopal Church and school in Pennick, founded and built by Deaconess Anna Alexander, who has been elevated to sainthood by the Episcopal Diocese of Georgia. Her feast day is celebrated on September 24. (Photo by Jingle Davis)

former student, Samuel Holmes, said she came to his house before he started school to insist that the grownups teach him and his siblings the alphabet.

"They said, 'Sure will,' and after she left, Auntie said to Uncle, 'What that fool woman talking about, their ABCs?' She didn't know her ABCs either," Holmes remembered, laughing. Holmes said his family memorized groups of letters until everyone could read and recite the alphabet. "We'd go around hollering A-B-C-D-E-F. She'd come and check up on us," Holmes remembered. He and other former students appeared in a 2002 video made by the Episcopal Diocese of Georgia on the hundredth anniversary of the founding of the Good Shepherd Episcopal Church and school.

At a time when it was rare for rural blacks in the Deep South to attend institutions of higher learning, Alexander encouraged her students to attend college. She drove several students at a time to southeastern colleges that accepted blacks. Her former students excelled, many entering professions such as medicine, engineering, and teaching.

She also worked at Camp Reese, an Episcopal camp built on St. Simons in 1924 for white church members. Alexander cooked, did repairs, taught, and counseled campers. The camp on East Beach grew so rapidly and was so popular that it was described, in 1945, as "the powerhouse of the diocese." Alexander was one of the most popular staff members; her campers later built a servants' house at Camp Reese and named it in her honor.

In a letter written to Alberta Telfair Taylor of St. Simons in 1937, Alexander related some of her parents' stories of pre–Civil War days on the Butler plantations. Taylor, who was white, and Alexander were good friends and fellow Episcopalians, according to Taylor's granddaughter, Barbara Hasell Murrah, who lives on the island.

"She wrote the letter to Grandmother just to tell her about the old times. Deaconess Alexander corresponded with people all over, from the Orient and Europe. They sent her books," Murrah said. She and her mother found Alexander's letter a few years ago when they were cleaning out her late grandmother's house.

After naming Alexander a saint, the Episcopal Diocese of Georgia chose September 24 as her feast day.

CHAPTER VI   Peacetime and War

OON AFTER the causeway linking St. Simons to the mainland opened in 1924, the Detroit millionaire Howard Coffin purchased neighboring Sea Island as well as large tracts on St. Simons. Brunswick officials put the islands on the world stage by sponsoring a daring young pilot, Paul Redfern, to fly from Sea Island's beach to Rio de Janeiro, a distance even farther than Lindbergh's famous solo flight across the Atlantic. The Great Depression interrupted development of both islands, but in the 1930s, the federal government built a new airport on St. Simons as well as the Coast Guard station. The beachfront King and Prince Dance Club, soon converted to a hotel, opened on St. Simons just before World War II. In 1942, a German submarine torpedoed two merchant ships off St. Simons, killing almost two dozen merchant marines. Military installations opened a few months later at the new airport and the King and Prince Hotel. Thousands of workers poured into Glynn County to build Liberty ships (cargo vessels) at the Brunswick docks; housing was in such short supply that workers slept in shifts in beds vacated by other workers. Because gasoline and tires were rationed, military people and workers building Liberty ships often hitchhiked across the causeway to enjoy the beaches of St. Simons and Sea Island.

The Detroit automotive pioneer Howard Coffin and his young cousin Alfred W. Jones developed a small island adjacent to St. Simons in the late 1920s into one of the world's premier resorts, Sea Island. Although the Cloister Hotel is on Sea Island, some of the resort's amenities, including the Sea Island Golf Club and the Lodge, are located on neighboring St. Simons. (Courtesy of Sea Island Company)

The idea of building a causeway across four miles of marsh and five tidal rivers between Brunswick and St. Simons had surfaced years, perhaps even centuries, before the route was built. Some claim that Oglethorpe proposed a causeway in the 1730s as a way for his soldiers and colonists at Frederica to escape an enemy attack on the island. Through the years, the idea resurfaced from time to time, but proponents were daunted by the difficulty and expense of such a project. Boats had always been the easiest way to travel along the coast. On the coastal mainland, travelers had to cross rivers, inlets, and broad stretches of marsh to get from place to place. Well into the 1900s, there were few roads or bridges in coastal Georgia, and most were in poor repair. Until cars and better mainland roads came along, there was little incentive to build the causeway to St. Simons.

Howard Coffin, one of America's earliest automotive engineers, made his fortune by making affordable cars for the Hudson Motor Company and promoting the standardization of auto parts. In 1910, while attending a Savannah road race featuring cars he designed, Coffin and his wife, Teddie, fell in love with the sea islands. A number of their wealthy northern friends owned Georgia sea islands or belonged to the exclusive millionaires' club on Jekyll Island. Coffin bought the bulk of Sapelo and began spending time in the area. U.S. Highway 17 was under construction along the coast from New York to Miami. Once the highway was completed, Coffin knew that vacationers looking for resorts and homesites would follow. He began investing in coastal property.

Around 1920, a Brunswick promoter revived the idea of building a St. Simons causeway, attracted a few investors, and broke ground on the mainland. The project was abandoned because of financial and engineering problems before the road reached the edge of the marsh. In the meantime, automobile owners on the mainland had seen the light. They liked the idea of driving to the beaches of St. Simons in a few minutes instead of catching a ferry for the hour-long trip. Islanders were just as enthusiastic. There were year-round jobs available in the growing city of Brunswick, and a causeway would make commuting easy. A land link would give islanders faster access to mainland merchants, jobs, and medical care as well. There were no doctors on St. Simons at the time, and the island's only school was for Gullah Geechee children. Until the St. Simons Elementary School was built in 1944, white children attended school on the mainland.

City and county officials, thrilled by the prospect of development on St. Simons and the resulting broader tax base, issued joint bonds and hired Fernando J. Torras, an engineer and the longtime Brunswick city manager, to survey the route and oversee the project. Torras, a Georgia Tech graduate, had built roads, railroads, and bridges in the jungles

Harrington Graded School

The Harrington Graded School, built in the Gullah Geechee Harrington community, which was settled by former slaves after the Civil War, served the island's black students from the 1930s until public schools were integrated during the 1960s. The school is being restored as a historic site.

IN THE 1920S, the two-room Harrington Graded School opened in one of the island communities established by former slaves after the Civil War. The school was modeled after the famous Rosenwald schools, built by Julius Rosenwald, the part owner and president of Sears, Roebuck and Company. At the urging of Booker T. Washington, noted founder of the Tuskegee Institute, Rosenwald supported the cause of educating black children in segregated America. Over time, the Rosenwald Fund built five thousand public schools for black children, most in the South, as well as workshops and teachers' houses in rural areas. To foster cooperation between black and white communities, Rosenwald required city and county officials, almost all of whom were white, to commit public funds to the effort, and residents of communities served by the schools were asked to raise money. Students from all three Gullah Geechee communities on St. Simons attended the Harrington school through the eighth grade. After that, all island children traveled to segregated mainland schools.

Through the years, the two-room school served as a community center for potluck suppers and celebrations such as the annual plaiting of the Maypole. After area schools were integrated in the 1960s, a day-care center occupied the school building. Later abandoned, the structure fell into disrepair. The Georgia Trust for Historic Preservation included the building on its top ten list of Places in Peril in 2011. The school building was scheduled for demolition, but concerned islanders formed the St. Simons African American Heritage Coalition and hired an expert to survey the structure. Colin Chambers, a preservation architect with the Coastal Regional Commission, declared the building salvageable. Chambers said the school was so well crafted of old-growth heart pine by master African American carpenters that it might have been "meant to float." If preserved, Chambers said, it would qualify for listing on the National Register of Historic Places. The coalition raised funds to restore the building and preserve it as a historic site, an interpretive museum, and a stop on the Gullah Geechee Heritage Corridor, which runs from North Carolina into Florida. Restoration began in 2012.

of South America. After he mapped out a favorable route, construction began. Thirteen months and $418,000 later, the two-lane causeway, which crossed five wooden bridges, opened to the driving public with great fanfare in July 1924. On opening day, fifty-five hundred cars from all over Georgia and beyond, along with horse-drawn carriages and other conveyances, crossed to the island, where locals staged a historic pageant and served fried fish to thousands of people. Called the St. Simons Causeway for the next three decades, the route was renamed for Torras after his death in 1952.

The new causeway was not without problems. Delays were common. The center sections of the Frederica and Back River bridges pivoted to allow larger boats passage. When a captain wanted the bridge opened, he sounded three blasts of his horn. The bridge tender, after lowering barriers to keep motorists from driving into the river, hand-cranked the center span open, a slow and laborious task. After the boat traffic passed through, the bridge tender cranked the center of the bridge back into place and lifted the barriers.

The first bridges were later replaced by central lift-span bridges. Like giant elevators, the lift spans could raise and lower a section of the bridge on twin towers, thereby accommodating boat traffic. The mechanized metal-mesh lift spans meant faster and less work for the bridge tenders, but they were far from perfect. On windy, rainy days, the center sections became slick enough to send vehicles into wild skids. When the lift mechanisms malfunctioned, as they often did in the corrosive salt air, the spans invariably stuck in the up position, or so causeway commuters said. Since the county's only hospital was in Brunswick, pregnant island women near their due dates were often advised to move to the mainland in order to avoid the possibility of delivering on the causeway.

Islanders loathed getting stopped on the causeway by boat traffic. They learned to look for large vessels approaching one of the lift-span bridges. If they spotted the boat in time, they could step on the gas and beat the bridge. The two lift-span bridges were later replaced by the two concrete arches that now soar sixty-five feet over the Back and MacKay Rivers and allow even sailboats to pass underneath. The high bridges offer panoramic views of the tidal estuary: the marshes, creeks and rivers, the sound and the distant ocean. During radical moon tides, the marshes are submerged and the causeway seems to float on the flood tide.

The causeway linking St. Simons to the mainland.

In the era of the two-lane causeway, people fished, crabbed, and threw cast nets off walkways attached to the sides of the narrow wooden bridges. Drivers learned to swerve to avoid fishing tackle as anglers swung back over the traffic lanes to make their next cast. Older people have fond memories of the loud rumble made by the heavy timbers of the original wooden bridges whenever a vehicle crossed. Island children drowsing in the backseat of the family car after a trip to the mainland knew the rumble meant they were almost home.

Stretches of the causeway often flooded during storms and the high tides of the full and new moons. Every spring, hundreds of diamondback terrapins crossed the route in search of nesting sites. Scores of the saucer-sized terrapins were crushed by vehicles and left to bake in the sun. Islanders endangered themselves and other drivers when they swerved to miss the terrapins or stopped, got out of their cars, and carried one of the slow-moving creatures to safety. Signs now warn travelers to watch for terrapins, but many of the slow-moving reptiles still fall victim to causeway traffic.

For more than seventy-five years, everyone paid a toll to cross the causeway. One toll-booth was located in the middle of the Back River bridge in the eastbound lane, requiring

drivers to stretch across the width of the front seat—and cars were wider then—to hand over the toll money. Children always begged to give the money to the amiable toll takers, which led to many a fumble. The dropped coins usually rolled through the lift span's steel mesh and disappeared into the murky river.

Unless they are in private school, older students from St. Simons still attend middle school in Brunswick and move on to Glynn Academy, the public high school founded in 1788. It is the second-oldest public high school in Georgia and the fifth oldest in the United States. Island students who commuted by car often got stranded on the mainland without toll money. Since the toll takers knew everyone on the island, the teens were allowed to leave wristwatches, bracelets, and other trinkets at the tollbooth, to be redeemed on their next trip. The toll was removed in 2003, after the causeway had paid for itself many times over.

In 1925, a group of Brunswick investors bought a sand spit called Long Island, separated from St. Simons by a short stretch of marsh and Black Banks River. The island's first known name was Fifth Creek Island, perhaps a legacy of Creek Indians who moved into coastal Georgia after the native Guale and Mocama fled. Or the island might have been located on the fifth creek crossed between the island and the mainland. Naturally fenced by tidewaters and marshes, the small island served as a pasture for St. Simons planters, who kept cows, goats, and pigs there. The Brunswick investors formed the St. Simons–Long Island Company, and the county built a short causeway connecting Long Island to its larger neighbor. After bulldozing streets through Long Island's leafy tangle of palm trees, grapevines, and palmettos, the company offered lots for sale. Some went for as little as $200. The company sold more than 100 lots, but nobody built houses and the company eventually went broke.

Howard Coffin, who already owned most of Sapelo Island, purchased Long Island in 1926 and renamed it Glynn Isle, then Sea Island Beach, and finally, Sea Island. The automotive pioneer had visited upscale Florida resorts designed by Addison Mizner, America's best-known architect of the 1920s. Mizner was much in demand to design elaborate country houses for wealthy New Yorkers, especially after he designed a retreat in the Adirondacks used by President Calvin Coolidge as his summer White House. The books published in the mid-1920s about Spanish missions in coastal Georgia may have influenced Coffin's decision to hire Mizner, who was famous for designing buildings in the Spanish Colonial style, to design the Cloister Hotel. Coffin formed the Sea Island Company and recruited his young cousin and protégé, Alfred W. Jones, who was working with him on Sapelo, to help develop and manage the resort.

The two men realized that Sea Island was too small to accommodate all the amenities they planned to offer. Neighboring St. Simons, three times larger, provided the perfect place for the overflow. The company bought Retreat Plantation on the south end of St. Simons and began building the Tolomato Golf Club, later renamed the Sea Island Golf Club, on the property. It built the Sea Island Yacht Club on Gascoigne Bluff just south of the Frederica River bridge. Later the company purchased most of the north end of St. Simons. It established the Sea Island Stables on Frederica Road and a large nursery on Gascoigne Bluff to supply trees, flowering plants, and shrubs to Sea Island's landscape department.

T. Miesse Baumgardner, the young landscape architect hired by the company, created the now-legendary Sea Island look: that of a well-groomed jungle with carefully tended flower gardens set like jewels amid the native foliage. Baumgardner landscaped many public buildings and private houses on St. Simons; his style still defines upscale land-scaping on the Georgia coast and in Florida and South Carolina.

To accommodate guests until the hotel on Sea Island was completed, Coffin and Jones bought the refurbished warship *Amphitrite*, which had patrolled the Atlantic coast during the Spanish-American war. They docked it at their new yacht club on St. Simons and billed it as a floating hotel, with such modern conveniences in the staterooms as telephones and electric fans. One of Mizner's earlier projects, called The Cloister, had gone bankrupt, but he liked the name and persuaded Coffin and Jones to adopt it for their new "friendly little Georgia hotel," which opened its guestrooms to the public in October 1928. President Coolidge was among the guests at Christmas that first year.

Mizner designed the forty-seven-room Cloister with arched colonnades, secluded courtyards, and a lovely public room called the Spanish Lounge, which had watery blue and green leaded-glass windows and a beamed ceiling. The hotel was topped by a signa-ture roof of red Ludowici tiles, first manufactured in the small southern Georgia town of Ludowici from alluvial red clay deposits along the nearby Altamaha River.

Coffin and Jones wanted to keep the approach to Sea Island beautiful all the way from U.S. Highway 17 in Brunswick. They lobbied for a county zoning ordinance that would prevent the type of development that had blighted other seaside resorts in the early twentieth century. While the two were not above trying to attract tourists with carnival-type exhibitions, they aimed for a more refined resort, "where ladies and gentlemen are served by ladies and gentlemen." At the time, state law permitted zoning only by cities of a certain size; Georgia counties were not allowed to enact zoning ordinances. With the

The Sea Island Company, which built its first golf course on the grounds of Retreat Plantation on south St. Simons, preserved the picturesque avenue of live oaks that led from the main road to the plantation house overlooking St. Simons Sound.

backing of the Sea Island Company, Glynn County successfully challenged the law and passed one of the earliest county zoning ordinances in the United States.

After the Torras Causeway was finished, the Sea Island Company paved more than twenty miles of roads on St. Simons, including Kings Way, which arrows southeast from the Frederica River bridge to the pier section, and Retreat Avenue, which led to the new golf club. Coffin and Jones preserved the picturesque arch of live oaks leading to the plantation buildings, several of which they adapted for golf course uses. Kings Way opened south St. Simons to new development.

Coffin often invited northern friends and business associates to the Georgia coast. Many liked it well enough to build vacation cottages on Sea Island. In 1927, one of Coffin's closest friends, the automotive and aircraft pioneer Eugene Lewis of Detroit, purchased Hamilton Plantation on Gascoigne Bluff. Lewis and his wife restored a sawmill-era house as well as the plantation's outbuildings and extensive grounds. The Lewises salvaged handmade bricks from abandoned island houses to build walkways, terraces, and the floor of a tabby slave cabin that had stood on Gascoigne Bluff since 1805. The cabin became their recreation room; it is now used by Epworth by the Sea. The Lewises were noted for giving lavish parties; among their guests on St. Simons were such luminaries as Henry Ford.

As homage to the plantation once described by the British actress Fanny Kemble as "the finest on the island," the new owners planted a large part of Hamilton with vegetables: cabbages, cucumbers and cauliflower, peas and peppers, lettuce and tomatoes. At harvest time, a hundred workers—most of them Gullah Geechees from St. Simons— were hired to pick and pack the produce and ship thousands of crates of vegetables to northern markets. When they bought the plantation, the Lewises discovered that oleander trees imported from the Mediterranean and Asia were growing on the property. Baumgardner, Sea Island's landscape architect, propagated and planted the colorful and hardy ornamentals all over St. Simons and Sea Island. With their abundant blooms and dark foliage, oleanders are beautiful, but every part of the plant is poisonous. Island children were warned from birth never to roast marshmallows or hotdogs on oleander branches or even to breath the smoke if oleanders cuttings were being burned.

Like Lewis, Coffin was a pioneer in the aeronautics industry: he had advised the federal government on building airplanes and standardizing aircraft parts during World War I. Coffin invited the Detroit-born aviator Charles Lindbergh to visit his mansion on Sapelo Island. Coffin used his aviation contacts to help publicize Sea Island when he

Oleanders are lovely, but every part of the plant is poisonous. (Photo by Jingle Davis)

In 1927, Paul Redfern, a young aviator, was offered $25,000 by the Brunswick Board of Trade to fly from Sea Island's beach to Brazil shortly after Charles Lindbergh made his famous solo flight across the Atlantic. Redfern's venture ended in tragedy. (Courtesy of the Coastal Georgia Historical Society)

invited another young aviation pioneer to begin his own journey into history from Sea Island's beach.

Three months after Lindbergh made his solo flight across the Atlantic in May 1927, Paul Redfern began a flight to South America from the Georgia coast. Aviation was still in its infancy, and everybody wanted to cash in on the publicity created by record-setting flights. The Brunswick Board of Trade offered a prize of $25,000—a fortune at the time—to any pilot who could fly nonstop to Rio de Janeiro, Brazil, a thousand miles farther than Lindbergh's flight from New York to Paris. The board members hoped Redfern's journey in an airplane named the *Port of Brunswick* would put the coastal city, as well as St. Simons and Sea Island, on international maps. Coffin and Jones knew the flight would publicize their fledgling resort. Newspapers, newsreels, and magazines all over the world would carry stunning photographs of Sea Island's gleaming beach, swaying palms, and the Cloister Hotel, then under construction.

Several thousand people gathered on the beach on a hot August day to watch Redfern take off. His monoplane was painted green and yellow, the colors of Brazil. Redfern's own family described him as a dreamer who believed he could do anything. Yet even Eddie Stinson, the manufacturer of Redfern's brand new Stinson sm-1 Detroiter, thought flying solo for forty-six hundred miles across open ocean and South American jungle was probably impossible and certainly ill advised. Redfern's flight would take fifty-two hours; Lindbergh's had lasted only thirty-three, and he admitted to falling asleep several times on the journey.

Redfern's small plane had no radio. His only navigation equipment was a compass and a map. He flew at the peak of hurricane season. In pre-satellite days, the most reliable way to know a bad storm was approaching was to see dark clouds and feel the leading edge of the wind. Redfern would fly through two pitch-dark nights; there would be no moon to illuminate the ocean or jungle below. The pilot's seat was so cramped by extra fuel tanks that Redfern had to either use a periscope or lean out the side window to see what was in front of him.

With his wife, Gertrude, and thousands of others waving and cheering, Redfern taxied down the hard-sand beach and lifted off over the Atlantic at 12:46 p.m. The excited onlookers included a young student from the Massachusetts Institute of Technology named Edgar H. Langston Jr. of Dublin, Georgia, who had a summer job as a roofer at the Cloister Hotel. The hotel, now surrounded by large trees and lush foliage, was built on filled marsh and offered a clear view to the beach at the time of Redfern's flight. Langston, who settled permanently on St. Simons in the 1940s with his wife and daughter, said he and the other roofers had ringside seats for the takeoff. He remembered cheering and clapping as Redfern soared over the shrimp boats trawling offshore and disappeared into the clouds at the astonishing speed of eighty-five miles an hour.

The following morning, Redfern buzzed a ship and dropped a weighted note to the crew, asking for directions to South America. The sailors signaled back that he was about two hundred miles north of the continent, exactly where he thought he was. The next sighting came that same afternoon over land. An American working in Venezuela identified Redfern's plane by its tail numbers as it passed low overhead, trailing a wispy plume of smoke.

There were no other reported sightings. The crowd waiting in Rio, including the president of Brazil and the actress Clara Bow, who was starring in the new flight film *Wings* (winner of the first Academy Award for Best Picture), were ready to welcome the twenty-five-year-old hero with a huge Rio-style celebration. Redfern never landed in Rio. He failed to drop a scheduled flare over a Brazilian town near the mouth of the Amazon River during his second night in the air. In the following decades, more than a dozen well-publicized search parties set out to find the pilot in the 2,500-mile stretch of dense jungle where his plane was presumed to have gone down. One group

sold "Redfern Rescue" stamps to finance its mission; members of another search party claimed they were driven back by hostile Indians. Several searchers died in the jungle or drowned in the Amazon.

Redfern rumors circulated, each more fantastic than the last. One told of a white man living in an Indian village, married to a native woman and father of her children. Over the years, the rumors faded. The people of Rio de Janeiro honored Redfern by naming a street for him. The small grass airstrip then on St. Simons was named Redfern Field. Today Redfern Village, an enclave of restaurants, bars, and shops on Frederica Road, occupies the site of the island's first airfield.

Hundreds of stories circulated for years after the young pilot was lost. The Redfern saga still surfaces from time to time, always shining a spotlight on the Georgia coast where Redfern waved a final good-bye to his wife and other well-wishers. Redfern's tragedy did publicize Brunswick, St. Simons, and Sea Island all over the world, although not as Coffin, Jones, and members of the Brunswick Board of Trade had wished.

In the mid-1930s, Coffin began to lobby for a larger airport on St. Simons. Redfern Field, flanked by marsh on one side and Frederica Road on the other, had no room to expand. Coffin wanted an airport large enough to handle commercial flights for the convenience of resort visitors. Coffin donated part of Retreat Plantation for the project, and county officials assembled the rest of the needed land. Glynn County Commission chairman Malcolm McKinnon, for whom the airport is named, persuaded the federal Works Progress Administration to fund the project. He also promoted paving projects on St. Simons, where most roads were still covered with crushed oyster shells from old Indian mounds.

Coffin died before the airport was finished. In 1937, in ill health and suffering from the loss of his beloved wife, Matilda, or Teddie, Coffin shot himself. The visionary engineer who helped forge the nation's automotive and aviation industries and played a major role in bringing prosperity to the Georgia coast had lost much of his fortune during the Great Depression. Sea Island, his dream resort, was struggling to survive. The death of the seventy-seven-year-old Coffin left Alfred W. Jones, his young cousin and longtime associate, to take over the company reins. Three generations of Jones family members ran the resort in succession until 2010, when Sea Island filed for bankruptcy during the global recession. The company's holdings were purchased by investment groups that

Next stop, North Africa

Members of the Civil Air Patrol volunteered to fly donated planes during World War II to patrol for enemy submarines off the coast. (Picture courtesy of Winn Baker)

now own and operate the Cloister Hotel and Sea Island's other resort amenities as well as upscale residential developments on both islands.

During the early stages of airport construction, a bulldozer unearthed a skeleton identified as that of a Native American. The Sea Island Company and the Works Progress Administration funded an eight-month exploration of the site by the Smithsonian Institution. The archaeologist Preston Holder, who led the dig, discovered the remains of a large prehistoric Indian village, which yielded postholes marking the site of houses and other structures. The team identified more than one hundred burials and collected more than twenty thousand artifacts.

With the completion of the airport, the causeway, and newly paved roads, the population of St. Simons continued to grow, bringing some of the problems that always come with growth. In the late 1930s, the elderly rector of Christ Church was shot to death as he sat at his desk in the rectory. It became one of the island's most widely publicized murders. Some say gambling sparked the crime. Small-time gambling had always been a popular pastime on the sea islands. Gullah Geechees played bolito, a type of lottery, placing penny, nickel, and dime bets at barbershops, beauty salons, cafés, and juke joints. Whites played bingo for cash prizes at church social halls, the VFW hall, and the Cloister Hotel on Sea Island. But when two prominent island brothers opened clubs that offered the sort of gambling then associated in the public mind with organized crime, some islanders objected. After the Reverend Charles H. Lee, the seventy-one-year-old rector of Christ Church and a cousin of Robert E. Lee, spoke out against the clubs, he was murdered. George Clayborn, a black island resident, was charged with the crime. Clayborn told authorities that the club owners, who were white, gave him a pistol to commit the murder and paid him and another black man to kill Lee. The club owners were arrested, but after authorities spent a week interrogating Clayborn at jails around southern Georgia, he recanted. He was convicted and sentenced to life in prison, but the club owners were never indicted or tried.

During Prohibition, boatloads of whiskey were smuggled into Georgia through the maze of tidal waterways that wind through the marshes to remote bluffs on the islands and the mainland. The nation repealed Prohibition in 1933, but the ban on alcohol sales in Georgia continued for two more years. Later, marijuana became the smugglers' drug of choice. So many bales washed up on island beaches that locals nicknamed them "square grouper." On the night of July 28, 1978, an eighty-foot shrimp boat was tied up at a private dock on the Frederica River in the West Point subdivision while the crew

unloaded a cargo of marijuana and stashed it in a rented house near the dock. U.S. Customs agents arrested thirteen people and seized more than thirty tons of marijuana, the shrimp boat, three smaller boats, a tractor-trailer, motor homes, and smaller trucks.

Coastguardsmen based on St. Simons proudly decorated the hulls of their cutters with marijuana-leaf decals crossed out with red *X*s to indicate the number of marijuana boats they captured. One load was stored at the Coast Guard's lifeboat station on East Beach. Eight coastguardsmen trying to make off with some of the marijuana were arrested after their transport truck backed into an old septic tank. Islanders joked afterwards that the septic tank should get a marijuana leaf decal x-ed out in red. The Coast Guard station on East Beach was built by the Works Progress Administration during the 1930s, along with a dock for larger craft on the Frederica River. During World War II, the Coast Guard facilities were adapted for wartime use. In addition, the navy converted the recently opened King and Prince Hotel into a training center for sailors learning such new technologies as air traffic control and radar. The navy quartered officers at the hotel and leased McKinnon Airport, which was already playing a role in the war effort. In December 1941, President Franklin D. Roosevelt called on civilian pilots to fly private planes on reconnaissance missions, especially during weather so bad that "the crows

The Coast Guard station, built by the Works Progress Administration at the base of the East Beach peninsula in the 1930s. The station has been decommissioned and is now a museum.

were walking," as the volunteer pilots were fond of saying. Civil Air Patrol Unit 6 was organized at McKinnon. A visiting army officer from Atlanta who saw the unit in action was impressed. He noted the pilots were too busy flying missions to eat regular meals and were flying planes in poor repair, since parts were hard to come by. Commenting on those handicaps, the officer nicknamed Unit 6 the "Sandwich and Suicide Squadron."

When the navy leased the airport from the county in 1942, the military added runways and a drainage system for the field, finished paving projects, and constructed new buildings, including a control tower and barracks. Commercial flights were limited to one a day, and most of the passengers were military personnel. Since the Coastal Air Patrol had been left homeless by the navy takeover, Sea Island offered the use of land nearby so that Unit 6 could continue flying. The men and women of the unit built the base camp themselves, without missing a single mission.

Navy pilots stationed on St. Simons during World War II flew several types of fighter planes, including these cc-f6 Hellcats. (Navy Institute photo, courtesy of the Glynn County Airport Commission)

An aerial photograph of the Malcolm McKinnon Airport on St. Simons during World War II (Photo from the collections of Larry Wade, courtesy of the Glynn County Airport Commission)

The navy brought in Hellcats, dive-bombers, Avengers, and other aircraft for training, and young pilots were soon practicing over the ocean. The planes had been used and abused in combat. Given the combination of pilot trainees and worn-out planes, accidents were inevitable. One plane crashed in marsh at the edge of the Sea Island Golf Club; the pilot, in danger of smothering in the mud, was dragged out of the cockpit and revived with oxygen. Another plane crashed after hitting trees adjacent to Demere Road on takeoff, killing the two pilots. Ned Egbert of St. Simons, a flight instructor, was forced to land in the ocean when his plane's propeller fell off. After being rescued, he kept flying missions.

Francis A. "Sam" Baker of St. Simons was second in command at the training school. On submarine-spotting patrol over the ocean near Cumberland Island, Baker saw what he thought was an odd-looking sailboat. When he descended for a closer look, the boat submerged, leaving the sails floating behind in the water. Since Baker's plane was unarmed, all he could do was notify the air base of a German submarine in the area.

Scheduled commercial flights now land at the Brunswick–Golden Isles Jetport on the mainland, but McKinnon is still a busy little airport. So many Sea Island cottage owners and guests fly in for the weekend on private jets that St. Simons residents refer to the traffic as the Sea Island Air Force.

The U.S. Navy took over the newly constructed Malcolm McKinnon Airport on St. Simons during World War II. The airport's tower and terminal were both built by the navy, which made other improvements to the facility. (Photo from the collection of Allen Wilson, courtesy of the Glynn County Airport Commission)

Islanders were introduced early on to the horrors of World War II. Soon after the bombing of Pearl Harbor, German submarines began prowling Atlantic coastal waters, targeting American merchant ships loaded with fuel, food, and other goods destined for Allied forces. The U-boats at first met little resistance from a nation scrambling to assemble troops to guard its borders and join the fighting overseas. One of the deadliest enemy submarines, *U-123*, sank dozens of American merchant ships between New York and Florida. So many ships were torpedoed on the Atlantic Coast that a Florida historian described the attacks as the "Atlantic Pearl Harbor."

During the predawn hours of April 8, 1942, *U-123* hunted in Georgia waters. The *Esso Baton Rouge* and the ss *Oklahoma*, both civilian oil tankers, were heading north past St. Simons, running dark. The submarine lay submerged a few miles off the coast, waiting for the first ship to pass between it and the islands. Blackouts had been advised, but many coastal houses and businesses still kept their lights on at night. When the bulk of the *Oklahoma* appeared in the U-boat's periscope, backlit by the glow from St. Simons and Sea Island, the captain unleashed a torpedo, which struck the tanker between the engine room and the crew's quarters. Most of the seamen aboard were asleep when the torpedo hit. They woke up floundering in fuel-fouled saltwater on a sinking ship. The explosion was loud enough to shake buildings and rattle windows on nearby islands and wake people as far away as Brunswick.

Shortly after the *Oklahoma* attack, *U-123* torpedoed the *Esso Baton Rouge* a few miles away. The ship went down fast in about thirty feet of water. At least two men, who were trapped below decks, drowned; the rest boarded two lifeboats. The submarine surfaced, and a voice speaking German-accented English ordered the lifeboats to pull alongside. The seamen instead flattened themselves in the lifeboats, fearing that the submarine crew planned to machine-gun them. Searchlights from the submarine played over the lifeboats, but the anticipated gunfire never came. The men watched as the U-boat disappeared into the darkness.

U-123 sank a third merchant vessel, the *Esparta*, a refrigerator ship owned by the United Fruit Company, the next night off sparsely populated Cumberland Island. Rumors circulated that injured survivors were savaged by sharks and barracuda, but the *Esparta*'s only casualty was a seaman who panicked and drowned; the other crewmen were rescued. The German submarine then proceeded to Florida, where it sank more merchant ships before returning to base in occupied France. For weeks after the torpedo attacks off St. Simons and Cumberland, southern Georgia beaches were covered with gobs of oil, dead fish and seabirds, frozen turkeys, whole hams, rolls of bologna, mattresses, lifejackets, bars of Ivory soap, shoes, gloves, crates of oranges and cabbages, and other debris from the sunken ships.

Survivors abandoned the *Oklahoma* in lifeboats, but when they heard screams from the tanker, the ship's master and three others climbed back onboard. They found a critically injured officer, who died later in the lifeboat. They also rescued a number of crewmen trapped in quarters below decks. Meanwhile, the submarine circled the stricken ship, firing its deck gun and hitting the *Oklahoma* five times. The U-boat did not fire at the lifeboats, however.

The first rescuer to reach the *Oklahoma* and the *Baton Rouge* was Olaf H. Olsen Sr. of St. Simons, an experienced seaman who captained a yacht for the millionaire Candler family of Atlanta at their summerhouse on Cumberland Island. His daughters, Sonja Olsen Kinard and Thora Olsen Kimsey, spent more than six years compiling and editing material from declassified and other military sources, personal letters, photographs, and oral histories for their book detailing the events of World War II in Glynn County. The book includes an account of Olsen's rescue of the men from the ships.

Familiar with local waters, Olsen took a shortcut through the shoal waters of Portuguese Slough in front of the King and Prince Hotel; Coast Guard cutters followed more slowly by way of marked navigation channels. Olsen took three lifeboats in tow and headed for St. Simons. On the way, he pulled alongside a Coast Guard vessel to pick up a doctor to treat the wounded. After the injured seamen were transferred to the cutter, Olsen towed the lifeboats to the Coast Guard's Frederica River dock. The seamen arrived nearly naked and shivering from shock. A small yellow dog, the mascot of one of the torpedoed ships, was among the rescued.

Twenty-two seamen died in the attacks, either in the initial explosions or later in the fuel-slicked water. Their bodies were recovered over the next several days. Five badly burned victims who could not be identified were buried in Brunswick's Palmetto Cemetery as unknown seamen. In 1998, the five were identified, although only one was claimed by family members and returned to his hometown to be reinterred. Relatives of the others have never been located.

Olsen received several commendations for rescuing the seamen and for assisting the military with his extensive knowledge of coastal waters and tides. The merchant ships were raised and towed into St. Simons Sound until they could be taken to port in Brunswick for repairs. Local boaters went out to see the damaged tankers, returning with awed descriptions of the damage. After the ships were repaired, both were returned to service. They were again torpedoed, this time in deeper water, and lost for good.

During the war, when beach erosion threatened the King and Prince Hotel, the navy built a massive seawall to protect the property. As erosion progressed, land on either side of the hotel washed away, leaving the King and Prince on a rectangular peninsula for decades until the beach was rebuilt. The charming old hotel has long since been expanded and renovated. Its original arched stained-glass windows, depicting scenes of St. Simons, were preserved and showcased in the hotel's oceanfront dining room.

The Coast Guard Auxiliary asked islanders to volunteer as air wardens and plane spotters during the war. Some spotters were stationed on top of the King and Prince and on Sea Island's administrative building to watch for enemy aircraft. In a few embarrassing incidents, inexperienced spotters called in excited reports of enemy aircraft that turned out to be turkey vultures or other large birds. Volunteers also walked, rode horseback, or drove jeeps, trucks, and cars along the beaches of the sea islands, looking for invaders. Trained dogs accompanied some of the beach patrols. Marsh tackies, horses that had run wild on St. Simons and other sea islands for centuries, were preferred mounts for beach patrols. Thousands of the sturdy horses were captured, trained, and deployed on the beaches of the southeastern coast during the war.

The beaches of St. Simons were off limits to civilians from dusk to dawn, except for those with official business. Islanders often heard rumors that English-speaking Germans from the U-boats sometimes paddled ashore on rubber dinghies at night to buy cigarettes and candy at island markets or to offload spies and saboteurs. At least one enemy submarine sent spies ashore on a northern Florida beach. The spies were captured in Atlanta and later executed.

Edwin Fendig, the islander who later became chief harbor pilot of the Brunswick port, was a teenager during the war. Fendig was out one night with a coastguardsman and one of the many locals who volunteered themselves and their boats to patrol the coast. They anchored in the mouth of the Hampton River just north of Sea Island, hoping to spot any enemy boats that might be prowling offshore. Fendig stood first watch.

"The wind was blowing, but I heard an unusual noise and woke up the others," he said. After listening for a few minutes, the coastguardsman identified the noise as the sound of a submarine charging its batteries. Having no radio, Fendig and the others sped back to dock to report a German U-boat off the coast.

Fendig said people from all over Georgia came to see the torpedoed merchant ships anchored in St. Simons Sound. The enterprising teenager offered to row spectators out in his bateau to see the big holes in the ships. Fendig said the passengers usually rewarded

Marsh Tackies

FERAL HORSES called marsh tackies (also spelled taki or tacky) have roamed the sea islands for centuries. Some may be descendants of Spanish horses; others are probably descended from antebellum plantation stock. Slaves who developed the unique Gullah Geechee culture on isolated coastal plantations in Georgia and the Carolinas gave the horses their memorable name: marsh tackies. Taki is a Gullah Geechee word for horse.

Descendants of horses brought to the coast by Spanish and British settlers and antebellum planters once ran wild in the marshes and woods of St. Simons. Named marsh tackies by the Gullah Geechees, the sturdy horses were employed for beach patrols during World War II. (Courtesy of Dwain D. Snyder)

Marsh tackies are similar in appearance to the horses brought over by the Spanish: they are small, with deep, narrow chests and forelegs that connect to the chest in an inverted V-shape. Their small feet are ideal for negotiating marsh mud.

Guerrilla troops who rode with South Carolina's famed "Swamp Fox," Francis Marion, during the Revolutionary War were often mounted on marsh tackies, whose ability to navigate the marshes and swamps gave them an advantage over larger, heavier British horses.

Children who learned to ride at the old Sea Island Stables on St. Simons were thrilled when Marvin Long, the stable manager and riding instructor for decades, said anyone who could put a rope on a marsh tacky could claim it. It is doubtful any child ever roped one of the fleet-footed horses, although adults corralled a few in the days when St. Simons was still rural. Older islanders still talk of seeing the shaggy-coated horses grazing in the high marsh, running on the beach, and swimming in the ocean to escape biting flies. One island native has a vivid childhood memory of watching a small herd of marsh tackies run out of a thick fog onto the Sea Island Causeway early one morning. They were like magical horses emerging from the mists of Avalon.

The marsh tackies of St. Simons are gone now, and the breed is considered critically endangered. Only about 150 genetically distinct marsh tackies have been identified to date in the United States. The Carolina Marsh Tacky Association, which aims to protect and expand the breed, successfully lobbied the South Carolina legislature in 2010 to name the marsh tacky the state's official heritage horse.

him with nice tips. The Coast Guard got wind of the enterprise, however, and shut him down because he was not licensed to transport passengers.

It has long been a tradition of the Brunswick harbor pilots to sound three blasts of a ship's horns when they pass the pier. Fendig said the blasts were originally to let the dispatchers know the location of the ships in the days before modern communication equipment. In days past, whenever people on the south end heard a ship's horn, they hurried to the beach to watch the big boats pass by and to wave to Captain Fendig at the helm. Even after Fendig retired, the harbor pilots continued the tradition of sounding the ship's horn as they passed his house a few blocks from the pier.

Fendig and his wife, Betty, still live in the family's waterfront house, originally a summer cottage remodeled several times over the years. Summer people usually returned to the mainland on Labor Day. But in 1928, after his parents spent a blissful summer at the cottage, Fendig's mother refused to leave. "My father said, 'Babe'—that's what he called my mother, Babe—'it's time to go back to Brunswick,' and she sat there in the rocking chair and waved at him. He stayed right there with her."

Five months after the merchant ships were attacked off St. Simons, construction began on the Glynco Naval Air Station, an airship base north of Brunswick. To house eight of their lighter-than-air craft, the navy built two enormous hangars, said to be the largest wooden buildings in the world. Towering almost three hundred feet high, well above the mainland tree canopy, the hangars were visible across the Marshes of Glynn from the causeway and the western shore of St. Simons. The wooden structures were the length of six football fields and so cavernous that they created their own weather. It often rained inside the hangars when the sun was shining outside. Trains that carried supplies into the hangars looked like children's toys inside the massive buildings.

The airships, armed with depth charges and bombs, escorted navy convoys and hunted down enemy submarines. Glynco was rated one of the most effective antisubmarine bases of World War II, putting a halt to U-boat attacks off the southeastern seaboard without losing a single aircraft, although many took fire. Island children loved waving to the gray flying elephants and chasing their giant shadows as they floated low over the beach. Sometimes a crewman in the gondola would delight the youngsters by hailing them on the loudspeaker. The airships and the hangars are gone now. The rotted wooden buildings were torn down after the war, a task so hazardous that even the contractor who built them declined to bid on the job.

The wartime population of Brunswick exploded after a small shipyard was selected to build a fleet of Liberty ships, mass-produced behemoths whose sole purpose was to carry

A fleet of giant airships operated out of the Glynco Navy Base in Brunswick, where three-hundred-foot-tall hangars, visible from the western shore of St. Simons and the causeway, towered above mainland trees. The craft patrolled coastal waters for enemy ships. (Courtesy of the Coastal Georgia Historical Society)

Thousands of workers flooded into the area during World War II to build Liberty ships, which carried supplies to U.S. forces fighting in Europe. Many of the workers settled in Brunswick and on St. Simons after the war. (Courtesy of the Coastal Georgia Historical Society)

supplies to Allied forces. The average Liberty ship was 441 feet long and 57 feet wide, meant to carry about nine thousand tons of cargo in five cavernous holds. Most were routinely overloaded with ammunition, weapons, food, hardware, tools, trucks, jeeps, and anything else needed by the Allies. Extra cargo was lashed on deck. The first Liberty ships were unarmed and vulnerable, but later ones were equipped with antiaircraft guns, small cannons, and machine guns.

The simplified British-based design of the vessels allowed the shipyard to hire workers with no prior experience and still turn out Liberty ships in record time. They were welded instead of riveted whenever possible, because riveting required more skill. Their lines were straight instead of curved to minimize the amount of metal the novice workers were required to bend. The plan worked; by the end of the war, the Brunswick shipyard had turned out eighty-five Liberty ships, plus fourteen other cargo vessels. The Liberty ship program was a huge success, but decades later a number of shipyard workers and members of their families were diagnosed with mesothelioma, an incurable cancer of the lung lining caused by exposure to asbestos. Workers recalled the blizzards of asbestos insulation that swirled around inside the ships whenever the material was being installed. When they carried the insulation home on their clothing, they exposed family members.

Once the Liberty ship project was up and running, sixteen thousand workers—more than Brunswick's prewar population of fifteen thousand—signed on to build ships. They and their families flooded in from all over the Southeast, eager for work after the Depression had left so many Americans jobless and destitute. Brunswick's population soared almost overnight to seventy-five thousand. Spillover newcomers crossed the causeway to St. Simons.

The government condemned every scrap of vacant land in Brunswick and threw up wartime housing. Existing boardinghouses, hotels, and apartments were packed to the rafters. Area residents rented out spare bedrooms, attics, and garages. People lived in their cars until they could find better lodgings. Workers on different shifts often shared the same accommodations, joking about bunking down in "hot beds" still warm from previous occupants.

The shipyards operated around the clock, seven days a week. When workers were criticized for laboring on Sunday, the standard response was "Our troops are fighting on Sunday; the least we can do is help them get supplies." New industries opened to support the shipyards, including Dixie Paint and Varnish Company, which supplied paint for the Liberty ships and varnish for the floors of wartime housing. The founders,

J. O. Hice and W. Q. Walker, mixed their first batches of paint in old wringer washing machines.

Glynn County public schools were overrun, requiring the board of education to schedule double shifts until dozens of new teachers could be hired and classroom space built or rented. White island children who had ridden buses to elementary school in Brunswick attended classes on St. Simons at a church camp on East Beach until an elementary school was built on the south end of the island. German POWs who worked on airport construction helped build the school, which is only a short block from the beach. For years, island children walked to school barefoot on the beach, and teachers took their students to the beach at recess.

Because of the housing shortage, two wartime subdivisions of small single-family houses were built on St. Simons to house shipyard workers. Kings Terrace, near the pier section, and Oglethorpe Park, off Frederica Road, are still popular island residential areas.

Many mainlanders who came to the area during the war had never seen the ocean. The only other Georgia sea island then accessible by causeway was Tybee, a small island east of Savannah; the causeway to Jekyll Island was not built until the 1950s. Vehicles whose owners were able to get rationed gas and tires always stopped to pick up people hitchhiking between the mainland and the islands. Sea Island began offering weekend package deals to soldiers on leave from the sprawling Fort Stewart Army Base between Brunswick and Savannah.

After the war, the military installations on St. Simons shut down. The shipyard closed. McKinnon Airport reopened to civilian traffic; the King and Prince Hotel hosted guests once again. Coastguardsmen resumed their efforts to aid boaters and swimmers instead of rescuing oil-covered survivors of torpedoed ships. Islanders, however, were ready to take advantage of the wartime economic boom, which ended the Great Depression and brought prosperity to St. Simons.

Drivers unfamiliar with the island's radical tides sometimes got caught when the tide flooded in. (Courtesy of the J. Hice family album)

Cars were once allowed to drive on St. Simons beach. (Courtesy of the J. Hice family album.)

Rachel Carson

THE WOMAN WHO LAUNCHED the postwar environmental movement in the United States spent a few months on St. Simons in the spring of 1952. Rachel Carson, the famed writer-naturalist, came to the island with her mother, Maria, and their orange cat, Muffin, a high-energy adolescent feline. They settled into an old beachside apartment near the lighthouse. Carson was already well known and respected in academic circles by the time she came to St. Simons. Islanders familiar with her books took her on boat trips to out-of-the-way places where rare sea- and shorebirds nested, including Pelican Spit, a large sandbar off the north end of Sea Island. On one trip, an island woman accompanying Carson found a pair of fledgling seabirds in a nest consisting of a shallow scrape in the sand. The nest and the fledglings were so well camouflaged that the woman almost stepped on them. For reasons she could never later explain, she took one of the fledglings home. The little bird died, as Carson warned it might. In later years, the islander often commented on how guilty she felt for taking the fledgling from its nest.

Carson was generous about sharing her knowledge of the seashore. She often took two St. Simons children on beach walks and introduced them to sea pansies, *Renilla muelleri*. Small, purple, and flowerlike, they lay under a thin layer of muddy sand at the waterline. Carson explained that each sea pansy was a colony of tiny animals that lived together, each doing a different job. After dark, she said, the small animals would glow with a bright green light. Walking the high-tide line with Carson another day, the children collected dried sea whips, *Leptogorgia virgulata*, to make a bouquet for their mother. Stiff and branching, sea whips come in a variety of colors: yellow, orange, white, lavender, and dark red. Carson said the whips were also colonial animals, with thousands of tiny creatures living on a single stalk. The children remembered Carson years later as a quiet woman with sun-freckled skin. Her mother, Maria, was more outgoing. She often invited the children to the apartment to play with Muffin, the cat, who loved racing after them and batting at their bare feet. Muffie, as they called him, was happy to dispose of some of the sea creatures Carson carried back to her rented quarters in jars and buckets for further study.

In her best-selling book *The Edge of the Sea*, Carson describes her time on St. Simons. She discusses the hidden life of the low-tide beach, the myriad burrows of small creatures marked by inconspicuous holes or tiny tubes protruding just above the damp sand.

The naturalist and writer Rachel Carson spent several months on St. Simons in 1952 while doing research for one of her books. Carson sometimes took the author and other island children on beachcombing expeditions. (U.S. Fish and Wildlife Service)

Carson captivates readers with her descriptions, such as when she relates the lives of millions of sea creatures invisible to the naked eye—water mites, crustaceans, sea worm larvae—that swim, breathe, reproduce, feed, and die in worlds too small to imagine: the thin film of water surrounding each grain of beach sand.

Many scientists and environmentalists today oppose beach renourishment in part because it destroys the habitat of so many plants and animals, visible and otherwise. Changes to natural beaches caused by dredged sand can disturb the life cycles of larger sea creatures too, including the giant loggerhead sea turtles that nest on Georgia beaches during summer months. The sex of loggerhead hatchlings is determined by the temperature of the sand in which the eggs are incubated. Renourished beaches tend to produce nests of all-male loggerheads, while natural beaches produce more females, an imbalance that affects the long-term survival of the species.

During Carson's visit to St. Simons, she would have noticed island children playing an exciting game they invented during the war: chasing the fogging machine. Trucks and jeeps began spraying on St. Simons during World War II to control the mosquito population and protect military personnel from malaria, then still endemic on the southern Georgia coast. Because there were so many military bases in the region, the federal government established a center in Jacksonville, Florida, called the Office of Malaria Control in War Areas, to fight malaria by attacking mosquitoes. The agency later became the renowned Centers for Disease Control and Prevention in Atlanta. The pesticide the military and, later, civilian governments used to kill mosquitoes was DDT, atomized in diesel fuel by using smoke-screen technology developed for the war. The vehicles that carried the sprayers were trailed by thick plumes of chemical-scented fog as well as scores of delighted children who loved running in and out of the fog. Before her St. Simons visit, Carson had expressed concern about widespread use of DDT. A decade later, she published *Silent Spring*, her landmark book that alerted the world to the dangers of the pesticide and led to its ban.

CHAPTER VII A Time to Grow

[1946–Present]

Growth brought environmental problems to St. Simons. The island's once-wide beaches had begun eroding rapidly during the war because of military dredging. Postwar development of the Brunswick ports exacerbated the problem, especially on south St. Simons and north Jekyll. Although many islanders found good jobs working in mainland industries that paid high wages year-round, industrial pollution fouled the air, tidewaters, and marshes of the coast. New businesses opened on St. Simons, two in abandoned navy buildings at McKinnon Airport. Sea Island rapidly became one of the area's major employers.

Subdivisions proliferated like weeds, replacing the dense woodlands that once flanked Frederica Road. St. Simons and Sea Island continued to grow as popular tourist destinations. Locals were puzzled that the majority of visitors to St. Simons came during summer months, while winter was neighboring Sea Island's high season. On St. Simons, winter belonged to islanders, who amused themselves by fishing, hunting, holding oyster roasts, and telling ghost stories. In pretelevision days, islanders were entertained by the area's most popular radio personality, who delivered the drive time morning news in a special style. St. Simons residents were invited to turn out at McKinnon Airport

A beach house in a losing battle against the Atlantic Ocean (Courtesy of the J. Hice family album.)

to greet a royal couple on their way to a Sea Island vacation. Islanders were excited for weeks about the visit. As St. Simons and Sea Island developed over the years, the two islands began to go their separate ways, and the close relationship they once shared came to an end.

During the war, the federal government dredged to deepen and extend the natural channel in St. Simons Sound to ease the passage of Liberty ships launched at the Brunswick shipyards. Once the dredging began, erosion on the beaches of St. Simons and Jekyll Islands accelerated. When residents complained, the navy assured them the beaches would rebuild themselves after the war, when the dredging stopped. Instead, the Brunswick Port Authority and the Georgia Ports Authority continued the dredging in order to make the ports more attractive to commercial shippers. New cargo terminals expanded port facilities in Brunswick and on Colonel's Island near the Sidney Lanier Bridge. The ship channel continues to be dredged to accommodate huge cargo ships that carry new cars, agricultural products, wood pulp, animal feed, paper products, machinery, and other goods. The ports boost the local and state economies, but experts say the ongoing dredging contributes to the loss of beaches on sea islands flanking the sound.

Beachfront development compounded erosion problems. When erosion threatens buildings close to an eroding beach, property owners lobby for government-funded seawalls, groins, jetties, and renourishment to protect their often-considerable investments. Sea Island continues to renourish its badly eroding beach, but residents of St. Simons have fought such projects because they are expensive, need repeating every few years, and damage the natural beach. Advocates of renourishment argue that it is preferable to building hard structures on the beach, which interfere with natural exchanges of sand between dunes, beaches, and sandbars. Seawalls and renourishment have negative consequences for wildlife too. For example, seawalls block the passage of loggerhead sea turtles, which lay their eggs in the warm sand at the edge of the dunes above the high-tide line.

For most of its length, the beach on St. Simons is armored by a seawall of large granite boulders known to islanders as the Johnson Rocks. The rocks were brought in after Hurricane Dora gave the island a glancing blow in 1964, flooding low-lying neighborhoods near the marsh and washing away a few cottages on Beachview Drive that were already teetering on pilings. The storm caused severe beach erosion south from the King and Prince past the pier and beyond the Sea Island Golf Club. The north end of East Beach at Gould's Inlet also eroded badly. Jekyll's already-eroding north beach

suffered additional damage from the hurricane. President Lyndon Johnson, who was running for election at the time and, no doubt, hoping to garner Georgia votes, toured storm-damaged beaches on St. Simons, Sea Island, and Jekyll and ordered the rocks installed. Many private property owners, including the Sea Island Company, have built seawalls at their own expense or augmented the government-funded seawalls.

After World War II, many islanders began commuting to Brunswick to work in mainland businesses and industries. Several larger industries discharged toxic waste into the air, waterways, and marshes, which for decades served as a cheap, convenient, and legal dumping ground. Hercules Inc., which operated a chemical plant near the mainland entrance to the Torras Causeway, began manufacturing the pesticide toxaphene shortly after the war to kill boll weevils on cotton plants and maggots on cattle. The company funneled wastes from the manufacturing process into a waterway leading to Terry Creek, the westernmost of the five tidal rivers crossed by the causeway. Although the creek was flushed by daily tides, shrimpers docked their boats there because toxaphene residue in the water was potent enough to kill barnacles and other marine growth on the boats' bottoms, saving the shrimpers the trouble and expense of hauling their boats out to scrape the hulls. Toxaphene, labeled one of the "dirty dozen" in the long lexicon of toxic chemicals, was banned for all uses in the United States in 1990 because it was found to cause cancer and birth defects. Nearby marshes, onto which material dredged from Terry Creek was dumped, along with the area around the plant and a government-approved toxaphene waste dump on the

Islanders refer to the seawall of granite boulders that lines most of the beach on St. Simons as the Johnson Rocks because former President Lyndon Johnson ordered the rocks installed after Hurricane Dora in 1964.

Shrimpers once docked their boats in the calm waters of Terry Creek, where industrial pollution killed barnacles and other growth on their boats' hulls. (Photo by Jingle Davis)

mainland, were named federal Superfund sites. Superfund dollars have helped pay to clean up some of the most heavily polluted areas in the United States. More than three decades after toxaphene was banned, fish, shellfish, and bottlenose dolphins in the coastal estuary miles from Brunswick still harbor the pesticide in their tissues. Other Brunswick-based industries contributed to the pollution. In 1998, three executives and the environmental health and safety manager of the Hanlin Group's LCP Chemicals plant west of Brunswick were convicted and sentenced to prison for discharging 150 tons of toxic mercury into tidal marshes and waterways. At the trial, plant workers described wading through knee-deep water contaminated with mercury at LCP, which was also designated a Superfund site. Mercury has been found in endangered wood storks on St. Simons and in other birds and wildlife in the area. Superfund money helped clean up Brunswick Wood Preserving, a mainland plant that produced tele-phone poles and dock pilings treated with poisonous creosote. Glynn County had the dubious distinction of having five Superfund sites, more than any other county in Georgia. Although the official cleanups have all been done, experts have no idea how long residual toxins will persist in the environment.

Howard Coffin and Alfred W. Jones, founders of the Sea Island Company, helped launch Georgia's pulp and paper industry, which brought prosperity to the coast and many other parts of the state. Especially in the poorer counties of South and Middle Georgia, landowners planted hundreds of thousands of fast-growing pine trees, which were harvested for the pulp mills to process into paper. Brunswick Pulp and Paper Company (now Georgia Pacific), which operated the large mill on the Turtle River, for many years produced noxious odors that often caused tourists traveling on U.S. Highway 17 to describe Brunswick as "the little city that stinks." The skunk-like smells continued until pulp mills nationwide were required to curtail their sulfur dioxide emis-sions. Whenever pulp-mill workers heard complaints about the bad smells pouring from the plant's smokestacks, they always retorted, "That's the smell of money." And so it was. For many years, the pulp mill paid some of the area's highest wages.

Much of the postwar development on St. Simons and Sea Island was designed to entice ever-increasing numbers of visitors to the coast. Before Interstate 95 became the major coastal highway, tourist promoters lured migrating snowbirds off U.S. 17. They decked out the mainland entrance to the Torras Causeway with a charming Spanish-style visitor center, a cutaway model of a Liberty ship, an iron pot in which, promoters claimed, the first Brunswick stew was cooked, and large lighted signs pointing the way to St. Simons and Sea Island.

One of the few remaining old beach cottages on St. Simons. Most of the others have been razed to make room for beachfront condominiums.

Middle-class people from all over Georgia continued to be the summer mainstay of St. Simons, as they had been since the late 1800s. Islanders who catered to the tourist trade in earlier and leaner postwar decades counted on three months' worth of summer business to carry them through the rest of the year. They complained loudly about low-budget visitors who brought food from home, camped in their cars, bathed in the ocean, and used public bathrooms. Islanders involved in tourism-related businesses always said the low-budget visitors arrived with a clean shirt and a dollar bill and stayed for a week without changing either.

Most visitors did spend money on the island. They rented casual, sandy-floored beach cottages or stayed at the old Golden Isles Hotel, Winn Gables, or the three-story Arnold House. The island's first modern motels opened in the 1950s: Queen's Court near the pier, the Sailfish on Beachview Drive, and Craft's Ocean Court by the Coast Guard station. Wealthier visitors stayed at the upscale King and Prince Hotel, which offered fine dining, a beachside pool, and summer dances on the patio. The King and Prince was originally built as a private dance club by the wealthy financiers Frank Horn and Morgan Wynn after the two were kicked out of the Cloister Hotel for being drunk and disorderly. Sea Island did not tolerate such behavior. In their new club on St. Simons, the two men offered adult entertainments such as boxing matches and extravagant floor shows. Big-name dance bands, including those led by Glenn Miller and Sammy Kaye, played at the club, first called The King and The Prince, the nickname friends had given Horn, who was tall and heavyset, and Wynn, who was short and slim. After fire twice destroyed the place, the partners rebuilt the club as a hotel, which opened in 1941, shortly before the navy took it over for wartime use.

The heart of St. Simons for vacationers and locals has always been the pier section and Neptune Park, now called collectively the Pier Village. In summer, the park featured a Ferris wheel, a children's train, and a miniature golf course. In winter, the attractions shut down. The Old Casino in the park housed a small segregated movie theatre. Gullah Geechees had to drive across the causeway to see movies at the Roxy, the theatre in Brunswick for black people. At the Casino Theatre, Georgia McKendree, the longtime manager and a multitasking genius, sold tickets at the box office, vended candy from the tiny concession stand, ushered patrons to their seats, and chaperoned young people in the audience. Movies for adults were shown at night; serialized matinees, including *The Durango Kid* and *Perils of Nyoka*, drew children in on Saturdays. Mrs. McKendree was quick to act in loco parentis if she saw an adolescent boy drape his arm across the back of a girl's theatre seat. She would hurry down the aisle and shine her flashlight on the offending youngsters, hinting that she might call their parents unless they behaved themselves. The Casino Theatre no longer shows movies but for many decades has been home to The Island Players, a dedicated community group that presents several plays a year and hosts a summer workshop for children.

There were no public swimming pools on St. Simons until after World War II. Before the New Casino and its giant pool opened in Neptune Park, white people swam in the ocean or at the employees' pool on Sea Island, where towels rented for a dime. Islanders could also buy pool memberships at the King and Prince or at some of the island motels. In the days before integration, many black islanders never learned to swim because they were banned from public beaches and swimming pools on St. Simons. Deep tidal creeks with slippery mud banks that often concealed sharp oyster shells were not ideal places for swimming lessons. Among the nonswimmers were Gullah Geechees who worked on the water every day as crabbers, oystermen, and shrimpers. Nonswimmers sometimes fell overboard and drowned.

When the county built the New Casino in about 1950 between the older casino and the lighthouse, the two buildings were thereafter known as the Old Casino and the New Casino. The New Casino was designed in the then-modern International Style, and its public rooms were equipped with huge metal-framed windows that rolled up like garage

doors around the large downstairs recreation room and the oak-floored skating rink on the second floor. As teenagers danced to early rock tunes—"Maybelline" by Chuck Berry and the wild, wop-ba-ba-lu-bop of Little Richard's "Tutti Frutti"—skaters glided to the sedate strains of organ music in the rink upstairs. Anyone not dancing, playing Ping-Pong, swimming in the pool, or skating sat on the New Casino's wide windowsills, talking, eating, smoking, and watching the action. Community meetings, Halloween carnivals, and other big events were held for many years at the New Casino, which also served for a time as the polling place for south-end residents.

The New Casino pool opened for summer the day school let out. Swimmers were required to walk through a chemical footbath and an anemic spray of cold water before entering the pool. For years there were no swim teams or organized activities, but divers practiced flips and cannonballs from the high and low boards while younger swimmers played alligator, trying to swim past the designated alligator to the deep-end wall while dodging the divers. When the lifeguards drained the pool for cleaning, they warned swimmers to avoid the deep-end corner where giant open drains funneled the pool water into pipes leading under the beach to the ocean. Island boys dared each other to swim through the whirlpool created by the suction of the drains. The whirlpool proved too strong for one youngster, Jeb Hanley, who was swept feetfirst into a drain. He grabbed the sides of the opening before being sucked into the pipe; he held on until lifeguards, muscles straining, pulled him out. The youngster was bruised but otherwise unharmed.

The bowling alley moved from the Old Casino to the new, and the St. Simons Library moved into the vacated space. The library, founded in the 1930s by the daughter of a former sawmill superintendent, was privately funded by islanders for decades. It was one of the coziest places on the island, with comfortable furniture and friendly, helpful librarians: Fraser Ledbetter, Lillian Knight, Frances Kane, and others. Among the stacks of books were treasures donated by islanders, including gnarled pieces of sun-silvered driftwood, turtle shells and skulls, and pale sea glass. A large collection of local seashells was displayed in a glass case. There was no better place than the library to spend a rainy afternoon when black clouds hung low over the ocean, lightning flashed, and waves crashed against Neptune Park's seawall a few hundred feet away. Ledbetter, the head librarian for more than forty years, was a talented genealogist who helped many patrons trace their ancestors. She was also knowledgeable about island history, captivating locals and visitors with her stories of old St. Simons. The library is now part of Georgia's public library service and the PINES electronic network.

In the 1950s, the St. Simons Jaycees staged the first Sunshine Festival in Neptune Park. The annual festival soon became the area's most anticipated summer event. Thousands of locals and visitors thronged the park to eat hot dogs and cotton candy and throw softballs to dunk a Jaycee in a tank of water. A navy minesweeper docked at the pier, and visitors were invited aboard. Early festivals featured a beauty contest. Contestants paraded around the New Casino pool in bathing suits and high heels while spectators cheered their favorites from the rooftop sundeck. The winner, crowned later at ceremonies in the park, was given the title of Miss Sunshine, later changed to Miss Golden Isles when the pageant officially became part of the

Early Sunshine Festivals in Neptune Park featured beauty contests. Carole Langston was crowned the winner in 1958. Her daughter, Kim Askin Beckum, and her husband, Henry, now live in the old Langston cottage on south St. Simons. (Courtesy of Bill Strother)

Fireworks fountain over St. Simons Sound on Independence Day. Thousands of people gather in the village, in Neptune Park, and on the beach (if the tide is low) to watch the display. Boaters congregate in the sound for ringside seats.

Miss Georgia and Miss America contests. The festival's grand finale has always been an elaborate fireworks display launched from the end of the pier. Thousands of spectators crowd the Pier Village and Neptune Park, spilling onto the beach at low tide, and hundreds of boats congregate in St. Simons Sound.

The New Casino building and pool deteriorated over the years, and the county had it torn down, over the objections of many islanders. It was replaced in 2010 by the Neptune Park Fun Zone, which includes a playground, a shallow pool with waterslides for young children, and a deeper pool for older swimmers, along with a paved patio, new lighting and landscaping, and a wall where people can sit and enjoy ocean vistas.

Neptune Park overlooks St. Simons Sound, where migratory right whales once congregated in great numbers. One of Neptune Park's more recent additions is a stunning life-size sculpture of a right whale and her calf. The sculpture, by Keith Jennings, honors the now-endangered whales that calved every winter in the sound.

By 1960, the population of St. Simons had grown from a few hundred people before the war to more than five thousand year-round residents, a number that soared on summer weekends. The entire nation was enjoying post-Depression, postwar prosperity, and people were eager to build new houses and take vacations. The real estate and resort businesses began booming on St. Simons and Sea Island. Coffin and Jones, founders of the Sea Island Company, always wanted the smaller island to be perceived as an upscale winter resort and residential enclave for wealthy people. While Sea Island was being promoted as a winter resort, St. Simons was marketed as a place for summer visitors, even though air and water temperatures were identical on the two islands, which are separated only by a narrow wedge

The new Neptune Park Fun Zone replaced the New Casino, built during the 1950s in the International Style.

One of the island's oldest beach cottages was named Tillandsia by a former owner after Spanish moss, *Tillandsia usneoides*, which grows wild all over St. Simons.

Swimmers enjoy the Atlantic Ocean
(Antique postcard courtesy of Freddie Pilgrim)

of marsh and a tidal creek. St. Simons residents were amazed that so many northern visitors to Sea Island swam in the ocean in January and February, when water temperatures hovered in the midfifties.

Famous people vacationed regularly on Sea Island, including U.S. presidents Calvin Coolidge, George H. W. Bush, and Jimmy Carter, as well as foreign heads of state, all of whom were invited to plant commemorative live oaks on the grounds of the Cloister Hotel. In 1952, Sea Island asked residents of St. Simons to help welcome a royal couple to the area. Queen Juliana of the Netherlands and her husband landed at McKinnon Airport on their way to a Sea Island vacation. The queen was greeted at the airport with flowers, dignitaries, speeches, and cheers. In pretelevision days, islanders were eager to get a look at a real queen. One little girl who expected to see a monarch dressed in a ball gown and jeweled crown was crushed when Her Majesty stepped off the plane wearing ordinary street clothes.

Right Whales

ST. SIMONS SOUND once hosted so many North Atlantic right whales, *Eubalaena glacialis*, that people could walk to Jekyll on their broad backs, or so the legend goes. Early Spaniards nicknamed the sound the Bay of Whales and called Jekyll the Island of Whales, according to the right whale expert Hans Neuhauser, who says that early maps mistakenly identify St. Andrews Sound, between Little Cumberland and Jekyll Islands, as the bay where the whales congregated. The critically endangered descendants of the fifty-foot-long whales still swim south from New England to calve during winter months in the warm shallow seas off southern Georgia and northern Florida, most within fifteen miles of shore, although they no longer bear their young in coastal sounds.

The first of the great whales to be hunted commercially, right whales were so named by whalers because they were the right whales to hunt. They swam slowly, favored shallow near-shore waters, and floated after they were killed because of their thick layers of blubber, making them easier to beach or bring aboard ship. Whalers rendered the blubber into oil and, in later centuries, sold baleen from the whales' mouths for corset stays, umbrella ribs, and horsewhips, which led to such colorful colloquialisms as "I'm going to whale the tar out of you." Tar was a nickname for a rowdy seaman. At one time, a small whaling industry operated out of Fernandina, Florida, and Brunswick. In the late 1800s, crews of passing ships hunted right whales when they happened to encounter them. About eighteen or nineteen right whales were killed by the opportunistic whalers; thousands were taken by whalers in the North Atlantic over several centuries.

By the twentieth century, right whales had been hunted to near extinction. They are now threatened primarily by collisions with large ships that travel the same routes as the migrating whales. The federal government is considering a proposal to relocate shipping lanes farther offshore in order to protect the rare marine mammals. In addition, right whales fall victim to illegal drift nets launched by commercial fishing boats. The nets, resembling giant tennis-court nets, have floats along the top and weights along the bottom so that they hang upright in the water and entangle whole schools of fish. Before laws were changed in the 1960s, some commercial drift nets were more than thirty miles long. Drift nets were efficient at catching fish, but they also entangled and killed whales, dolphins, sea turtles, and other wildlife. In 1992, the United Nations banned drift-net fishing worldwide because of damage to the environment, but some commercial fishermen continue the practice. Lost or abandoned drift nets, many made of synthetic material that does not biodegrade, are still floating in the ocean, and they continue to catch, entangle, and kill sea creatures.

North Atlantic right whale and calf. The highly endangered whales migrate south each winter to calve in the warm shallow waters off the southeastern coast. (Courtesy of the National Oceanic and Atmospheric Administration)

Buildings at the airport that had been abandoned by the military after the war were occupied by new enterprises. The Atlanta artists Bill Hendrix and Erv Davis opened the island's first art school in 1950 in the old navy barracks. Davis's tenure was brief, but Hendrix stayed on, teaching art for decades and attracting students from all over Georgia and beyond. St. Simons has long been a magnet for artists and photographers, who say the island's pure golden light, reflected off the ocean and filtered through semitropical foliage, resembles the light that draws artists to Provence, in the south of France. The quality of the light may have prompted the sea islands' memorable nickname: the Golden Isles. Sir Robert Montgomery of Scotland proposed to create what he called the Margravate of Azilia along the coast in 1717, well before Oglethorpe founded Savannah. The nobleman published pamphlets advertising the project and inviting Europeans to invest. The pamphlets included an illustration believed to be the earliest art done in America to promote land speculation. Sir Robert's project never got off the ground, but the nickname he coined is still popular. He referred to most of Georgia's sea islands as the Golden Isles, but the name is now often used only for the islands of Glynn County.

In 1948, the St. Simons entrepreneur Jaxon O. Hice, one of the founders of Dixie Paint and Varnish Company on the mainland, conceived the idea of freezing fresh Georgia shrimp and fish and shipping it to distant markets. SeaPak Corporation, founded by Hice, James J. Meadows, and J. Roy Duggan, took over the large walk-in freezer built by the navy at McKinnon Airport. Barefoot children accustomed to warm sea island winters ignored warnings to stay out of the freezer. They had to be rescued when their feet stuck to the icy concrete floor. SeaPak rapidly became a pioneer in the frozen-seafood industry. Hice and his partners developed fish sticks, the

St. Simons is one of the famed Golden Isles of Georgia, so named by an early would-be developer. Artists claim the island's golden light, reflected off the ocean through the dense semitropical foliage, is similar to the light that drew so many artists to Provence, in the south of France.

Georgia white shrimp are prized in northern markets for their size and delicate flavor. Shrimpers today struggle to compete with imported pond-raised shrimp and to cope with the rising cost of doing business, including soaring prices for diesel fuel.

A striker, or crew member on a shrimp boat, sorts the catch. Otter trawls, the nets used by Georgia shrimpers, are fitted with devices to exclude endangered sea turtles but still scoop up fish, crabs, stingrays, and many other coastal species as well as shrimp.

flash-freezing process, and individually quick-frozen shrimp. The company hired scores of Gullah Geechees and other islanders to process and pack frozen seafood. SeaPak created a new market for Georgia shrimpers' and fishermen's catches. In the days before freezer trucks crisscrossed the nation, Hice, a private pilot, began shipping SeaPak products by air from McKinnon Airport to markets all over the United States. He served as company president until he resigned to pursue other ventures. Until his death in 1985, Hice continued to develop seafood-related businesses and invent new products. After more than sixty years, the company he started on St. Simons, now Rich-SeaPak, maintains its executive offices at the small island airport.

After the war, the old airship base north of Brunswick became Naval Air Station Glynco. Many Glynco officers and their families bought or rented houses on St. Simons, commuting across the causeway to work. One of the island's first subdivisions opened just north of the old Sea Island Stables at Frederica Road and the Sea Island Causeway. After a scattering of small frame houses went up in the 1930s, the project stalled through the lean years of the Depression. Initially named Sylvan Springs Glynn Haven, the development embraced a spring-fed pond called Sylvan Springs. The subdivision's name was soon shortened to Glynn Haven. For many years, Glynn Haven was one of the island's poorest neighborhoods, but it grew over the years into a popular subdivision offering attractive houses.

Glynn Haven's original developer was a colorful character known to everyone as Mighty Fine because the phrase defined his lexicon. Mighty Fine, whose name was Daniel Cowart, ended every sentence, answered every question, and described anything and everything as "mighty fine," even if tragedy and death were involved. Cowart built his own house on Frederica Road in Glynn Haven and opened an adjacent country store that sold kerosene lamps, dry goods, seeds, underwear, candy, staple groceries, and many other necessities of island life. The unassuming frame building was covered with colorful advertising signs and featured a waterwheel next to the parking lot, much to the joy of island children, who begged their parents to stop at Mighty Fine's so they could watch the dripping wheel turn slowly around and around, reflecting the leisurely pace of island life more than half a century ago.

Another of the island's early subdivisions was Epworth Acres, which adjoins Epworth by the Sea on Gascoigne Bluff. Part of the bluff includes an oak-shaded county-owned park and a public marina, the St. Simons Boating and Fishing Club, along with a new fishing dock near the Frederica River bridge. In antebellum times, Hamilton Plantation occupied the bluff as well as hundreds of acres of adjacent land. Epworth by the Sea has

Jaxon Hice Jr., born on St. Simons in 1947, was always an avid fisherman. (Courtesy of the J. Hice family album)

expanded over the years. Its six motels, dozen family apartments, and thirteen youth facilities can accommodate one thousand guests. Lovely Lane Chapel, built during the sawmill era, sits near Epworth's entrance gates. It is the island's second-oldest church building. Two fishing piers jut into the Frederica River from Epworth's grounds. Both are great places to watch winter sunsets over the marsh. One pier also boasts an exceptional fishing drop. Fish are attracted to the large pile of ballast stones dumped there by sailing ships more than a century ago.

The Arthur J. Moore Methodist Museum and Library, established in 1965 by its namesake, a former Georgia Methodist bishop, sits on the grounds of Epworth but is owned and operated by the South Georgia Methodist Conference. The facility offers tours, lectures, and exhibits from early days on St. Simons. Among the museum's treasures are letters written by John Wesley. The library's collection of six thousand books is available to genealogists and scholars.

For many years, residents of Epworth Acres lined the subdivision's yards, walkways, and streets with luminarias in the weeks before Christmas. Thousands of the luminarias, each consisting of a candle in a small brown paper bag weighted with sand, gave the subdivision a warm, magical glow that delighted island children and attracted visitors from nearby islands and the mainland who drove slowly, lights off, through the neighborhood before taking their children to the village pier to greet Santa Claus.

Well into the late twentieth century, poverty continued to plague the island's three segregated Gullah Geechee neighborhoods, where small, uninsulated frame houses were heated by fireplaces, woodstoves, or kerosene heaters. One tiny house on Demere Road in the Harlem/South End neighborhood was built entirely of corrugated tin. Gullah Geechee women took in ironing to help make ends meet. In winter, the garments came back smelling pleasantly of woodsmoke and kerosene. Black women found jobs on St. Simons and Sea Island as maids, housekeepers, and cooks. In 1960, a full-time domestic earned about $25 a week plus toting privileges, meaning the worker was allowed to take leftover food home to her own family. Sea Island became and remains one of the area's largest employers. Sea Island's landscape crew alone numbered more than a thousand workers, the majority of them black. Now, as more and more Gullah Geechees move up the economic scale, Sea Island employs Hispanics to groom the grounds of its resort buildings and private cottages. No matter how large or lavish, houses on Sea Island are always called cottages. The northern millionaires who founded the exclusive Jekyll Island Club always referred to their island vacation houses as cottages to distinguish them from the mansions they owned elsewhere. Sea Island's founders continued the tradition.

As integration proceeded during the 1960s, more and more Gullah Geechees began commuting across the causeway for better jobs on the mainland. Many continued to augment their incomes by fishing, hunting, and planting large vegetable gardens, often growing corn and other row crops that required large tracts of land on island roadsides and other public rights-of-way. Gullah Geechee men, who had intimate knowledge of island woodlands and tidewaters, hired out as fishing and hunting guides. Members of the Sullivan family in the Harrington community established a popular fish camp on a high-tide creek at the end of South Harrington Drive. Sullivan's Fish Camp was called Cusie's by locals because Cusie Sullivan ran the camp. He, his brother Ben, and other family members were descended from the Muslim slave Salih Bilali, who was owned

The islanders Jack and Jean Hice and J. Roy Duggan show off a large catch of speckled trout and spottail bass landed near Little Cumberland Island back in the days before saltwater fishing was regulated. Jack Hice and Duggan were two of the founders of SeaPak Corporation, a pioneer in the frozen-seafood industry. (Courtesy of the J. Hice family album)

by the Coupers of Cannon's Point. Cusie Sullivan was one of the best fishing guides on the Georgia coast. He knew when and where the fish were biting, what bait to use, how deep to fish, and whether high or low ebb would yield a mess of speckled trout or spot-tail bass. Like many other islanders, he spoke rapid-fire Gullah Geechee creole, which is incomprehensible to most outsiders. One of the island's most avid anglers, a young white woman from Dublin, Georgia, who moved to St. Simons in the 1930s, made it a point to acquire enough of the Gullah Geechee language so that she could learn the finer points of saltwater fishing from the knowledgeable guide.

Taylor's Fish Camp off Lawrence Road on the north end of St. Simons was another favorite boat-launch site for longtime islanders. The Taylors are one of the old island families, related to Captain Charles Stevens of Denmark, who immigrated to the United States in 1836. Stevens became a "coasting captain," sailing up and down the Georgia coast while carrying produce to and from Savannah. Stevens purchased five hundred acres on the Frederica River, where he operated a plantation. The land included the ruins of Fort Frederica and most of the colonial town. Stevens was one of the few white people who stayed on the island during the Civil War. He joined the Confederate army in 1864 and was captured by Union forces. He was sent to a northern prison camp, where he died. One of his descendants, Isabelle "Belle" Stevens Taylor, was born in 1850 at Frederica and lived all her life in the family home place, which was built on top of the fort's tabby ruins. She and her siblings inherited the property at Frederica. In 1903, Belle Taylor donated her share to the Georgia Society of the Colonial Dames of America, whose members wanted to preserve the British colonial fort and town. The federal government acquired the property in 1945, condemning and purchasing adjacent land owned by other family members, several of whom still are still unhappy about the governmental takeover. Some Taylor family members relocated to the fish-camp property on the other side of the island.

The landing at Sullivan's Fish Camp at the end of South Harrington Road is still in use, although the fish camp run by Cusie Sullivan is long gone. Sullivan, a descendent of the Muslim slave Salih Bilali, was one of the area's most knowledgeable fishing guides. The fish camp was in one of three historic island communities settled by Gullah Geechee people after the Civil War.

Taylor's Fish Camp on the north end of St. Simons was another popular boat launch for island fishermen. Large parts of the movie *Conrack*, based on Pat Conroy's book *The Water Is Wide*, were filmed in a one-room schoolhouse built near Taylor's dock for the film about Gullah Geechee children on a remote South Carolina barrier island. Many Gullah Geechees from St. Simons were cast in the movie.

Not far from the fish-camp dock, the remains of a one-room wooden schoolhouse sit in a weedy field. The school was built as a set for the movie *Conrack* (1974), based on Pat Conroy's book *The Water Is Wide*. A number of scenes from *Conrack* were filmed at Taylor's, and many Gullah Geechee children from St. Simons played roles as Conroy's students in the movie. The Taylors later sold the property to the Sea Island Company.

A commercial strip mushroomed in the 1950s along Frederica Road near its intersection with Demere Road. The strip included a drive-in theatre, a string of nightclubs, and the Wayside Grill, which stayed open all night. The grill offered Chicago-style pizza, the island's first, and pinball machines that paid off in nickels to players with the highest scores. Islanders and visitors partied on the strip for decades. The Washboard Band, a wildly popular quartet of Gullah Geechee musicians, performed regularly at a nightclub on the strip called The Oasis. A number of Atlanta people drove the three hundred miles to St. Simons on summer weekends just to go to The Oasis and hear the Washboard Band, which took its name from one of the instruments. Nathan Jones wore thimbles on his fingers and strummed an old-fashioned tin washboard; he also played the kazoo. Robert Ivory was one of the guitarists; his son, Charles, played bass. Among the band's most celebrated offerings were "Old St. Simons," "Who Threw the

Whiskey in the Well," and "The Sheik of Araby," which featured the refrain, "With no pants on." The refrain, rendered in falsetto by the guitarist Smitty "Shorty" Feimster, always brought down the house. Whenever the Washboard Band played, The Oasis was mobbed. Although band members appeared on *The Garry Moore Show* and recorded several popular albums, Evelyn "Bootie" Gowen Wood, an island native, remembers when band members went door-to-door in wintertime to serenade island residents. The tips they received helped them survive until bookings picked up the following summer. The nightclubs have been replaced by upscale shops, office buildings, condominiums, and shopping centers, including one named for Paul Redfern, the pilot who took off from Sea Island beach and was lost on his solo flight to Rio de Janeiro.

The Washboard Band was one of the island's major musical attractions from the 1930s through the 1960s. The band often entertained at the train depot in Brunswick when Sea Island visitors were expected. They played on summer weekends at the Oasis, a nightclub on Frederica Road. The group released an album titled *Scrubbin' & Pickin'*, which featured some of their most popular songs. (Memorabilia collection courtesy of Freddie Pilgrim)

Alphonza's Old Plantation Supper Club in Harrington was a popular steak-and-seafood restaurant that featured an a cappella singing group called the Friendly Stars. Alphonza Ramsey, a Gullah Geechee whose family has lived on the island for centuries, closed the restaurant after being shot during a burglary. The interior remains just as it was when the restaurant closed years ago.

North of the strip, Frederica Road was flanked by dense forests that reclaimed the island's plantation fields after the Civil War. In the Gullah Geechee Harrington community, a small freshwater lake was called Obligation Pond. There are two explanations regarding the origin of the pond's name. One theory offered by the late historian Margaret Davis Cate is that the pond, which was used for baptisms, was where the newly baptized accepted their obligations to God. The other theory, offered by old islanders, is that the pond was a mandatory stop for people riding up and down the island on horseback or in wagons or other animal-drawn conveyances. They considered it an obligation to stop and allow their animals to drink at the mid-island watering hole. Both theories may be true. Obligation Pond was filled in by developers years ago. In predevelopment days, Frederica Road under the live oak canopy at night was a dark tunnel all the way to Christ Church. In 1954, Bennie Gentile built Bennie's Red Barn on Frederica Road in Harrington. At the restaurant, Gentile strung lights in the live oaks, and diners parked at random under the trees, as they still do. For years, the Barn was a beacon in the darkness along the island's main north-south route. The restaurant featured steaks, fresh seafood, and garlicky salads made in a huge and reputedly never-washed wooden bowl. Now owned by Gentile's son Don, Bennie's Red Barn is the island's oldest privately owned restaurant. For years the Barn, along with the King and Prince dining room and three now-defunct restaurants—two yacht clubs and the Deck, a seafood restaurant on the Torras Causeway—were special-occasion places for islanders. Alphonza Ramsey, a Harrington resident who had worked with Gentile, opened his highly successful Alphonza's Olde Plantation Supper Club nearby in Harrington. A popular a cappella group of Gullah Geechee singers called the Friendly Stars entertained diners as they feasted on oysters Alphonza, peppery collard greens, and other specialties of the house. Ramsey closed the restaurant after being shot during the last of several burglaries at the supper club. Frederica Road is now lined with subdivisions, shopping centers, and other development, and the dense woodlands that once flanked the road are gone.

Winters were quiet on St. Simons. Traffic thinned on narrow island roads, and mosquitoes and sand gnats disappeared along with the tourists and oppressive summer humidity. Winter was the best time to catch speckled trout in tidal creeks and to hunt marsh hens in the vast fields of spartina grass. Lucky islanders owned wooden boats handmade by the Brunswick craftsman Willie Harris, whose descendants continue the fine boatbuilding tradition.

Nobody on the island had television; video games and computers were still decades away. Brunswick's only daily newspaper, the *Brunswick News*, was an evening publication, so islanders tuned in to local radio stations every morning to hear the overnight news. The area's best-known and best-loved radio personality was the late John Lane, who reported at different times for Brunswick's two AM radio stations, WMOG (Marshes of Glynn) and WGIG (Golden Isles Georgia). Lane was a well-informed, intelligent man with an amazing memory for details of the stories he reported. He was most famous, however, for his malapropisms. Lane rose every morning long before daylight to check the crime blotters at the city and county police stations. He reported all major and minor crimes, referring, for example, to suspects with "reddish red hair" who eluded the police in "wooden" (wooded) areas. He once referred to the Horse Stamp Church of Camden County as the Horse Dump Church. When announcing the meeting of a local club, Lane said all "interesting" people were invited to attend. After a funeral, "intimate" would be in Greenwood Cemetery. At Christmas, he announced that lights on Jekyll Island would be "eliminated" over the weekend instead of illuminated. Area residents adored him; he was also respected in his profession. In 2012, Lane was inducted posthumously into the Georgia Radio Museum and Hall of Fame, which preserves the history of radio in Georgia and honors its outstanding men and women.

The late Willie Harris of Brunswick built fine wooden boats coveted by islanders and others who valued them for their craftsmanship. Many Harris-built boats are still on the water. His son carries on the boatbuilding tradition.

Oyster Roasts

OYSTER ROASTS ON St. Simons were ceremonial events as well as meals. Before the guests arrived, the host would build a roaring oak fire in a pit outside, adding driftwood to make the flames burn purple and green from the phosphorous soaked into the wood from seawater. While the fire was burning down, guests and hosts opened dozens of oysters and ate them raw. After the fire reached the proper point, the host and his helpers laid a heavy sheet of tin or a metal grate over the glowing coals. When the tin was smoking hot, somebody spread it with the first of many bushels of oysters. As soon as the mollusks began to pop, they were shoveled onto plank-and-sawhorse tables under the live oaks. Guests gathered around the crude tables, shucking and eating oysters as fast as they could pry the hot shells open to get at the succulent mollusks. Some people were squeamish about eating the small commensal crabs that often shared shell space with the oysters, but longtime islanders usually gobbled them down whole. People also found pearls inside the shells, but unlike pearls that come from shellfish in waters elsewhere, those of the southern coast are fragile and have no monetary value. At fund-raisers, volunteers always stood by the tables, opening oysters by the bushel for children and others who needed help. Wealthier islanders hired Gullah Geechees for the job. Islanders considered it good manners to bring their own oyster knives

Oysters have been a favorite seafood on St. Simons for thousands of years.

and heavy gloves to the roasts. Those who forgot the gloves could always grab a clump of Spanish moss to protect their hands from the hot, sharp shells. Hosts usually augmented the oysters with baked beans, coleslaw, homemade cocktail sauce, melted butter, lemon slices, and saltines, but purists rarely ate anything but oysters. After all the shellfish were eaten and the guests had gone home, hosts spread the empty shells on sandy island roads and driveways. For many years, driveways paved with anything but oyster shells were rare on the island. In gentler times, family oyster roasts did not include alcohol, but ice-cold beer is now considered an essential accompaniment.

One of the finest winter traditions on the island, and one that continues today, was the oyster roast. St. Simons residents did not hold low-country boils as they do now. Everyone knew South Carolina's coast was the low country, not Georgia's. Islanders hosted oyster roasts to entertain friends and family members, and island churches, Scout troops, civic organizations, and businesses regularly held oyster roasts as fund-raisers. City Market, then located on St. Simons near what was then called the pier section, sold oysters by the bushel, but enterprising islanders with access to a boat could also gather the tasty mollusks free off riverbanks at low tide. The tidewaters around St. Simons and Brunswick have long been closed to shellfish harvesting because of pollution from Brunswick industries and runoff from roads and parking lots. Oysters safe to eat were available from the waters of neighboring Camden and McIntosh Counties, neither of which were as developed as Glynn County. McIntosh, which consistently ranks as the poorest of Georgia's six coastal counties, had no large industry, but it did have clean waterways, especially around Blackbeard and Sapelo Islands, where an oyster cannery operated during the early twentieth century. Blue Point oysters from Sapelo were famous.

St. Simons is now popular year-round. Canadians spend winter months on the island, and retirees buy or rent upscale houses and beachfront condominiums. Among the new-comers are "half-backs," northerners who retired to South Florida, got tired of crowds, traffic, and high-rise condominiums, and moved halfway back home. St. Simons has become more and more expensive through the years, something for which many island-ers give credit or blame to the Sea Island Company, which built many high-end devel-opments on its larger neighbor, including the new gated subdivisions along Lawrence Road and the one called Hawkins Island, which is built on several hammocks (small marsh islands) west of St. Simons. Environmentalists now oppose hammock develop-ment because runoff from cars, parking lots, and fertilized lawns damages the marsh.

Egrets settle into their rookery on a small hammock in the Marshes of Glynn. Hammocks, or islands in the marsh, are one of the last refuges of coastal wildlife.

Hammocks are one of the last refuges of coastal wildlife. Egrets, ibis, and endangered wood storks often nest in hammock trees. When the birds settle into their rookeries at dusk, their white feathers glow like candles against the dark foliage.

As rapid—some say rabid—growth continued through the 1980s and 1990s, many longtime islanders and newcomers began begging for relief. People plastered their cars with bumper stickers saying, "Save St. Simons—Blow the Bridges." The northern third of St. Simons remained largely undeveloped until the early twenty-first century because most of the land was owned by the Sea Island Company, traditionally a slow and careful developer. Under the stewardship of the Jones family, Sea Island helped control the pace, density, and quality of growth on St. Simons. A company-owned north-end tract called Pike's Bluff was zoned for 6,000 houses. At Sea Island's request, the property was down-zoned to accommodate just 350. Before the recession hit in 2010, estate-sized lots in Pike's Bluff were selling for as much as $2 million. The lower density helped keep already-congested Frederica Road from being overwhelmed by traffic, at least for the short term. Nowadays, other developers are targeting tracts on the north end.

Through the years, the Sea Island Company made many contributions to St. Simons in land, money, and such services as landscaping to beautify the causeways, the traffic circle at Frederica and Demere Roads, and the entrance to St. Simons at Gascoigne Bluff. Even more important were the people the company brought to St. Simons through the years. Sea Island hired hundreds of top-flight professionals from all over the world as chefs, landscape designers, accountants, and instructors who taught golf, tennis, swimming, diving, sailing, riding, and ballroom dancing. Most of them made their homes on St. Simons, joining civic organizations and churches, sending their children to island schools, and adding their diverse cultures, talents, and accents to the community.

Sea Island's assets were purchased by investors after the company declared bankruptcy in 2010. Members of the St. Simons Land

The new Cloister Hotel on Sea Island, which opened in 2006, replaced the smaller hotel built by resort founders eighty years earlier.

Trust and others quickly began lobbying to protect one of the assets from development: historic Cannon's Point. The point embraces more than six hundred acres of maritime forest, prehistoric archaeological treasures such as shell rings, and the ruins of John Couper's antebellum plantation, as well as the old Taylor's Fish Camp tract. Wells Fargo, which owned the point, agreed to hold it in reserve while the St. Simons Land Trust raised $25 million to pay for it. The sale was completed in October 2012. Henry Paulson, a former CEO of Goldman Sachs and former U.S. treasury secretary, and his wife, Wendy, were major contributors to the project, as were Pete and Ada Lee Correll. Pete Correll is a Brunswick native who served for years as chairman and CEO of Georgia Pacific. The Paulsons, who have helped preserve natural lands all over the world, are now the majority owners of Little St. Simons Island, which lies just across the Hampton River from Cannon's Point. Ben Slade, the land trust's president, said the point will be opened to the public for education and low-impact recreation, with bike trails, hiking paths, and interpretive signs.

The tip of Hampton Point, opposite Cannon's Point on the north end, was developed as a subdivision in the 1980s, with houses, condominiums, a public marina, and a golf course. There are antebellum tabby ruins on Hampton Point visible from the development's main road. Until recently, Hampton Point was the only subdivision on the north end. Now, gated subdivisions where houses are marketed for millions of dollars line Lawrence Road. Development along the once-deserted road where many island teens learned to drive includes churches, a new park with a soccer field, sidewalks, and a fire station.

As property values on St. Simons soared, real estate taxes climbed. Many lifelong islanders relocated to the mainland because they could no longer afford island life, including Gullah Geechees whose ancestors were brought to St. Simons as slaves in the 1700s. In the late twentieth century, the island's three Gullah Geechee neighborhoods were invaded; real estate agents and developers went door-to-door in Harrington, Jewtown, and South End/Harlem, asking people to sell their property. Many people were so offended and tired of being harassed that they posted bright yellow signs in front of their houses: "Don't Ask, Won't Sell."

The Jewtown community on Demere Road between the causeway and Frederica Road has been especially hard-hit by growth. One of the first large intrusions into the neighborhood was a mixed-use development called Plantation Village. Jewtown residents and many other islanders, including a sitting federal judge, spoke against the project at a Glynn County Commission meeting in 1984, pointing out, among other things, that the development was not compatible with the carefully crafted St. Simons Master Plan. Commissioners approved the project anyway. Plantation Village opened the floodgates to a deluge of development along the once-quiet stretch of road. Jewtown residents are now hemmed in by condominiums, apartments, fast-food restaurants, shopping centers, a car wash, and other commercial enterprises. In part because of so many of the spot zonings on St. Simons were made by a county government dominated by mainlanders, island residents have lobbied in recent years to incorporate St. Simons in order to gain more control over future development.

Growth has brought many good things to the island: better-paying jobs, new schools, playgrounds, parks, and entertainments such as evening concerts in summer on the lighthouse grounds. Islanders no longer have to cross the causeway for emergency medical care; there is an emergency clinic near Gascoigne Bluff, and a number of doctors have houses and offices on St. Simons. It is inevitable that battles over development,

Historic Cannon's Point will be open to the public for historic and nature tours.

Ruins of the Couper Plantation
at Cannon's Point

incorporation, seawalls, and renourishment will continue on St. Simons, the largest of
Georgia's developed sea islands and the only one that still has significant vacant land.
St. Simons, Sea Island, and Jekyll, three of the four sea islands linked to the mainland
with causeways, are in Glynn County. Tiny and heavily developed Tybee Island, east of
Savannah, is the fourth. State-owned Jekyll limits building on the island. Sea Island,
only five miles long, is nearing development capacity. Prices for houses in Sea Island's
cottage colony and in the newer Ocean Forest development are out of reach of all but
the very wealthy. The northern tip of Sea Island, which fronts on the Hampton River,
was developed in recent years as the beyond-exclusive Ocean Forest Golf Club, a gated
community within gated Sea Island. Ocean Forest, where cottages routinely sell in the
multimillion-dollar range, is off-limits even to Sea Island residents and visitors.

In years past, Sea Island and St. Simons enjoyed a more intimate relationship. People
from St. Simons participated in many Sea Island activities, including Easter egg hunts
on the Cloister grounds, the lighting of the Christmas yule log in the hotel's lovely
Spanish Lounge, Wednesday-night bingo, alfresco buffet lunches at the Beach Club,

and dress-up dinners in the Cloister's elegant dining room. Some still do, if they hold a Sea Island membership. But as the population of St. Simons increased and the cottage colony and resort facilities expanded on Sea Island, the smaller island became less and less welcoming to outsiders. At one time, the county owned property on Sea Island. In the 1950s, county commissioners traded four county-owned parks on Sea Island for part of the Massengale tract on St. Simons, where beachfront Massengale Park is now located. When Sea Island hosted President George W. Bush and other world leaders in 2004 at the annual G8 summit, it limited access to the island. Not long afterward, the company repurchased roads on Sea Island that had been dedicated to the county long ago so that they could be paved at government expense. With the roads back in private ownership, Sea Island closed the causeway to outsiders entirely, ending the easy relationship between the neighboring islands that began almost a century ago.

Root, Mouth, and Mojo

AFRICAN SLAVES brought their own religious beliefs and practices to the south-eastern coast centuries ago. In times past, a Gullah Geechee root doctor, often called Dr. Buzzard in coastal Georgia, used root (blue root was the worst), bad mouth, and mojo to cast spells to aid his customers and often to punish the customers' enemies. Dr. Buzzards also used herbs, other plants, and folk remedies to cure illnesses, treat wounds, set broken bones, ease the pain of childbirth, and relieve other medical problems in the days when rural people, black and white, had limited access to doctors and good medical care, especially in the Deep South.

The once high-profile root doctors have disappeared, but mojo, mouth, and root are still alive and well on the Internet. Hundreds of websites offer such items as High John the Conqueror Root candles, for attracting love, power, and prosperity; Goofer Dust, made of graveyard dirt, rattlesnake skins, ground-up spiders, and sulfur, for jinxing enemies; and Court Case Powder, a mixture of deer tongue leaves and calendula flowers, to sprinkle on court documents or around the courtroom for favorable verdicts. Mojo bags and bundles contain bones, fingernails, hair, dried frogs, plant material, and feathers dyed green for money, red for love, orange for change, and blue to soothe the spirit. Website practitioners offer to interpret dreams, everyday events, and unusual occurrences. Some offer conjure vigils in which the practitioner lights special candles and prays over them to achieve a customer's desired outcome.

Sometimes coastal mojo takes an unexpected turn. In 1984, a seventy-three-foot-long shrimp boat owned by the veteran shrimper Lawrence Jacobs of McIntosh County was fixed with bad mojo. While cleaning the deck freezer on his boat one day, Jacobs pulled out a strange bundle tucked into the bottom of a plastic soda bottle. The bundle contained the skull of a small animal, perhaps a cat, arranged on top of bones, dried vegetable material, and dirt that Jacobs later learned probably came from a grave-yard—perhaps the grave of a convicted murderer.

A native of coastal Georgia, Jacobs had heard all his life about mojo, mouth, and root. He knew many people who still believed it worked. But Jacobs, a Christian with his own beliefs, decided another shrimper had planted the bundle in his freezer as a joke. He tossed the thing overboard. Soon afterward, his boat, the *Tornado II*, was plagued with a rash of problems: the engine broke down, the boat ran aground, the

An Episcopal priest from Darien performed an exorcism on a shrimp boat after the owner found a mojo bundle on board.

nets got hung on underwater snags. The mishaps continued through the fall shrimping season until a Gullah Geechee woman told Jacobs's wife, Gay, that someone had fixed the *Tornado II* with bad mojo. Jacobs remembered the strange bundle he had found in the boat's freezer.

The Jacobses, who are white, discussed the matter with each other and then with their white Episcopal priest in Darien. The priest obtained permission from his bishop to perform a rite of exorcism on the shrimp boat. The ancient religious rite, with its overtones of magic, is designed to cast out demons.

The couple and the priest later talked to a reporter about the ceremony, which was attended by the Jacobses and their three grown children. According to the Jacobses, the sky above the dock turned dark and menacing. The wind rose and kicked up whitecaps on the tidal river as the priest sprinkled holy water and oil blessed by the bishop over the *Tornado II*. The priest read aloud from a small book, but Jacobs said the howl of the wind snatched the exorcist's words away. After the ceremony ended, the priest gave Jacobs a bottle of holy water to keep onboard the boat. As extra insurance, Jacobs installed a cross in the wheelhouse. Afterward, Jacobs said, his shrimp boat's problems abruptly ceased.

CHAPTER VIII   A Time for Island Tales

[Long Ago–Now]

STORIES ARE THE SOUL of St. Simons. Old islanders still tell stories about slaves who could fly. Others talk about the work of root doctors who could cure people or harm them with folk medicine and mojo. Some of the most popular stories feature the doings of island ghosts—restless spirits whose footsteps echo in the lighthouse tower or prowl the few remaining lonely island roads, cemeteries, and moonlit marshes. Stories brought over on slave ships recount the humanlike antics of animals—trickster rabbits, clever spiders, persistent tortoises—and are designed to teach moral lessons as well as entertain. One famous story rooted in the history of St. Simons is the true but tragic tale of the wealthy New Yorker who rebuilt Christ Church after the Civil War. His story was made famous by a northern novelist who fell in love with St. Simons and adopted the island as her home.

As development continues, the old tales are no longer as popular as they once were. But like the natural beauty of the island itself, the stories endure, reminding natives and newcomers that St. Simons is a unique but fragile treasure that deserves and requires protection, now and in the future.

Stories involving mojo in modern times still circulate on the Georgia coast, even on developed St. Simons, although islanders rarely discuss those beliefs and practices with outsiders or even with people they know well and respect. Ministers preach against mojo, calling it the work of the devil, much as the Franciscan friars at the seventeenth-century Spanish missions preached against the beliefs and customs of coastal Indians, convinced they were devil inspired.

The Gullah Geechee people brought stories from Africa and passed them down to children, black and white, through the years. One of the main characters was Brother Rabbit, or Br'er Rabbit, a conniving trickster whose ego often got him into trouble. He was always saved by his own cleverness. Overconfidence caused Br'er Rabbit to lose a race to a slow-moving but persistent tortoise because the hare stopped to take a nap while the plodding tortoise lumbered across the finish line. In another well-known story, Br'er Fox tried to capture Br'er Rabbit one day by sculpting the figure of a baby out of tar. When Br'er Rabbit encountered the Tar-Baby, it offended him by refusing to speak. He hit the effigy with all four paws and got stuck in the tar, just as Br'er Fox had planned. But when Br'er Fox came to eat Br'er Rabbit, the rabbit saved himself by begging the fox not to throw him in the briar patch, his favorite habitat. Sometimes a spider, or Nancy (*anansi* in the Ashanti language of West Africa, and Nancy in Gullah Geechee) played the role of the intelligent trickster in the stories. A number of writers, including Joel Chandler Harris, a reporter at the *Atlanta Journal and Constitution*, collected and published the stories in the 1880s, calling his elderly black narrator Uncle Remus. The well-known author Zora Neale Hurston collected Gullah Geechee folktales on St. Simons in the 1930s, too.

One St. Simons story features a famous root doctor who moved to the island a few years after the Civil War. Mazinga, as he was known in his home country, was about seventeen when he, his pregnant mother, and other family members were captured and brought to Jekyll Island in 1858 on the notorious slave ship *Wanderer*, one of the last, perhaps the very last, illegal slave ships to land in the United States. Although slavery was legal at the time, the federal and state governments had long since banned the importation of slaves directly from Africa. The law was routinely broken. The *Wanderer*'s owner, the outspoken secessionist Charles Augustus Lafayette Lamar, the scion of a prominent Savannah family, conspired with members of the wealthy DuBignon family, who then owned Jekyll Island, to land the slave ship's human cargo on Jekyll. Mazinga's mother gave birth to a daughter in squalid conditions in the hold of the crowded ship; the baby miraculously survived. She was later named Clementine DuBignon, indicating she had

The notorious slave ship *Wanderer* landed on Jekyll Island to unload its human cargo in 1858. Tom Floyd, one of the captives, later built a home on St. Simons and practiced as a root doctor.

been sold to the DuBignons or possibly given to them in payment for their part in the *Wanderer* scheme. To prevent federal authorities from finding and confiscating the captives, the conspirators quickly moved most of the slaves out of Glynn County and sold them up and down the coast. A group of captives were sold in the Edgefield district of South Carolina, where they were employed before and after the Civil War in area potteries that produced the first alkaline-glazed stoneware in North America. Edgefield pottery, some of which shows artistic influences from the *Wanderer*, commands high prices today. Mazinga was sold away from his family to Captain Henry Floyd of Camden County, Glynn County's neighbor to the south. Floyd renamed the teenager Tom and taught him carpentry. After the war, Tom took the surname of his former owner and built a house in the South End community on St. Simons, where he practiced root doctoring, as his ancestors had for centuries in Africa. Floyd probably retained vivid memories of his home country when President Lincoln signed the Emancipation Proclamation five years after the *Wanderer*'s landing on Jekyll.

The following accounts were published, in different centuries, about Tom Floyd and a direct descendant who was born on St. Simons in the 1930s. The first, Floyd's obituary from 1883, illustrates white attitudes common during Reconstruction regarding root doctoring in particular and the Gullah Geechee people in general. The second, published almost a century later, celebrates the career of Floyd's great-grandson, the famed Cleveland Browns running back Jim Brown.

Brunswick Advertiser and Appeal
Saturday, 22 December 1883
   St. Simons Department—Tom Floyd, a noted African, died very suddenly in a convulsion last week. Tom was one of the cargo of Africans on the schooner Wanderer, about which such an excitement was produced in Brunswick waters, and the trial and the acquittal of her captain before the United States Circuit Court at Savannah. Tom was also famous among his deluded class as a "medicine man" and manipulator in voodooism and other humbuggery.

Pro Football Hall of Fame
Jim Brown
Class of 1971
Fullback —— 6–2, 232
(Syracuse)
1957–1985 Cleveland Browns

James Nathanial Brown . . . Syracuse All-American, 1956 . . . Browns' No. 1 draft pick, 1957 . . . Awesome runner, led NFL rushers eight years . . . All-NFL eight of nine years . . . NFL's Most Valuable Player, 1957, 1958, 1965 . . . Rookie of the year, 1957. . . Played in nine straight Pro Bowls . . . Career marks: 12,312 yards rushing, 262 receptions, 15,459 combined net yards, 756 points scored . . . Born February 17, 1936, in St. Simons, Georgia.

Tom Floyd's great-great-granddaughter Karen Brown Ward, the daughter of Jim Brown, now occupies the house her *Wanderer* ancestor built on St. Simons well over a century ago. The house, many times remodeled and expanded, is one of the oldest on island and one of the few of similar vintage still occupied by members of the original owner's family. Ward said her father was nine years old when he moved with his mother from St. Simons to New York but still had vivid memories of his childhood on the island. Jim Brown did not remember interacting with white islanders; in fact he said there were none on St. Simons when he was growing up. Considering the Jim Crow laws and racial prejudices of the time, Brown's mother and other relatives probably kept the youngster in the relative safety of the all-black South End community. He still visits the island from time to time, but Ward said she usually travels to California to see her famous father, who became a successful film actor after his football career ended.

Karen Brown Ward, the great-great-granddaughter of Tom Floyd, still occupies the home her ancestor built more than a century ago. Her father is Jim Brown, the famed NFL running back.

Decades after Tom Floyd died, his cousin Floyd White praised his prowess as a root doctor. At the time, White lived in a tabby slave cabin on the part of Retreat Plantation called Newfield, most of which is now occupied by McKinnon Airport. White's former residence is now the Tabby House, a gift shop at Retreat and Frederica roads.

White was interviewed in the 1930s by writers with the Works Progress Administration, one of many federal agencies created by President Franklin D. Roosevelt to help lift the country out of the Great Depression. Besides conducting cultural studies, WPA workers built post offices, parks, roads, bridges, and many other public buildings. Members of the Savannah Unit of the Georgia Writers' Project interviewed Gullah Geechees in coastal Georgia, including several on St. Simons, before writing their landmark book *Drums and Shadows: Survival Stories among the Georgia Coastal Negroes*. In the book, White described one of Tom Floyd's medical treatments.

"He could cut you with a knife and cop you," White said, referring to a procedure practiced for thousands of years by medical doctors. Called bleeding and cupping, it involves placing a heated cup on the patient to create a vacuum that raises the skin inside the cup. The cup is removed, and shallow cuts are made on the raised skin. The cup is reheated and replaced; the resulting vacuum draws out blood. Bleeding and cupping is still practiced around the world in developed and developing countries, often as a remedy for pain.

Many coastal Georgia residents, black and white, now identify themselves as Christian or Muslim, but many older people also believe, at least a little bit, in the power of mojo. They tell stories about magical events that they say they or others have witnessed. Gullah Geechees like Floyd White often recounted stories of slaves and root doctors who could fly, including a group of rice slaves on Butler's Island who rose en masse while performing a circle dance called a shout. According to the story, the slaves flew back to Africa to escape further whippings on Major Pierce Butler's rice plantation. White said he knew a root doctor on Butler's Island named Alexander. According to White, some of Alexander's friends who were traveling by boat to Savannah invited him to come along. Alexander said he would meet them at the dock instead, "and he was there to catch the line," White reported.

St. Simons offers the perfect setting for spooky stories. Ghost stories rooted in the island's history are still told at night around driftwood fires on the beach or on shadowy porches lit only by the green-gold winks of lightning bugs signaling their Morse code messages for mates. The air is scented with the perfume of gardenias, honeysuckle, and Confederate jasmine and the pervasive salty smells of the tidewater environment.

When cool night air settles on sun-warmed tidewaters and marshes, heavy fog drapes the island, making it the ideal venue for ghost stories.

When cool night air settles on sun-warmed marshes and the ocean, as it often does, St. Simons is shrouded in heavy fog. Wisps of fog tangle in the twisted limbs of live oaks and mimic the gray scarves of Spanish moss draped limply over tree limbs, fences, and utility lines. In the distance, a bell buoy tolls its mournful warning to boaters in the sound. Even the powerful beam of the lighthouse vanishes in heavy fog, leaving an eerie glow that dances through the treetops as the beam sweeps over the island.

The Ghosts of Ebo Landing

ON THE WEST SIDE of St. Simons, Dunbar Creek meanders through the marsh to a bluff called Ebo Landing, where a group of newly imported slaves from the Ebo tribe of Africa died. Some say the slaves had been gathered on the creek bank in chains when their leader, rather than submit to slavery, led them into the deep tidal creek, where they all drowned. Another, no less tragic version of the story was offered by the late historian Malcolm Bell Jr. of Savannah, who wrote about five generations of Major Pierce Butler's family. Major Butler, a wealthy planter, owned Hampton Point on north St. Simons and diked islands on the Altamaha Delta, where he grew rice. Bell found documents indicating that a cargo of Ebo slaves newly imported from Africa in 1803 were brought to Savannah and sold, some of them to the St. Simons planters John Couper and Thomas Spalding. As the boat bringing them to the island entered Dunbar Creek, the slaves "rose" against the boat captain and the two other crew members. The three jumped overboard and drowned, according to a letter written to Couper by William Mein, the Savannah slave trader who sold the Africans. Mein said the Ebos took to the marsh, and "ten or twelve" drowned. Survivors were "salvaged" at a cost of $10 a head, he noted.

Whether the slaves died by suicide or drowned by accident after trying to escape, both accounts illustrate the determination of the Ebo people to be free. On St. Simons, the name is rendered as *Ebo* and pronounced with a long *e*, but the proper name of the

In the early 1800s, a group of Ebo slaves were brought to a landing on Dunbar Creek, where a number of them drowned. The historic site, called Ebo Landing, is now on private property.

Africans is Igbo; the *g* is silent. Before colonization and the slave trade, the Igbo did not have a cohesive identity, but they are now concentrated in southeastern Nigeria. Planters in the antebellum South considered Ebo people rebellious and prone to suicide, traits that lent credence to the legend of Ebo Landing. Well before Glynn County located its sewage-treatment plant on Dunbar Creek near the historic site, many longtime islanders did not fish at the landing, either out of respect for the drowned Ebos or because the creek is haunted by their ghosts, who, some say, can be heard clanking their chains at night. Though the landing is now on private property, it can be seen from the Dunbar Creek bridge on New Sea Island Road.

The Lighthouse Ghost

THE LATE Annie Svendsen, a longtime island resident, was well acquainted with the ghost of the St. Simons lighthouse. She was the wife of Carl Olaf Svendsen, who tended the light from 1907 until his death in 1935, just a few years after the kerosene lamps that served as the beacon were replaced by a 1,000-watt electric lightbulb. The beam from the electric light today, magnified by antique French Fresnel lenses, is visible twenty-five miles out to sea on clear nights. The beam sweeps once every minute over the island's tree canopy.

The Svendsens occupied the redbrick light keeper's house adjacent to the tower; the house, built in the late 1800s, is thought to be the oldest brick building in Glynn County. Before the lighthouse was electrified, the keeper climbed the spiral staircase many times every night to refill the kerosene lamps, trim the wicks, and polish the sooty glass chimneys. Every seventy-five minutes, the keeper rewound the clockwork weights that kept the light turning. Many nights at suppertime, Mrs. Svendsen heard steps descending the staircase. She put food on the table, but by the time her husband arrived much later, supper would be cold. The Svendsen children and the family dog, Jinx, also heard the ghostly footsteps. When Jinx heard the steps, he barked but turned his head away from the sound.

The Svendsens' son, Carl Jr., was so annoyed by the footsteps that he threw his shoes up the tower stairs one night, yelling for the ghost to go away and let him sleep. The Svendsen family always considered the ghost a friendly spirit and never feared it. Mrs. Svendsen, however, was terrified of the water moccasins and rattlesnakes that sometimes took up residence in the tower.

Carl Svendsen served for years as keeper of the new St. Simons lighthouse, rebuilt after the original was destroyed by retreating Confederate troops during the Civil War. His family often reported hearing ghostly footsteps in the tower. (Courtesy of the Coastal Georgia Historical Society)

The new St. Simons lighthouse, rebuilt a decade after the first tower was destroyed during the Civil War. The architect and several workers died of malaria before the tower was completed.

The lighthouse ghost is said to be that of a former keeper killed more than a century ago. Frederick Osborne was shot to death on a Sunday morning in March 1880 by John W. Stevens, the assistant keeper, after the two men argued. The argument, which continued over several days, may have involved rogue chickens kept by Mrs. Stevens that raided Osborne's garden. Stevens "threatened to chastise" Osborne for his comments to Mrs. Stevens. When Osborne threatened Stevens with a pistol, Stevens returned to his upstairs quarters, got his double-barreled shotgun, went back outside, and shot Osborne.

Stevens fetched a doctor, then rowed to the mainland to turn himself in. Released without posting bond, he rowed back to St. Simons and resumed his duties as keeper, working around the clock until another assistant was hired. Stevens was never prosecuted for the shooting. No one else was available to tend the light, which may account for the leniency of the authorities. He continued as lighthouse keeper for three years, then built a house on the island and farmed. He served on the Glynn County Commission and as a vestryman at Christ Church.

Some say Osborne's ghost inspects the beacon every night. Many people have reported seeing his ghost in the tower and on the surrounding property. Several keepers and their families claim to have heard Osborne's ghostly footsteps on the tower stairs.

The Bloody Walls of Pink Chapel

A SMALL TABBY CHAPEL near Fort Frederica was known for more than a century as Pink Chapel because its tabby walls were colonized by a rosy lichen, *Chiodecton sanguineum*. Built after a young planter named John Armstrong Wylly was shot to death by his neighbor, the chapel was said to be haunted by Wylly's ghost. The neighbor was Dr. Thomas Fuller Hazzard. The doctor and his brother owned adjacent plantations: West Point and Pikes Bluff. The brothers enjoyed hunting with their pack of dogs and entering their boats, *Comet* and *Shark*, in racing competitions, with plantation slaves manning the oars.

In 1838, Dr. Hazzard and his young neighbor, John Wylly, argued over the boundary between their properties. The dispute escalated. A dueling challenge was issued and accepted. Articles of battle specified that the opponents were to use firearms and wear white paper targets over their hearts. The winner was to have the privilege of cutting off his dead opponent's head and placing it on a pole on the disputed boundary.

The would-be duelers met by chance on the porch of the Oglethorpe Hotel in Brunswick on December 3. Wylly hit Hazzard with his cane, but onlookers broke up the fight. The same day, Wylly and Hazzard met again in the hotel's doorway, and Wylly spat in Hazzard's face. Hazzard drew his pistol and shot Wylly through the heart, killing him. Hazzard, who was justice of the peace at the time, was tried for manslaughter and acquitted.

Wylly was well connected on St. Simons. His youngest sister, Caroline, married James Hamilton Couper, the son of John Couper of Cannon's Point. The Coupers, father and son, were prominent regional planters and horticulturists. People sympathetic to the Wyllys cold-shouldered Hazzard and his family at Christ Church, the center of island social and religious life, so the doctor built the small chapel on the grounds of West Point to avoid censure from the other planters. Later, Dr. Hazzard was restored to the good graces of the congregation; a former Christ Church rector said the doctor donated money toward the purchase of a new church organ.

Over the years, the Pink Chapel's roof collapsed and its walls weathered. Islanders said patches of the lichen, whose species name derives from the Latin word *sanguineus*, meaning "blood" or "bloody," were put on the chapel's walls by Wylly's ghost to remind people of his murder. John Armstrong Wylly was just thirty-two when he died. He is buried in Christ Church Cemetery. His grave is marked by a broken white obelisk to represent his broken life. Hazzard family members are buried at Christ Church, too.

A St. Simons artist who owned the chapel property had a replica built on the site after the old tabby chapel deteriorated. The replica has not been colonized by the lichen, although longtime islanders still call the structure Pink Chapel. It is now on private property and is not open to visitors.

The Ghost of Mary the Wanderer

MARY DIED IN 1824, but her ghost still wanders the island's south end with a flickering lantern held high. Mary, the ward of an island planter, fell in love with the planter's son, and the two planned to marry. The young man left for the mainland one morning in a small boat, promising Mary he would return before nightfall. That same day, the hurricane of 1824 struck St. Simons. During a lull in the storm, Mary took a lantern and went to search for her sweetheart. When she saw his rowboat overturned in the raging surf, she ran into the water and drowned. Ever since, she has roamed the island's south end, dressed in white, carrying her lantern and searching for her lost love.

Many old islanders have seen the ghost, including a longtime third-grade teacher at St. Simons Elementary School. The teacher, the late Caroline Butler, lived in the King City subdivision on the south end. A small patch of marsh, since filled in, was a few blocks down the road. Butler was outside one night with her dog Boots. She felt cold air embrace her and looked toward the marsh, where she saw a gossamer figure dressed in white and holding a lantern aloft. Butler ran inside, but Boots fled the neighborhood and refused ever to return, the teacher said.

Similar stories have been told for decades by islanders who have seen the ghost, often called Mary de Wanda or Mary Wan by Gullah Geechees in earlier days. A road in Jewtown was named Mary Wan Road because it marked the route the ghost traveled. Most of the road was destroyed when the Island Club Golf Course was built, but a short unpaved section existed until the late twentieth century, when it too was lost to rampant island growth. It was the only known road in Georgia named for a ghost.

One famous island ghost, Mary the Wanderer, is said to have thrown herself into a raging surf after her lover drowned in a boating accident. Also called Mary de Wanda or simply Mary Wan, she is said to walk the south end of the island with a lantern held high. A Jewtown road named in her honor has been lost to development in the historic neighborhood.

The Ghost of Christ Church Cemetery

THE YOUNG WIFE of an island planter was afraid of the dark and always slept with a candle by her bed. She made hundreds of candles from beeswax or from the berries of the wax myrtle trees that grow wild on the island. When she died, she was buried in Christ Church Cemetery. The grieving widower, unhappy that his wife would sleep through eternity in the dark, placed a lighted candle on her grave every night, continuing the custom for the rest of his life. Before the brick wall was built in front of the church and cemetery, people who drove past at night saw a ghostly light in the graveyard. Some said it was only car headlights mirrored by a white marble tombstone. Others claimed the dead planter's ghost was still placing candles on his wife's grave. In years past, teenagers crept into the cemetery at night, looking for the candlelit grave and shrieking in terror when wisps of Spanish moss or spider webs brushed their faces, or when their erstwhile friends drove off and left them alone in the dark.

The Crypt in the Marsh

THOMAS CATER, the planter who owned Kelvin Grove, was murdered by his wife and the plantation overseer. Cater had moved to the island with his wife and son in about 1798. Tragedy struck after Thomas's wife, Elizabeth, fell in love with Kelvin Grove's overseer. The plantation's head driver, Denbow, heard the three arguing. Fearing for the safety of the Caters' young son, Denbow carried the boy to the neighboring plantation, which was owned by William Page. After the murder, Elizabeth and the overseer fled the island. The two were never caught and brought to justice.

Benjamin Franklin Cater, the son, was reared by the Page family. He graduated from Yale, returned to St. Simons, married an islander, and for years ran his father's plantation, one of the largest on the island. Part of Kelvin Grove is now a subdivision of the same name adjacent to the Bloody Marsh Monument. Thomas Cater, the murdered planter, was buried on the plantation, close to a giant magnolia tree bordering the marsh. Some say he was buried standing up so he could avenge himself if his murderers ever returned; others claim he was laid to rest in a crypt in the marsh with a knife in his lifeless hand.

Graves in picturesque Christ Church Cemetery date back to the 1700s.

On summer nights, in the deepening shadows of live oak trees, islanders tell the story of a murdered man buried in a crypt somewhere in the marsh. The victim's name is not given as Thomas Cater, but some details of the story are similar. The storytellers claim that a group of teenagers once dared each other to wade through the marsh to the crypt where the planter was allegedly buried, then take the knife and stab the corpse in the heart. According to the story, one teen accepted the challenge and walked into the marsh, watched by his friends until the moon slipped behind a cloud. The waiting friends heard the screech of metal and knew the crypt's rusty gate was being opened. Moments later, they heard a horrible scream. The friends ran away and called police. The legend holds that authorities found the teen's body with a knife through his heart, but the crypt's original occupant was gone.

On nights when clouds shadow the moon, a lone figure is said to prowl the marshes near Bloody Marsh Monument. It is either the ghost of the murdered planter or the teenager's ghost, seeking revenge on the friends who abandoned him. If there ever was a crypt, it was long ago buried in marsh mud and lost.

One of the most famous true stories about St. Simons was told by the best-selling author Eugenia Price in her first novel, *The Beloved Invader*, published in 1965. The book and Price's subsequent historical fiction connected with readers all over the world and brought hoards of new people to the island. On a book-signing tour of Florida in 1961, Price, a native of West Virginia, and her longtime companion, Joyce Blackburn of Indiana, took a side trip to St. Simons, which neither had ever visited. After exploring Christ Church Cemetery, they heard the tragic but romantic story of Anson Green Phelps Dodge Jr., the young northerner who rebuilt the church after the Civil War. Price, already a successful writer of Christian nonfiction, had been looking for a story to spark her first novel. She and Blackburn rented an island house and spent several years doing research and listening to family stories told by descendants of Gullah Geechee slaves, planters, coasting captains, and other longtime islanders.

Price's novel recounts the true story of Dodge Jr. He was the son of the man who served as superintendent of the St. Simons sawmills owned by his wealthy family. Dodge Jr. came south to visit his estranged father at Christmas in 1879. The nineteen-year-old hoped to form a relationship with the man who had abandoned him and his mother in New York when he was six years old. And he wanted his father to know that he planned to marry his wealthy first cousin, Ellen Phelps Dodge, a marriage that other family members opposed for religious reasons. Perhaps young Dodge hoped to get his father's blessing.

His second day on St. Simons, he borrowed a horse and rode to Christ Church, captivated by the island's giant live oaks and the play of sunlight through the trees. The church was locked and the windows boarded over, but the battered exterior of the small frame structure touched his heart. He later learned that the interior had been ruined by black Union troops bivouacked at the church during the war. The windows had been shot out, part of the belfry blown away by cannon fire, and some of the pews carved with soldiers' names or chopped up for firewood. Pews had been overturned to serve as bunks, and the sanctuary floor was charred from fires built inside. The final insult was the condition of the pulpit, which had been used for butchering cattle.

When Dodge saw the church, it was probably in even worse condition than it had been thirteen years earlier when Fan Butler attended the funeral of the island planter James Hamilton Couper. Fan came to St. Simons the year after the war ended with her father, Pierce Mease Butler, to help him revive the family plantations. She recorded the appearance of the church when she saw it in 1866: "Here a most terrible scene of desolation met us. The steps of the church were broken down, so we had to walk up a plank to get in; the roof was fallen in, so that the sun streamed down on our heads; while the seats were all cut up and marked with the names of Northern soldiers, who had been quartered there during the war. The graveyard was so overgrown with weeds and bushes, and tangled with cobweb like grey moss, that we had difficulty in making our way through to the freshly dug grave."

Since the roof had fallen in, some of the damage Dodge observed was likely due to exposure. The island's humid, salty air has always been unkind to manmade structures. The church cemetery was still overgrown when Dodge saw it, and most of the graves remained untended. The few congregants left on St. Simons had no money to rebuild the church and no slaves to groom the grounds. The church's endowment, deposited in a Savannah bank, was lost when the bank failed during the war. Congregants were meeting for Sunday-evening prayers at the Gould house at Black Banks Plantation.

Young Dodge vowed to rebuild the church, become its minister, and build a house for himself and Ellen at Frederica. Just as the sawmills saved the island's economy after the Civil War, St. Simons and the church project saved Anson Dodge Jr. When he returned to Rose Cottage, his father was packing to leave the island and his only son for good. Although Dodge Sr. always supported his wife and son, he claimed he was not cut out to be a family man.

Dodge Jr. consoled himself with plans for the future and the company of close friends he soon made, including Horace Bunch Gould, whose father built the island's first lighthouse. Dodge's mother, Rebecca, and his fiancée, Ellen, both came to the island for Christmas and were delighted by St. Simons and by Dodge's plan to rebuild Christ Church. Back in New York, he enrolled in the General Theological Seminary; six months before graduation, he eloped with Ellen.

The couple left for a three-year around-the-world honeymoon. Dodge planned to complete his religious studies after they returned, then move to St. Simons with his bride. He hired an architect to draw up plans for the sixteen-room modified Queen Anne house at Frederica where he and Ellen would live. Dodge refused to have an artesian well or indoor plumbing installed because he wanted to live as his poorer congregants did.

In India on their honeymoon, Ellen contracted cholera from contaminated fruit and died. Dodge had her body embalmed and shipped to St. Simons in a lead-lined vault.

The Dodge burial plot at Christ Church Cemetery

St. Ignatius Episcopal Church on Demere Road in the Jewtown community was one of the mission churches for Gullah Geechees built on St. Simons by Anson Dodge Jr. in the late 1800s. Services are still held at the church on Sunday evening. Two other Dodge-built mission churches on the island have been lost to time.

He finished seminary six months after her death and was ordained in Atlanta in May 1884. Using $200,000 left him by his wife, along with part of his own fortune, Dodge rebuilt Christ Church and dedicated it to his young wife. Her body, in an ebony coffin with a glass top "in position for the body to be seen when it was taken out," was ensconced in a vault under the altar, where it remained until her husband died. Dodge had promised Ellen she would not be buried until he could share her grave. Ultimately, both were interred in plain pine coffins; Dodge, who died at age thirty-nine, refused to be embalmed, believing his body and Ellen's should return to dust as soon as possible.

Sharing the Dodge cemetery plot are Anson's second wife, Anna Gould Dodge, and their son, Anson III, who was killed in a carriage accident at age three. Dodge asked that Anna be buried alongside him and his first wife, Ellen, but she declined, yielding that spot to his mother. Anna is buried at the far end of the Dodge plot, next to her little boy. Anna did honor her husband's request that she dress in white for his funeral, although mourners at the time usually wore unrelieved black. After his death, she started the Anson Dodge Home for Boys at Frederica, a project she and her husband had planned together in memory of their son. The home operated on St. Simons until the late 1950s. Some longtime island residents grew up there; other islanders remember playing as children with the boys who lived at the home.

During his lifetime, Dodge Jr. founded the first Episcopal cathedral in India and the Georgia Mission Society. He funded and preached at mission churches in a number of South Georgia towns. At age twenty-four, he built three mission churches on St. Simons: St. Ignatius Episcopal in Jewtown, Transfiguration on the south end, and St. Perpetua at German Village off Lawrence Road. Transfiguration and St. Perpetua have been lost to time, but St. Ignatius still holds services on Sunday evenings.

Dodge rebuilt Christ Church in 1884 on the cornerstone of the original church. It was designed to resemble an inverted ship's hull, symbolizing the ship of faith. The tall belfry and steep roof are typical of the severe Gothic style, but the wood trusses, pews, and walls, along with the glowing stained glass, give the small sanctuary a warm, intimate feel. Over the years, church members dedicated the stained-glass windows as memorials to loved ones. The window opposite the main entry is an unsigned but authenticated masterpiece by Louis Comfort Tiffany featuring the two red dots characteristic of the artist's work. Other windows depict Oglethorpe and Tomochichi, the Wesley brothers, scenes from church history, and the life of Christ. An Italian marble bust depicts Anson Dodge Jr. as a boy.

The cross topping the steeple was hand-carved from a single block of wood by craftsmen from Portugal who lived on St. Simons for several years during the 1980s while doing cathedral-quality plasterwork on a house being built on Sea Island for a Brunswick millionaire. The Portuguese enjoyed both islands and their edible wildlife; they trapped squirrels, marsh rabbits, and other small game and roasted them over barrel fires at the Sea Island construction site and the apartment building they rented on St. Simons.

The oldest marked grave in the Christ Church Cemetery dates to 1803; documented burials date to the late 1700s. Behind the church is the grave of the Reverend Edmund Matthews, the first rector of the original church. His monument is designed in the shape of an altar table. When he was buried, altar tables in cemeteries were used as places to feed poor people.

When it was published, *The Beloved Invader* (1965) became an international best seller. Eugenia Price wrote two more books in her St. Simons trilogy, *Lighthouse* (1972) and *New Moon Rising* (1969), best sellers that focused on the Gould family and featured other people and events from the island's past. She then moved on to other historical fiction set on the southeastern coast. All of Price's novels sold millions of copies in the United States and around the world.

Launched as a novelist, Price settled on the island with Blackburn, who wrote a picture-book series for young children as well as fiction and nonfiction for young people and adults, some based on island history. Her books won numerous awards and are still popular with readers and educators. Blackburn's St. Simons books include *James Edward Oglethorpe* (1970), a biography of Georgia's

Christ Episcopal Church is one of the most-visited sites on St. Simons. Former presidents, including Jimmy Carter, have worshiped at the old church during visits to Sea Island and St. Simons.

Gully Hole Creek, the site of a battle between Oglethorpe's troops and Spanish invaders from Florida. The small creek is sometimes used as a dumping ground.

Wading birds stretch and preen at sunrise.

founder; *Phoebe's Secret Diary: Daily Life and First Romance of a Colonial Girl* (1993), an account of life at the town of Frederica; and *The Bloody Summer of 1742: A Colonial Boy's Journal* (1984), which describes the battles of Gully Hole Creek and Bloody Marsh.

Just as the protagonist of Price's first novel had done, the two writers built an elegant house near Christ Church, which they named "The Dodge." Price described it as "our home in the sun-and-shadow streaked woods." They were nature lovers, and a floor-to-ceiling window beside the toilet in their first-floor bathroom overlooked the house's secluded and beautifully landscaped grounds, where deer, raccoons, and dozens of species of birds came to feed.

Price and Blackburn became environmental activists, lending their names, time, and financial support to groups opposing projects that threatened the island's environment, historic sites, and people. They sponsored the Georgia Sea Island Festival, a summertime celebration of Gullah Geechee culture that has been held since 1989 on St. Simons. Price wrote a nonfiction account of her life on St. Simons with Blackburn. Called Genie by friends, Price died in 1996 and is buried at Christ Church Cemetery, a few yards from where Dodge Jr. is buried with other family members under the marble slab that covered Ellen's body in the church vault. Joyce Blackburn died in 2009 and is buried beside Eugenia Price.

Afterword

ISLANDERS NOWADAYS often wonder whether St. Simons will survive the tsunami of growth and development that has washed over the island since the 1980s. According to the 2010 census, about twenty thousand people live year-round on St. Simons, although visitors often boost that number to thirty thousand and beyond. That figure seems modest for a twelve-mile-long island, but sandy, ever-shifting sea islands cannot support the heavy development possible on islands such as Manhattan, which are underpinned by bedrock. Rapid growth on St. Simons stalled during the recession of the early twenty-first century, but development is likely to keep pace with the economic recovery. The more the island grows, the more difficult it will be to allow natural beaches to build and erode. More people will put pressure on old island neighborhoods and roads, especially Frederica Road, the island's only major north-south route. Turning lanes have relieved some of Frederica's congestion, but widening it and other heavily traveled island roads would require cutting more of the iconic old live oaks, something most islanders oppose.

When Hurricane Floyd threatened coastal Georgia in 1999, it took many hours to evacuate people on St. Simons and Sea Island. Once the evacuees reached the mainland, they were caught in the largest evacuation—and the largest traffic jam—in United States history as millions of Georgia and Florida residents took to the interstates, highways, and byways to escape what weather forecasters believed would be a major storm. Stores, gas stations, restaurants, and motels were overwhelmed. Vending machines were

Azaleas bloom all over St. Simons every spring.

Three-year-old Anson Galland practices his fishing skills on St. Simons beach.

Southern Soul Barbecue, owned and operated by third-generation islanders near the Malcolm McKinnon Airport, offers Brunswick stew, pulled pork, and burnt ends.

stripped bare. Stalled vehicles were pushed to the side of the road, where they languished for weeks before their owners could retrieve them. Emergency vehicles were tangled in traffic, helpless to reach people who needed them. In the capricious nature of hurricanes, Floyd bypassed Florida and Georgia and devastated the Carolinas instead. Had it struck the lower Georgia coast, however, many refugees from St. Simons and elsewhere might have died in their cars trying to escape the path of the storm. Improvements have been made since then to mainland evacuation procedures, but the length of time required to move people off St. Simons and Sea Island still concerns emergency officials and islanders. Proposals have been made for constructing a second causeway from the mainland to the north end of St. Simons; it would open another evacuation route and also alleviate heavy traffic on Frederica Road, made worse by all the new north-end development. The financial cost and environmental damage involved in building a causeway to the island today would be staggering.

The pier on the south end of St. Simons is usually crowded with fishermen, crabbers, and others who come to stroll and enjoy the ocean breezes and magnificent sunsets.

Even with the fast-paced development of recent decades, St. Simons remains a lovely place to live or visit. It routinely enchants newcomers with its natural beauty, historic treasures, and amenities such as golf courses, tennis courts, white-sand beaches, island and boat tours, fishing expeditions, good restaurants, the pier and Neptune Park, and the variety of shops and stores that cater to island residents and visitors. The pace of island life remains leisurely. When traffic backs up on Frederica Road, as it does almost every day, islanders tend to shrug and wait for the snarl to work itself out. Even with all the second homes and rental properties, St. Simons still feels more like a community than a resort, perhaps in part because it has never been privately owned by a single family or treated as a millionaires' club.

St. Simons was one of the first places in the country to have settled communities. At least 4,500 years ago, ancient Indians congregated year-round in island villages, abandoning the nomadic lifestyle of their predecessors. The early Indians built giant shell rings on St. Simons that some experts believe were among North America's first large community architectural projects. In the early 1600s, Franciscan friars established the

A tugboat stranded on the
beach of Little St. Simons, a
privately owned nature resort
across the Hampton River from
St. Simons

island's Mocama mission in the Indian village of Guadalquini. It operated for almost a century on the south end of St. Simons as a blended Spanish-Indian community. British-built Fort Frederica was a town as much as a fortification. During antebellum days, wealthy planters and slaves formed strong communities on the island from a diverse mix of people from England, France, Ireland, Scotland, the Caribbean, and dozens of African countries who came, willingly or not, to St. Simons, bringing their cultures with them. In the late 1800s, island communities, black and white, grew up around the sawmills of Gascoigne Bluff. Many of the military personnel and Liberty ship builders who lived on St. Simons or visited during World War II settled permanently on the island after the war ended. Many vacationers have chosen to relocate full-time to St. Simons, joining old communities and building new ones.

Nature is still an ever-present part of everyday island life. Bottlenose dolphins cruise the tidal waterways, and endangered wood storks stalk beach seiners, looking for handouts. Platoons of pelicans fly in tight formation past the pier, skimming the ocean swells. Flocks of seagulls halo the shrimp boats as the fleet chugs toward port at sunset. Bald eagles, brown pelicans, and osprey, once all but wiped out by DDT, are again nesting on St. Simons. The giant live oaks that canopy so much of the island are enduring and strong, fitting symbols for the people who have put down roots in the sandy soil and stayed to make a life and a history on a southern sea island. The island is ruled more by the natural rhythms of seasons and tides than by clocks and calendars.

At least for now, St. Simons still runs on island time.

Bibliography

Bagwell, James E. *Rice Gold: James Hamilton Couper and Rice Plantations on the Georgia Coast.* Macon, Ga.: Mercer University Press, 2000.

Bailey, Cornelia Walker. *God, Dr. Buzzard, and the Bolito Man: A Saltwater Geechee Talks about Life on Sapelo Island.* With Christina Bledsoe. New York: Doubleday, 2000.

Bannon, John Francis, ed. *Bolton and the Spanish Borderlands.* Norman: University of Oklahoma Press, 1964.

Bartram, William. *Travels of William Bartram.* New Haven, Conn.: Yale University Press, 1958.

Bell, Malcolm, Jr. *Major Butler's Legacy: Five Generations of a Slaveholding Family.* Athens: University of Georgia Press, 1987.

Bolton, Herbert E., and Mary Ross. *The Debatable Land: A Sketch of the Anglo-Spanish Contest for the Georgia Country.* Berkeley and Los Angeles: University of California Press, 1925.

Brown, Gillean. *The Franciscan Missions of Coastal Georgia: The Cause of the Georgia Martyrs.* Boston: St. Anthony's Shrine, 1985.

Carolina Marsh Tacky Association. 2009. Accessed August 20, 2012. http://www.marshtacky .org/.

Carson, Rachel. *The Edge of the Sea.* Boston: Houghton Mifflin, 1955.

Cate, Margaret Davis. *Early Days of Coastal Georgia.* Illustrated by Orrin Sage Wightman. St. Simons, Ga.: Fort Frederica Association, 1955.

———. "Mistakes in Fanny Kemble's Georgia Journal." *Georgia Historical Quarterly* 44 (March 1960): 2–16.

———. *Our Todays and Yesterdays.* Brunswick, Ga.: Glover Brothers, 1979.

Clinton, Catherine. *Fanny Kemble's Civil Wars: The Story of America's Most Unlikely Abolitionist.* New York: Simon and Schuster, 2000.

———. "Susie King Taylor: 'I Gave My Services Willingly.'" In *Georgia Women: Their Lives and Times*, edited by Ann Short Chirhart and Betty Wood, 1:130–46. Athens: University of Georgia Press, 2009.

Coastal Georgia Historical Society. *Historic Glimpses of St. Simons Island, 1736–1924*. St. Simons: Coastal Georgia Historical Society, 1973.

Colquitt, Dolores B., Margaret Davis Cate, Mary Wylie McCarty, and Sidney Lanier. *Flags of Five Nations: A Collection of Historical Sketches and Stories of the Golden Isles of Guale*. Sea Island, Ga.: The Cloister, n.d. [c. 1946].

"Constitution: America's Ship of State." Official U. S. Navy site. Accessed August 20, 2012. http://www.history.navy.mil/ussconstitution/.

Cook, Fred C. "The Kent Mound: A Study of the Irene Phase on the Lower Georgia Coast." Master's thesis, University of Florida, 1975.

———. "A Tale of Two Mini-sites: A Mast Processing Location and a Game Processing Location on the Georgia Coast." The South Georgia Archaeological Research Team. Accessed 2011. http://thesga.org/category/georgia-archaeology-resources/georgia -archaeology-online/2011.

Cook, Jeannine, ed. *Columbus and the Land of Ayllón: The Exploration and Settlement of the Southeast*. Darien, Ga.: Lower Altamaha Historical Society, 1992.

Cooksey, Elizabeth B. "Dodge County." *New Georgia Encyclopedia*. November 17, 2011. Accessed August 20, 2012. http://www.georgiaencyclopedia.org/nge/Article.jsp?id=h-2322.

Davis, Jingle. "Ancient Sloth Bones Found: Amateur Hunters Uncover Fossils near St. Simons." *Atlanta Journal-Constitution*, March 10, 1992.

———. "Mojo Bundle Leads to Shrimpboat Exorcism." *Atlanta Journal-Constitution*, February 9, 1985.

Davis, Pablo J. "Robert Sengstacke Abbott, 1868–1940." *New Georgia Encyclopedia*. September 19, 2008. Accessed August 20, 2012. http://www.georgiaencyclopedia.org/nge/Article .jsp?id=h-3196.

Davis, Richard A., Jr. *The Evolving Coast*. New York: Scientific American Library, 1993.

Doster, Stephen. *Voices from St. Simons: Personal Narratives of an Island's Past*. Winston-Salem, N.C.: Blair, 2008.

Episcopal Diocese of Georgia. Interviews with Good Shepherd Episcopal Church congregants, Pennick, Georgia, 2008. Video.

Fairbanks, Ralph Betts, *Hawkins-Davison House, Frederica*. St. Simons: Fort Frederica Association, 1956.

Ferguson, T. Reed. *The John Couper Family at Cannon's Point*. Macon, Ga.: Mercer University Press, 1994.

Ford, James A., Marmaduke Floyd, and Thomas Spaulding. *Georgia's Disputed Ruins*. Edited by E. Merton Coulter. Chapel Hill: University of North Carolina Press, 1937.

Francis, J. Michael, and Kathleen M. Kole. "Murder and Martyrdom in Spanish Florida: Don Juan and the Guale Uprising." *American Museum of Natural History Anthropological Papers*, no. 95. New York: American Museum of Natural History, 2011.

Freedman, Samuel G. "Long Road from Come by Here to Kumbaya." *New York Times*, November 19, 2010.

Gannon, Michael. *Operation Drumbeat: Germany's U-boat Attacks along the American Coast in World War II*. New York: Harper Perennial, 1991.

Goodyear, Albert C. "On the Study of Technological Change." *Current Anthropology* 28 (1998): 320–23.

Graham, Abbie Fuller. *Old Mill Days: St. Simons Mills, 1874–1908*. Brunswick, Ga.: Privately printed, 1976.

Green, R. Edwin. *St. Simons Island: A Summary of Its History*. Charleston: History Press, 2004.

Groom, Winston. "The Lost Pilot." *Garden and Gun Magazine*, June–July 2011. Accessed August 20, 2012. http://gardenandgun.com/article/lost-pilot.

Hansen, David. "John Wesley Lecture." Moore Methodist Museum, Library, and Archives, St. Simons, February 19, 2012.

Harris, Juliette, and Pamela Johnson, eds. *Tenderheaded: A Comb-Bending Collection of Hair Stories*. New York: Pocket Books, 2001.

Harris, Thaddeus Mason. *Biographical Memorials of James Oglethorpe: Founder of the Colony of Georgia in North America*. Boston: Privately printed by the author at Freeman and Bolles, 1841.

Hoffman, Paul E. *A New Andalucia and a Way to the Orient: The American Southeast in the Sixteenth Century*. Baton Rouge: Louisiana State University Press, 1990.

Holder, Preston. "Excavations on St. Simons Island and Vicinity, Glynn County, Georgia." *Proceedings of the Society for Georgia Archaeology* 1 (1938): 8–9.

Hudson, Charles. *The Southeastern Indians*. Knoxville: University of Tennessee Press, 1976.

Hudson, Charles, and Carmen Chaves Tesser. *The Forgotten Centuries: Indians and Europeans in the American South, 1521–1704*. Athens: University of Georgia Press, 1994.

Hull, Barbara. *St. Simons Enchanted Island: A History of the Most Historic of Georgia's Fabled Golden Isles*. Atlanta: Cherokee Publishing, 1980.

"International Shark Attack File." Ichthyology at the Florida Museum of Natural History. January 30, 2012. Accessed August 20, 2012. http://www.flmnh.ufl.edu/fish/sharks/statistics/gattack/mapusa.htm.

Johnson, Edward A. "Building Liberty Ships in Brunswick." *Ships for Victory: J. A. Jones Construction Company and Liberty Ships in Brunswick, Georgia*. Digital Library of Georgia. August 20, 2012. Accessed August 20, 2012. http://dlg.galileo.usg.edu/liberty_ships/BuildingLibertyShips/?Welcome.

Jones, Bessie. *For the Ancestors: Autobiographical Memories*. Edited by John Stewart. Athens: University of Georgia Press, 1989.

Jones, George Fenwick. *The Germans of Frederica*. St. Simons: Fort Frederica Association, 1996.

———. *The Salzburger Saga: Religious Exiles and Other Germans along the Savannah*. Athens: University of Georgia Press, 1984.

Kebler, Martha L. *Seas of Gold, Seas of Cotton: Christophe Poulain DuBignon of Jekyll Island*. Athens: University of Georgia Press, 2002.

Kemble, Fanny, and Catherine Clinton. *Fanny Kemble's Journals*. Boston: Harvard University Press, 2000.

Kimsey, Thora Olsen, and Sonja Olsen Kinard, eds. *Memories from the Marshes of Glynn, World War II*. Decatur, Ga.: Looking Glass Books, 1999.

King, Anna Matilda Page. *Anna: The Letters of a St. Simons Island Plantation Mistress, 1817–1859*. Edited by Melanie Pavich-Lindsay. Athens: University of Georgia Press, 2002.

Landers, Jane. "Gracia Real de Santa Teresa de Mose: A Free Black Town in Spanish Colonial Florida." *American Historical Review* 95, no. 1 (1990): 9–30.

Lanier, Sidney. *Hymns of the Marshes*. New York: Scribners, 1908.

Lanning, John Tate. *The Spanish Missions of Georgia*. Chapel Hill: University of North Carolina Press, 1935.

Lauterbach, Preston. *The Chitlin' Circuit and the Road to Rock 'n' Roll*. New York: Norton, 2011.

Lear, Linda. *Rachel Carson: Witness for Nature*. New York: Henry Holt, 1997.

Legare, John Girardeau. *The Darien Journal of John Girardeau Legare, Ricegrower*. Edited by Buddy Sullivan. Athens: University of Georgia Press, 2010.

Leigh, Frances Butler. *Ten Years on a Georgia Plantation since the War*. London: Richard Bentley and Son, 1883.

Lewis, Bessie. "Patriarchial Plantations of St. Simons Island." N.p.: Privately printed, 1974.

Lyon, Edwin A. *A New Deal for Southeastern Archaeology*. Tuscaloosa: University of Alabama Press, 1996.

Martin, Harold H. *This Happy Isle: The Story of Sea Island and the Cloister*. Sea Island, Ga.: Sea Island Company, 1978.

McCann, Josh. "Writer on Board: Recalls Mansion's Journey up the Intracoastal Waterway." *Hilton Head (S.C.) Island Packet*, April 29, 2011. Accessed August 20, 2012. http://www.islandpacket.com/2011/04/29/1638083/writer-on-board-recalls-mansions.html.

McKay, Frances Peabody. *More Fun Than Heaven: Vignettes of Life in the Waycross Colony, St. Simons Island, Georgia, 1890–1934*. St. Petersburg, Fla.: Valkyrie Press, 1978.

McWhorter, Cameron. "Need a Job? Losing Your House? Who Says Hoodoo Can't Help? Tough Times Boost Sales of Spider Dust, Spells for Good Fortune, Mojo Powder." *Wall Street Journal*, December 28, 2010.

Milanich, Jerald T. "A Chronology for the Aboriginal Cultures of Northern St. Simons Island, Ga." *Florida Anthropologist* 30, no. 3 (1977): 140.

———. *Laboring in the Fields of the Lord: Spanish Missions and Southeastern Indians.* Gainesville: University Press of Florida, 2006.

———. *The Timucua.* Malden, Mass.: Blackwell Publishers, 1996.

———. "When Worlds Collided." Lecture on the history of Cannon's Point as part of a chautauqua sponsored by the Coastal Georgia Historical Society, St. Simons Island, August 18, 2011.

———. "When Worlds Collided: Native Peoples of the Caribbean and Florida in the Early Colonial Period." *Myths and Dreams: Exploring the Cultural Legacies of Florida and the Caribbean.* Accessed August 17, 2012. http://www.kislakfoundation.org/millennium-exhibit/milanich1.htm.

Montgomery, Robert, and John Barnwell. *The Most Delightful Golden Islands, Being a Proposal for the Establishment of a Colony in the Country to the South of Carolina.* Atlanta: Cherokee Publishing, 1975.

Moore, Francis. *A Voyage to Georgia.* London, 1744.

Morgan, Philip, ed. *African American Life in the Georgia Lowcountry: The Atlantic World and the Gullah Geechee.* Athens: University of Georgia Press, 2009.

Opala, Joseph A. *The Gullah: Rice, Slavery, and the Sierra Leone–American Connection.* Washington, D.C.: U.S. Department of State, 1987.

Parrish, Lydia. *Slave Songs of the Georgia Sea Islands.* 1942. Reprinted, Athens: University of Georgia Press, 1992.

Patrick, Bethanne Kelly. "Col. Robert Gould Shaw: Young Officer Led Union's First Black Regiment in Charge to Prove Themselves." Military.com. Accessed February 13, 2013. http://www.military.com/Content/MoreContent/1,12044,ML_rgshaw_bkp,00.html.

Ramey, Daina L. "She Do a Heap of Work: Female Slave Labor on Glynn County Rice and Cotton Plantations." *Georgia Historical Quarterly* 82, no. 4 (1998): 707–34.

Ray, Janisse. *Drifting into Darien: A Personal and Natural History of the Altamaha River.* Athens: University of Georgia Press, 2011.

San Miguel, Andrés de. *An Early Florida Adventure Story.* Translated by John H. Hann. Gainesville: University Press of Florida, 2000.

Sassaman, Kenneth E. *Early Pottery in the Southeast: Tradition and Innovation in Cooking Technology.* Tuscaloosa: University of Alabama Press, 1993.

———. *The Eastern Archaic, Historicized.* Issues in Eastern Woodlands Archaeology. Lanham, Md.: AltaMira Press, 2010.

———. *People of the Shoals: Stallings Culture of the Savannah River Valley.* Gainesville: University Press of Florida, 2006.

Savannah Unit, Georgia Writers' Project, Work Projects Administration. *Drums and Shadows: Survival Studies among the Georgia Coastal Negroes.* 1940. Reprinted, Athens: University of Georgia Press, 1986.

Schoettle, Taylor. *A Naturalist's Guide to St. Simons Island.* Illustrated by Jennifer Smith. Darien, Ga.: Self-published, 1993.

Sedberry, George R. "A Profile of the Charleston Bump." *Islands in the Stream 2001. NOAA Ocean Explorer.* Accessed August 17, 2012. http://oceanexplorer.noaa.gov/explorations /islands01/background/islands/sup11_bump.html.

Shaw, Robert Gould. *Blue-Eyed Child of Fortune: Civil War Letters of Col. Robert Gould Shaw.* Edited by Russell Duncan. Athens: University of Georgia Press, 1992.

Steele, Virginia W., and Mary R. Bullard, eds. *Journal of a Visit to the Georgia Islands, 1753.* Macon and Savannah: Mercer University Press and Georgia Historical Society, 1996.

Stewart, Mart A. *"What Nature Suffers to Groe": Life, Labor, and Landscape on the Georgia Coast, 1680–1920.* Athens: University of Georgia Press, 1996.

Sullivan, Buddy. *Early Days on the Georgia Tidewater: The Story of McIntosh County and Sapelo.* 4th ed. with revisions. Darien, Ga.: McIntosh County Board of Commissioners, 1995.

Swanton, John R. *Indians of the Southeastern United States.* Washington, D.C.: Smithsonian Institution, 1946.

Taylor, Susie Baker King. *Reminiscences of My Life in Camp with the 33rd United States Colored Troops, Late 1st S.C. Volunteers.* Boston: Self-published, 1902. Reprinted as *Susie King Taylor: An African American Woman's Civil War Memoir.* Athens: University of Georgia Press, 2006.

Thomas, David Hurst. *St. Catherines: An Island in Time.* Athens: University of Georgia Press. 2011.

Thomas, M. C. *Fossil Vertebrates: Beach and Bank Collecting for Amateurs.* Revised ed. Gainesville: Florida Paleontological Society, Florida Museum of Natural History, 1992.

Turner, Lorenzo Dow. *Africanisms in the Gullah Dialect.* 1949. Reprinted, Columbia: University of South Carolina Press, 2002.

Van Doren, Mark, ed. *Travels of William Bartram, from "A Diary of a Journal through the Carolinas, Georgia and Florida, from July 1, 1765, to April 10, 1766."* Philadelphia, 1942. Reprinted, New York: Dover, 1955.

Vanstory, Burnette. *Georgia's Land of the Golden Isles.* Self-published, 1956. Reprinted, Athens: University of Georgia Press, 1981.

———. "Ghost Stories and Superstitions of Old St. Simons." N.p.: N.p., n.d.

von Reck, Philip Georg Friedrich. *Von Reck's Voyage: Georgia in 1736; Drawings and Journal of Philip Georg Friedrich von Reck.* Edited by Kristian Hvidt. Savannah, Ga.: Beehive Press, 1980.

Wesley, Charles. "March 9–August 30, 1736." In *The Journal of Charles Wesley (1707–1788)*. Wesley Center Online. Northwestern Nazarene University. Accessed August 20, 2012. http://wesley.nnu.edu/charles-wesley/the-journal-of-charles-wesley-1707-1788/.

Williams, David S. *From Mounds to Megachurches: Georgia's Religious Heritage*. Athens: University of Georgia Press, 2008.

Wood, Virginia Steele. "The Georgia Navy's Dramatic Victory of April 19, 1778." *Georgia Historical Quarterly* 90, no. 2 (2006): 156.

Worth, John E. "Spanish Florida: Evolution of a Colonial Society, 1513–1763." University of Florida Faculty Home Page for John Worth. Accessed 2011. http://uwf.edu/jworth/spanfla.htm.

———. *The Struggle for the Georgia Coast*. Tuscaloosa: University of Alabama Press, 2007.

Index